PINK FLOYD

ALBUM BY ALBUM

MARTIN POPOFF

WITH

Roie Avin, Craig Bailey, Nick Beggs, Ralph Chapman, Robert Corich,
Dennis Dunaway, Heather Findlay, Steve Hackett, Lewis Hall,
Paul Kehayas, Ed Lopez-Reyes, Steve Rothery, Jordan Rudess,
Kyle Shutt, and Jeff Wagner

VOYAGEUR
PRESS

CONTENTS

INTRODUCTION
AND DISCOGRAPHIC NOTES 6

1. THE PIPER
   AT THE GATES OF DAWN 8
2. A SAUCERFUL OF SECRETS 22
3. MORE 36
4. UMMAGUMMA 46
5. ATOM HEART MOTHER 62
6. MEDDLE 76
7. OBSCURED BY CLOUDS 92
8. THE DARK SIDE OF THE MOON 106
9. WISH YOU WERE HERE 122
10. ANIMALS 138
11. THE WALL 154
12. THE FINAL CUT 174
13. A MOMENTARY LAPSE
    OF REASON 188
14. THE DIVISION BELL 204
15. THE ENDLESS RIVER 218

PHOTO CREDITS 230
ABOUT THE AUTHOR 231
ABOUT THE INTERVIEWEES 232
A COMPLETE AUTHOR BIBLIOGRAPHY 236
INDEX 238

INTRODUCTION

Reflecting on my listening experiences with Pink Floyd over the decades, my first instinct was to assume that most have been very deep and contemplative, befitting the gravitas of the band's famed Immersion box sets—deep psych sessions on Roger's couch, a little hypnosis thrown in for good measure, after which my personality was refracted in a new direction, likely toward the sullen, fatalistic, and cynical.

But then the memories began flooding back: educations from cousins and older brothers of friends as to the seriousness (and stoner sacrament) of *The Dark Side of the Moon* and *Animals*; that school band trip to Boise, Idaho, during which *The Wall* was played (at quite a low volume for once) at the back of the bus, we music heads mumbling along, seeing who could recite the next effect, discussing the storylines, ticking off band teacher Mr. White, who saw revolution on wheels in "We Don't Need No Education."

Later there were the university years and ruminations over *The Final Cut*, in conjunction with loving the new wave of British heavy metal and its more modest adjunct neo-prog movement. Later still it was *A Momentary Lapse of Reason* during my first job out of MBA school (with Xerox), followed by Floyd in hi-fidelity, heard from those way-back seats at the McLaughlin Planetarium next to the Royal Ontario Museum in Toronto.

Finally, I achieved a more sophisticated level of communion closer to the business end of Floyd when I began transitioning into the rock 'n' roll biz through an upstart heavy metal magazine with my buddy Tim Henderson. Here me an' the writer buds would ponder things like a 1994 with a new Pink Floyd studio album and where classic rock and metal and prog fit in a music industry in which grunge, techno, industrial, and various other forms of alternative rock were killing the careers of our heroes.

So, gosh darn it, despite the tendency to think one is alone and intense with one's Floyd—be it the massiveness of the band or the discussion-provoking concepts therein or even the sound effects and spoken bits—Pink Floyd has turned out to be an improbable meeting place of minds yearning for extra protein with their lunch, willing to take those long runs, relishing a good read of the lyric sheet, happy that the party got quiet.

And in that light, *Pink Floyd: Album by Album* became another one of those communal Pink Floyd experiences—specifically the interviews, which had the soothing effect of demonstrating the shared solitary contemplation of Floyd that I figured (but never really confirmed in direct conversation) millions of people share around the world.

But it was also deeply satisfying to witness what different fans emphasized when asked about Floyd. I heard excitement (mostly couched in reverence) across the board, touching down on guitar work, keyboards, album covers, concepts, and, most regularly, Roger's dense and intense lyrics. A few folks made it personal, or rather, wanted to make sure their personal connection with the band was told.

As a result, I emerged out the other end re-educated in whatever level of mastery of the catalog I thought I had (especially pre–*Dark Side*), as well as placated by the understanding that Floyd can be enjoyed alone and with a crowd, that the shared humanity of it all would be enough to shed any reclusive tendencies I might have had. Really, I couldn't have asked for a better crowd with which to share Pink Floyd, and I thank them one and all for making this book entertaining and informative on a readerly level and, on a personal level, making my relationship with Floyd that much richer.

And so, without further introductory musings, I hope this deep-tissue massage of Pink Floyd's fifteen studio albums does for you what it did for me, beginning with dusting off your collection in whatever format it resides for an enriched listen to the myriad facets you always knew were there but perhaps had not reflected o'er (like myself with some of these records) in a long, long time.

DISCOGRAPHIC NOTES

A few notes on the presentation of the album credits:

Credits and citations of all types, where available, are reproduced to be in the spirit of the earliest UK issue of album.

Song timings are cited per the earliest issue of the album from any territory—if not available on UK issue as was the standard, I deferred to the US or Canadian issue from the same year.

I've cited only last names, even if first names were used in the original issues. Where Gilmour was spelled "Gilmore" in original credits, I overruled and went with the correct spelling, even if I left the odd Dave vs. David (and it was *Nicky* Mason who played drums on *Piper*!).

Where there were discrepancies on writing credits or song spellings and punctuations, the back cover took precedent over the label (except for *Ummagumma*, where the record label made more sense); note that the official releases are wildly inconsistent with song title subsectioning.

Writing credits that distinguish between music and lyrics are not common with Pink Floyd, so the comma is used so as not to cause errors, especially when four names are listed; as well, the distinction is maintained where it has been made clear, such as on *The Division Bell*.

Performance credits are as cited per earliest issue (including the order of names and the exact wording), but where no performance credits were listed, I went with best estimates of personnel and instrumentation; however, some reordering has been done using the criteria of importance, especially when it comes to guest performances.

It is recognized that no further demarcation was cited for single-song performers or the occasional performance or vocal on a track, nor for producers of certain sessions (i.e., *The Endless River*). Songs are not in double quotes in this area of the book to promote neatness.

Obvious typos have been fixed (note the misspelling of Britannia Row in *The Division Bell*).

References to "the Pink Floyd" have been changed to Pink Floyd.

Other liberties were taken when the situation required it—complicated records, these are. Especially in the early years.

CHAPTER 1

THE PIPER AT THE GATES OF DAWN

WITH DENNIS DUNAWAY
AND PAUL KEHAYAS

SIDE 1
1. Astronomy Domine   4:08
   (Barrett)
2. Lucifer Sam   3:05
   (Barrett)
3. Matilda Mother   3:05
   (Barrett)
4. Flaming   2:44
   (Barrett)
5. Pow R. Toc H.   4:23
   (Barrett, Waters, Wright, Mason)
6. Take Up Thy Stethoscope and Walk   3:04
   (Waters)

SIDE 2
1. Interstellar Overdrive   9:38
   (Barrett, Waters, Wright, Mason)
2. The Gnome   2:02
   (Barrett)
3. Chapter 24   3:39
   (Barrett)
4. The Scarecrow   2:07
   (Barrett)
5. Bike   3:20
   (Barrett)

ISSUE VARIANCE NOTES: The US version consists of Side 1: "See Emily Play," "Pow R. Toc H." (as "Pow R. Toch"), "Take Up Thy Stethoscope and Walk" (as "Take Up My Stethoscope and Walk"), "Lucifer Sam," "Matilda Mother"; Side 2: "The Scarecrow," "The Gnome," "Chapter 24," "Interstellar Overdrive." "See Emily Play" was new to the US edition while "Astronomy Domine," "Flaming," and "Bike" were omitted.

Recorded at EMI Recording Studios, St. John's Wood, London

PERSONNEL: Syd Barrett—lead guitar, vocals; Roger Waters—bass guitar, vocals; Rick Wright—organ, piano; Nicky Mason—drums

Produced by Norman Smith

Released August 5, 1967 (UK); October 21, 1967 (US)

Wielded like a rainbow-refracting sword not a year into psychedelic rock's very existence, *The Piper at the Gates of Dawn* seemed to destine Pink Floyd for notoriety—which they instantly received, the press labeling them incendiary pied pipers making music for LSD takers. Psychedelia might have gotten off the ground stateside, with a trajectory that might include (using the Beatles as its base) Bob Dylan, the Byrds, the Beach Boys, Jefferson Airplane, the 13th Floor Elevators, and the Grateful Dead, but Pink Floyd served as the first complete package about London town, soon and forever to be psych's second office, after San Francisco.

The three architecture students (Roger, Rick, and Nick) and one art student (Syd) had been making music together as school chums since 1962, signing a deal with EMI on February 1, 1967, and one month later issuing their contentious "Arnold Layne" single. The band's £5,000 record deal, although spread over five years and without free studio time, allowed them complete control over their output, which, to the label's dismay, got stranger as time went on, culminating in 1969's *Ummagumma* and letting up only slightly with the release of *Atom Heart Mother* the following year.

The collection of songs issued in August 1967, *The Piper at the Gates of Dawn*, represented an intensifying UK response to the birth of psych on the American West Coast. The proceedings were led for the first and last time by Syd Barrett, sole penner of eight of the original UK issue's eleven tracks, and in on the full-band credit for two more (both instrumentals), with only "Take Up Thy Stethoscope and Walk" credited to Roger Waters alone. Additionally, Syd played all the guitar on the album and took the lion's share of the lead vocals, his accent lending it some distinction.

In the spirit of what the Beatles had already been pioneering, especially with *Revolver*, Pink Floyd recorded *Piper* with Beatles engineer Norman Smith at EMI Studios (later to become Abbey

ABOVE: A suitably psychedelic portrait of Pink Floyd from 1967. Clockwise from top left: Syd Barrett, Nick Mason, Rick Wright, and Roger Waters.

BELOW: Label from the UK mono pressing of *The Piper at the Gates of Dawn*.

An Italian pressing of *The Piper at the Gates of Dawn* from 1971, with Gilmour—not actually a member of the band at the time the album was made—erroneously pictured on the cover.

Road). As well, George Harrison's friend Vic Singh emphasized the new sartorial style of psych by finding crazy, colorful clothes for the band and then shooting the guys in triple vision with a prism lens to evoke an acid trip.

The cover art and the new *Wind in the Willows*–derived title (changed at the last minute from *Projection*) represented powerful messaging parallel to the band's already notorious reputation for trip-friendly live shows. The visuals helped focus the message, setting the Floyd up for success as the new hippies upturning the apple cart and freeing minds with their new full-length record, a field recording of the proceedings in Syd's head as the more responsible trio behind their acid-addled leader looked on in growing dismay.

The warning signs of Syd's descent into madness are all over the record. Against the idyllic and paisley "Flaming," "The Gnome," "Bike," and "Chapter 24," there are "Matilda Mother," "Lucifer Sam," "Interstellar Overdrive," and the harrowing "Astronomy Domine," a virtual sound-painting of brain drain. All told, one might conjecture that Pink Floyd's was the type of psych that was going to cause King Crimson, Van der Graaf Generator, and heavy metal, rather than that of Yes, Genesis, and the peaceful easy sounds of the country-rock Avocado Mafia taking over the Troubadour in L.A. Indeed, this darkness brought in by Syd on this record would linger and then metastasize inside of Pink Floyd after his exit, with Roger Waters as its new carrier and newcomer David Gilmour as sullen enabler.

The Piper at the Gates of Dawn hit #6 in the UK charts but stalled at #131 in the US and, quite shockingly, never garnered even gold certification in America (sure, neither did the next two, but *Piper* would have sounded fresh and distinct in 1967). Perhaps its fate was sealed by a disastrous attempt at a US tour in October and November 1967, in which Syd sabotaged all but a handful of appearances, his mind gone and his mates desperately trying to coax it back.

POPOFF: Could you please set this record up in terms of prehistory of the band? What is the pathway to *The Piper at the Gates of Dawn*?
KEHAYAS: Good grief. They were architecture students and then there was the artist. Cambridge is the place where it all comes together, and I guess they're like many other bands, formed by people who had a love of music. But Syd Barrett, obviously being the key figure in all of this, was pretty much not considering himself to be a musician. He was considering himself groomed to be working in the visual realm, but he was pretty good at rhythm guitar and he had a passion for things like Bob Dylan and the blues.

As with anybody else hanging out in university life in Cambridge, jazz, blues, a lot of dope, painting, young people, and probably girls all conspired. When they started using the name the Pink Floyd, it was in homage to the blues men Pink Anderson and Floyd Council. Then they go to London and get hooked up with the emerging scene and, in particular, the UFO Club, and they become sort of the house band around there.

I guess this band was doing R&B covers and soul covers and whatever else, badly. There are recordings that have cropped up, bootlegs and now official releases, of them doing "I'm a King Bee," and not well. They had to go somewhere else with it. Most of their live performance would be, I guess, extended jams while people danced, in late-night settings—the starting up of rave culture, really. They would go freeform. Eventually, one of these bits would turn into "Interstellar Overdrive" or some version of that.

I believe Syd was probably into Love. I think he was a record hound as well. And he was a huge Dylan fan. But the ramp-up to the record is that they become darlings of the London underground of '66, and if I'm not mistaken, Joe Boyd, the person behind the UFO Club, engineers their first single. Joe Boyd had done some engineering and producing with things like the Incredible String Band. He was an American who lived in London who has the greatest life. So, he takes the Floyd in and does their first single, "Arnold Layne" backed with "Candy and a Currant Bun."

POPOFF: Who is their competition in making this crazy psych music? Who is big on the scene, or are Pink Floyd essentially the first?

KEHAYAS: They are not. The spirit of '66 in London is very much music and art coalescing. There were other musicians who were kind of ahead of them, but not anything pop. AMM were an improvisational instrumental group in the London scene, and it's documented that Barrett used to go see these guys. They are very far out, very improv, very no rules. That would be the most far-out and forward-thinking.

Certainly, there was a jazz scene, and there would be the influence of the poetry scene. Again, a lot of dope. That's gonna open up a lot of minds and throw a lot of people's perception of what is and what means something into complete disarray. The Soft Machine from Canterbury are contemporaries of theirs. Soft Machine at that point were probably in San Tropez, so I don't know whether they were starting to play in London. But the people who were playing at the UFO were galvanizing what you would call the London "underground scene." But let's be realistic: there were other people who played but may not have done a single.

POPOFF: Let's step forward to this record. Tell me a little bit about the making of *The Piper at the Gates of Dawn*.

A pair of archival EP releases containing early Pink Floyd music: *1965: Their First Recordings* collects the earliest-known recordings by the band, then known as the Tea Set, while *London '66–'67* contains an extended version of "Interstellar Overdrive" and the previously unreleased "Nick's Boogie."

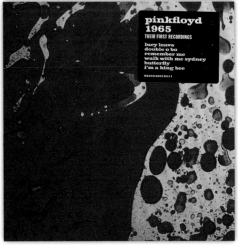

KEHAYAS: After the success of "Arnold Layne," obviously there was the idea to create a follow-up single and a full-length record. They signed a deal and the sad part of it is Joe Boyd was not asked to produce. They're now going to be using the EMI Studios, commonly called Abbey Road. Somewhere during the recording, stuff starts to shift for Syd, and in particular his brain starts to not work the same way.

So, it's fraught with trouble because, although he can come up with a single, he wants to push the living hell out of the engineers' and Norman Smith's patience. I don't think Norman had many good things to say about working with Syd Barrett. Probably because Norman wanted a hit, but there's tension.

But the band is so unified. The majority of the songs are Syd's. Everything has been written within a six- to eight-month stand. That's the creative life of Syd Barrett and Pink Floyd, that all these songs vomited out in one go. They go in and they make this record. Somewhere in the middle of it, Syd starts to lose focus because of whatever mental issues he's having, exacerbated by excessive LSD use, no sleep, and probably his growing hatred and distress over the pop mechanism.

The other guys are basically happy to do anything they are told to do, because this is their lucky break. Apparently, somewhere during the recording of "Getting Better," Norman brought his new group over to meet the Beatles, and they were completely daunted by it. Apparently, Syd Barrett was a huge John Lennon fan.

But everything centers around Syd for the first LP, because he's the writer, the lead singer, the charismatic presence. Although the other guys are incredibly talented, at this point, Rick Wright's contribution is mainly sort of Eastern modality solos, played on the Farfisa organ. I'd say Roger Waters's bass playing isn't exactly the deftest of all bass playing at this point, but he was fine. Let's face it, Nick Mason was a good pounder. They were a good unit, but there was a star.

Interestingly enough, at the time there were two mixes made of the album. Now you can find the mono mix that was out of print for so long, and I'm gonna be on record and say that the mono mix is one of the most radically different things I've ever heard in my life between stereo and mono mixes, more so than, say, *Sgt. Pepper*. And the mono mix is superior. It has the input of the writer because Syd was very much interested in mixing.

Anyway, it's a monumentally great record, and it crystallizes this moment in the life of a young man who obviously was looking back at the influences of his childhood. For example, the title comes from Kenneth Grahame's *The Wind in the Willows*. He was filtering his childhood memories through this new emerging prism of LSD.

The concept of acid, to me, tends to be about the loss of ego that one experiences when one takes it. When you look at a salt shaker and you're not on acid, you say, "That's a salt shaker and I'm obviously more important than that." But if you remove the sense of self, then it's not an unequal. It becomes exactly as important as you are. I have a feeling that this sort of childlike complete ego loss is what allows all Syd's influences from his childhood to come flooding back.

ABOVE AND OPPOSITE: Undated shots of the band performing at the UFO Club, London, circa early 1967.

POPOFF: Dennis, tell me about how you and your school chum, Alice Cooper, first interfaced with *The Piper at the Gates of Dawn*.
DUNAWAY: The way that I found out about Pink Floyd was Alice and I, way early on, before anybody had a clue who they were in America, we read this interview with Paul McCartney, and somebody asked him what British bands he liked, and he mentioned this new band called the Pink Floyd. So, Alice and I found a place and mailed away to England, and had to wait a long time for it to show up, but we got our *Piper* album, British copy, early on, before it was released in America. So, that was our first exposure. It was basically because a Beatle said that he liked it [*laughs*].

When I first heard it, I heard parallels with us. I thought we were kind of pioneering this direction that nobody else was doing. Even though what we were doing was more erratic and more in-your-face, there were definite similarities. We felt like we were kind of exploring outer space, and then we look over and somebody else is out there [*laughs*].

We had discovered Karlheinz Stockhausen and Morton Subotnick and his *Silver Apples of the Moon* album. Those were influences on us and I really wanted to bring that kind of feel to rock. Pink Floyd were doing things that had those same influences and we just loved it. It was the most psychedelic album of that era and it captured the feel of what was going on with LSD trips and whatnot. You have to remember the drug culture hadn't yet really run into the harsh realities that addictions would bring.

POPOFF: And where does this idea manifest itself most on the album for you?
DUNAWAY: I found the whole album to have that feel of going on a trip. It reflects a lot of what was happening at that time. The drug culture was in full swing. For example, the song "Chapter 24" was from the *I Ching*, and there were a lot of people into that . . . it was a big influence. To me, it was very confusing that they would decide what they were going to do by some sort of a chance [*laughs*]. Now, there might be more to it than I got out of it. But these Syd songs had a closeness where it's almost like you were in the same tiny room while he's singing to you. That's something that would change from the first album to the second.

With "Bike," you're going along, it's a happy song. But then all of a sudden it gets very spacey, and then it drops down and it's like time is stretched. That's where I get the feeling that it's like an LSD trip. Then there's a part where you hear footsteps. Somebody is walking on a wooden floor. Then it sounds like they open the door and suddenly this big blast of spacey music takes over. We'd put the headphones on and listen to stuff like that over and over. See, this was done at EMI Studios, where the Beatles recorded, and there's something to those Beatle albums and there's something to this, a similarity that draws you deep into the production. The harder you listen, the more it draws you in.

POPOFF: Let's drop down on a few of the key tracks. "Lucifer Sam" is one everybody loves on this record. It's not typical pastoral Syd, nor is it space rock.
KEHAYAS: One of my favorites, but first, I must stress with this record, everybody was really tensed out by the fact that Syd was hard to control in the studio and did not like to play the same thing twice. That wasn't just when he went bananas; that was from the word go—he hated the concept of rulemaking. So, yes, "Lucifer Sam"—best song about a cat of all time [*laughs*]. A Siamese cat. It's got the greatest guitar tones, plus that wonderful spy riff with the drums and the band speeding up oh so slightly behind it. Just amazing. As soon as that song starts, everybody's pulse quickens.
DUNAWAY: "Lucifer Sam" is three minutes and six seconds, but a lot happens in that period of time [*laughs*]. Immediately you've got the bass and the guitar playing a

OPPOSITE: Pink Floyd celebrates signing their first record deal outside EMI House, London, March 3, 1967.

BELOW: Another early portrait of the band, taken in the spring of 1967.

lick in unison to make it strong, but then when the vocals come in the whole thing changes. The bass drives through these quick, high melodic parts then lands on a whole note that seems to be dictated by the whims of Syd's vocal.

Then it goes to this spacey thing before it comes back to the riff. But I love the intro riff and the urgency of Syd's singing. It's only the second song, and already their style, with the heavy effects and unpredictable arrangement twists, is established.

POPOFF: It must be mentioned that the US edition of the album has a different track list, the most significant difference being the inclusion of a pretty famed single for the band, "See Emily Play." What is the significance of that song?

KEHAYAS: Besides being one of the greatest singles in the history of rock? It is the moment where they crystallize everything that was great in the early Floyd, and got it within three minutes. It's a cynical song, and people tend to miss that Syd was a cynic.

But it's filtered through childlike tendencies. I always look at Donovan, for example, as a wide-eyed childlike character, but rarely do you see a wink and gesture from him. But there's a lot of apprehension underneath many Syd Barrett songs, and "See Emily Play" is one of those. It's about a young girl, as I understand it, who was a dilettante on the scene, and it's perfect lyrically and musically, with the sped-up tracks and the piano bit, which, incidentally, XTC used on "Omnibus" from *Nonsuch*. They went, "Ah! We'll borrow this melody—it's perfect."

POPOFF: We'd be remiss if we didn't discuss "Astronomy Domine" and "Interstellar Overdrive," sort of the twin engines of the band's dark space sound we'd get more of next album.

DUNAWAY: When I dropped the needle on this record in 1967, "Astronomy Domine" was, of course, the first thing I heard, and my very first impression of this song, and of Pink Floyd, was the heavy use of echo effects, which sort of dominated the mix, although Syd's harmonies somehow cut through. I learned later that he did this with what was called ADT—automatic double tracking.

Now, that odd rhythm of the vocal phrasing, the way it breaks out into a catchy descending vocal thing, the Alice Cooper group did that on "Levity Ball" on our first album, *Pretties for You*. That song was our big tribute to Syd-era Floyd, in a way.

But back to "Astronomy Domine." Then the song stops abruptly and in comes this sparse organ part that reintroduces the song, but without vocals—very different from accepted song arrangements of that era. In that respect, I felt a kindred connection to what the Alice Cooper group were doing.

Original UK seven-inch pressings of Pink Floyd's first two non-album singles, "Arnold Layne" and "See Emily Play."

"Interstellar Overdrive" is a different style of song than the other songs that Syd wrote by himself. Man, our light show guy, Charlie Carnal, used to play that song over and over. I agree, it's more like the direction of the second album. So, you had this texture again, but also Syd's erratic guitar playing. Whenever he gets going, it's like total abandon, but still spacey.

You have to also keep in perspective when this is happening. Toward the tail end of the British invasion, a lot of bands—Soft Machine, Cream—were changing from the type of pop songs that the Beatles and the Stones were doing. This was also the era when electronic composers were becoming more well known. Just before *Saucerful of Secrets* was released, *2001: A Space Odyssey* came out. The soundtrack to that was very electronic music–oriented.

But I liked Floyd's harder-hitting songs the most, where the bass would lock in and there'd be that erratic, anxious feel mostly due to Syd's guitar playing. When he would do that, the other guys would kind of up the ante as well. For example, I liked "Pow R. Toc H." because it was heavier and more in-your-face. With a lot of the bass parts Roger didn't really use his low string very much and neither did I. And most every other bass player out there was trying to keep the bass down in this bigger, lower register. But like I say, it's hard to pick favorites because the feels would change rapidly from passage to passage, all within a short time, the time of a radio single, essentially.

TOP: Waters, Mason, Barrett, and Wright pose in front of a mixing desk at EMI Studios, London.

INSET: A special twelve-inch pressing of *Piper's* centerpiece, "Interstellar Overdrive," as released for Record Store Day 2017.

alexis korner
alex harvey
creation
charlie brown's
clowns
champion jack
dupree
denny laine
gary farr
graham bond
ginger johnson
jacobs ladder
construction co.
move
one one seven
pink floyd
poetry band
purple gang
pretty things
pete townshend
poison bellows
soft.machine
'sun trolley
social deviants
stalkers
the utterly incredible
too long ago
to remember
sometimes shouting
at people
marc sullivan
martin doughty
maureen pape
john pape
mike stocks
noel murphy
dave russell
christopher logue
barry fantoni
ron geeson
john fahey
mike horowitz
alex trocchi
mike kenshall
yoko ono
binder edwards
& vaughan
26 kingly street
the flies
robert randall

international times
free speech benefit
alexandra palace N.22
8pm saturday
29 april»sun30
tickets £1
in advance»only

indica better books colletts
dobells dave curtis 57 greek
st w.1 ger 1548 and main
it distributors
or your local agent

14 HOUR TECHNICOLOR DREAM

bus shuttle from wood green ⊖
highgate ⊖ 8:12pm

KEHAYAS: I think everybody involved didn't want "Interstellar Overdrive" to be on the album—except for the band. There are all sorts of really goofy things there, like the stereo panning, but we're dealing with a distillation and an edited version of what they would do live. I've talked to people that saw the Floyd live at that point, and they said their songs could last a half hour. So, "Interstellar Overdrive" is the closest thing to the live Floyd experience on *Piper*. It touches down on those improvisational bands like AMM I mentioned earlier. There's no song structure, so to speak, although in a sense it's very jazz, isn't it? There's a head and then the soloing and then it goes back to the head at the very end.

POPOFF: "The Gnome," "Chapter 24," "Scarecrow," and "Bike" almost seem like a set, like we're transitioning to a Syd Barrett solo album at this point. What do you think of that idea?
KEHAYAS: The album does come down off "Interstellar Overdrive" into that, so I guess that would be the whimsical side of the Floyd. Interestingly enough, the band supports it perfectly. Sure, I would probably say that if "Interstellar Overdrive" is the antithesis of the Syd Barrett solo experience, you're right. Perhaps these four songs form the core of the whimsical Syd Barrett, the same guy who later wrote "Effervescing Elephant."

And it's a decidedly English experience. This is the other thing we have to point out, is that, like Ray Davies, Syd gave an interesting voice to English youth. You don't have to be Roger Daltrey, who sounded like he desperately wanted to be a soul singer from Detroit. It's sung in the vernacular of the people who were making it as opposed to trying to sound like they were from another culture.

ABOVE: Rehearsing for the "Games for May" show at the Queen Elizabeth Hall, London, May 12, 1967. The concert would make use of quadrophonic sound.

OPPOSITE: A poster for the "14 Hour Technicolor Dream," which took place at Alexandra Palace, London, on April 29, 1967.

Wright and Barrett onstage at the International Love-In Festival at Alexandra Palace, London, July 29, 1967.

It's very European or British, which is interesting, coming from a band that basically had its roots in blues and jazz and R&B. To take that completely on its head and say, "I'm not going to do an approximation of that." It's the same thing that happened with the Fairport Convention. They so desperately wanted to be American and were covering Leonard Cohen and Richard Fariña. Interestingly enough, that was one of the bands Joe Boyd had a lot to do with. But Joe would say to them, "Okay, you're great, you do them okay, but you're not as good as the people you're covering."

It's interesting to note what gets leveled at progressive rock, that it's songs about gnomes and songs about fairies—that's what Syd is writing about. It's more fantastical than one would realize. Though the last one there, "Bike," has none of that. Some people think it's kind of sad because it sounds like a man kind of going crackers. But does it point the way to the kid's madness, or is this madness something that gets exacerbated with his adventures down the line? I know people who feel very weird listening to it. It's like Ian Curtis: they listen and read things into Joy Division records because of what eventually happened to him. But I believe wholeheartedly that these are things that interested Syd.

POPOFF: Dennis, any final tracks you wanted to point out as cool on here?
DUNAWAY: I like "Matilda Mother," which begins pretty mellow but is still sort of urgent. There's the Rick Wright organ in there, but it shifts into a Middle Eastern belly dance feel and then Syd's guitar segues right back into another verse. It's cool how it goes back to the original intimate feel as if you've been sent on a soaring journey and now you're being set gently back down.

Rick is a big part of "Flaming" as well, where there's that dissonant organ chord and a siren-like effect, but it's set against a pretty smooth vocal from Syd. And it's weird—the cuckoo clock sound makes the craziness of the album or Syd's world, however you want to take it, sort of lighthearted. Not so much that you want to be in that strange world, but it makes you feel comfortable enough to listen along from the outside.

Like I say, "Matilda Mother" is three minutes, "Flaming" is even less, and those are almost like Elvis Presley single lengths, like AM radio length. But, those songs go through so many changes that it seems like you're hearing a lot more than you're hearing in that short amount of time.

POPOFF: So, sum it up for me. How important is *The Piper at the Gates of Dawn* in rock history? How much should we care?
KEHAYAS: It's one of the few psychedelic records that bears repeated listening. The textures and sounds on the album are fantastic. Norman Smith basically outdid himself with getting a unique-sounding record. Compare the sound of this record to *Revolver*. Not many records were done in Studio 3, and *Piper* has the same sort of rocking tendencies that *Revolver* has.

Which is interesting. Geoff Emerick has basically said that Studio 2 was a cleaner-sounding studio, and that the difference between the recording of *Sgt. Pepper* and the recording of *Revolver* is the cleaner sound of the larger studio. *Piper* rocks in ways that it wouldn't have if they would've recorded it in a larger, different studio. So, it's four-track recording done at the same time that the Beatles were in the studio. I can imagine it was incredibly overwhelming for everyone involved, and most importantly for Syd.

I know that when I first started getting into Pink Floyd, *The Piper at the Gates of Dawn* was an album that was not talked about. It was out of print for a long time. It was available in a really strange form on *A Nice Pair*, because in Canada and the US they substituted "Astronomy Domine" with the live version from *Ummagumma*. It wasn't available for the longest time and it always got the lowest ratings out of any Pink Floyd record. There was always this slight bias toward later Pink Floyd and a bias against Barrett-era Pink Floyd.

Time has proven that there was an embarrassment of riches in *Piper*. I'm not one of those who listens only to Barrett-era Floyd. I listen to all periods of it, though I probably drop off after Waters leaves. But *Piper* is as valid as anything that came out. It's as valid as Tomorrow's first record, it's as valid as the Pretty Things' *S.F. Sorrow*, it's as valid as the Zombies' *Odessey and Oracle*. And *Sgt. Pepper*—I put it in that kind of company. I don't put it in Pink Floyd company—I put it in with the best of what we would consider to be psychedelic freakbeat. It's a monumental record.

Three more landmark releases from psychedelic rock's heyday: the Pretty Things's *S.F. Sorrow*, Tomorrow's self-titled debut, and the Zombies's *Odessey and Oracle*.

CHAPTER 2

A SAUCERFUL OF SECRETS

WITH CRAIG BAILEY AND
DENNIS DUNAWAY

SIDE I
1. Let There Be More Light   5:32
   (Waters)
2. Remember a Day   4:25
   (Wright)
3. Set the Controls for the Heart of the Sun
   (Waters)   5:19
4. Corporal Clegg   4:06
   (Waters)

SIDE 2
1. A Saucerful of Secrets   11:49
   (Waters, Wright, Mason, Gilmour)
2. See-Saw   4:29
   (Wright)
3. Jugband Blues   2:58
   (Barrett)

Recorded at EMI Recording Studios, St. John's Wood, London; De Lane Lea Studios, Holborn, London

PERSONNEL: Roger Waters—bass guitar, percussion, vocals; Richard Wright—piano, organ, Mellotron, vibraphone, xylophone, tin whistle, vocals; Nick Mason—drums, percussion, kazoo, vocals; David Gilmour—guitar, kazoo, vocals; Syd Barrett—guitar, vocals

Produced by Norman Smith

Released June 29, 1968

With only one Syd Barrett original ("Jugband Blues"), and his playing on the album occasional and inconsequential, *A Saucerful of Secrets* sounds much more like Pink Floyd's debut, with the spacier and more atmospheric direction that would mark the next three albums like a lazy comet.

The album was recorded in sessions during which Syd was still part of the band, as well as into spring 1968 when he was ousted, David Gilmour having been added in January to play parts while Syd wandered the stage. Then, on their way to a gig on January 26, the band asked, "Should we pick up Syd?" The answer at that point was why bother?

All told, Syd has part in three songs on the album: "Remember a Day," "Jugband Blues," and "Set the Controls for the Heart of the Sun," while David has part in five (although, really, to no discernible effect). Syd or not, the band was still writing very much in the vein of *The Piper at the Gates of Dawn*, believing against the rushing reality that they were still that band.

As for trivia, one of the songs that Gilmour appears on, "Corporal Clegg," a sort of heavy Beatles (kazoo notwithstanding), features a Nick Mason vocal. Nick, for his part, looks at the album fondly, if mainly for the reason that it marked a poetic and gradual transition from Syd to David. He might also ring chuffed about it because a studied spin reveals much vigor and note density from Mason all over the album. Also of interest, "Set the Controls for the Heart of the Sun," a hypnotic raga of sorts, is the only song where all five members are featured, serving as microcosm for Mason's view of the record. The track has become a perennial favorite—and how could it not be with a title like that?

"Set the Controls" was one of the first songs recorded for the album, at sessions on August 7 and 8, 1967, that also produced a non-LP composition called "Scream Thy Last Scream." Into the new year, organ from Rick was overdubbed onto the "Set the Controls" beds, as were vocals from Roger and eventually guitar from David. The track would be celebrated anew come *Ummagumma*, in live rendition, as would the title track, which here dominates side two, the Floyd turning in twelve minutes of instrumental demarcated into five parts, building on the debut's "Interstellar Overdrive" and setting a trajectory for longer epics to come.

The lead single was "Let There Be More Light," dark and haunting space rock similar to "Set the Controls" but slightly livelier. This was backed by "Remember a Day," one of the album's more pastoral songs and an outtake from the *Piper* sessions.

Toward the dark side of the record, those still attentive after the title track heard "See-Saw," perhaps the strongest telegraphing of Gilmour-era Floyd— not less melodic, exactly, but more obscure and challenging of melody. It's quite a contrast to album-closer "Jugband Blues," on which the kazoo returns, along with the Salvation Army band and those upright and evident Beatle-esque melodies for which Syd was known. The first-person lyrics and the cacophonous way it disintegrates into a false ending, followed by Syd isolated and fading with his acoustic, serve as a quiet and mindful closing of the door on Syd, two collaborative (of necessity) and sad solo albums notwithstanding.

POPOFF: The big story with Pink Floyd's second album is that it's the transition from the Syd Barrett era to what I guess we'll call the Waters-Gilmour era. Give me a little bit of detail on how that went down.

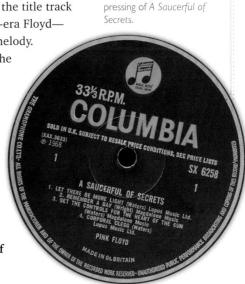

Label from the UK mono pressing of *A Saucerful of Secrets*.

BAILEY: Syd was the cofounder of the band, very big on *Piper at the Gates of Dawn*, but the cracks started to show early on. The consensus seems to be that he was prone to mental difficulties and that they were exacerbated by his drug use. In mid- to late 1967 it began to really be a problem; he was becoming unreliable and unpredictable. If you don't show up to a gig, that makes it difficult for your bandmates to move forward, be professional, and climb the ladder.

On the other hand, he wrote nearly everything and was the frontman. Ultimately, they decided that the only choice was to replace him. The first strategy was to maybe take a Brian Wilson approach where he would be a writer but he wouldn't tour. It didn't take long for them to figure out that wasn't going to work.

So, they brought in David Gilmour, who knew Syd since they were kids. For a very brief period, late '67 to early '68, they were a five-person band. There's one photo shoot, and in one picture, you see the four of them, and then standing in the back is Syd, and it's almost haunting, and obviously indicative of what was happening.

Syd and David were together in the band for a brief time, and *A Saucerful of Secrets*, interestingly, was smack in the middle of that. It was started in August of '67, and they finished it in May of '68. It seems to be that no one can say for sure which tracks Syd is actually on, although the consensus is "Set the Controls for the Heart of the Sun" includes both of them.

Syd writes only one track on *Saucerful of Secrets*, and it's really somewhat telling. It's like a little coda at the end of the album called "Jugband Blues." He says, "I'm wondering who could be writing this song." It seems to be a narrative of him acknowledging that he is in a difficult space and that he is being forced out of this band. There's a film clip that they made for that which is also quite haunting. Syd looks like a zombie. Well, for that matter, all of them look like zombies. Maybe they were trying to do that as an effect, but it's creepy to watch.

POPOFF: Dennis, you got to see this transition firsthand.
DUNAWAY: Yes, when they came to America, they stayed at our house. We lived in Santa Monica, because we played at this club in Venice, California, which was out on the pier—the Aragon Ballroom that Lawrence Welk made famous. We played there a lot, so we moved into a neighborhood that wasn't far from there.

Anyway, Pink Floyd stayed at our house, the five of them. We were pretty much all in the kitchen, both bands, Pink Floyd and Alice Cooper, with Neal Smith as well. Neal had just joined our group and we'd just become Alice Cooper at that point. I was sitting at a table and I was having a conversation with Syd Barrett, and he looked like he was completely hanging off every word I was

saying. When I would say something that solicited some kind of response, he wouldn't respond. Pretty soon I realized it was one of those kind of, you can wave your hand in front of his face and he doesn't move.

I went into shock. I had never seen that kind of a drug casualty before. He was a hero of ours. They had a roadie, Les Braden, and he walked up to me while I'm sitting there with Syd, and he said, "It's sad, isn't it?" and started talking about all of Syd's problems, right in front of him as if he wasn't there.

I saw his guitar, which was leaning in the corner in the kitchen, and it wasn't in the case. He had the strings set high because he played a lot of slide. But I went over and looked closely at it and everything was rusty. Les said that, as a roadie, he was in charge of making sure that Syd didn't wander off, because they couldn't find him a lot of times. He'd just walk away and Les found his guitar just laying out in the street in the rain.

We had an audition in L.A., the Alice Cooper group, at this club called Gazzarri's. We went down in the afternoon and played and our manager and the booker had left the room. There were tables and the only people there were Pink Floyd, without Syd. After we got done playing, we went over to the table and said, "Well, what did you think?" and Roger said, "It looks like a lot of fun." But their conversation was focused on, what are we going to do about Syd?

The first week or so of their tour was canceled, and they said it was because they hadn't gotten their work permits in order. Which may have been true, but I saw the show with Syd. He walked up to the microphone and he played for a while, but then at one point he walked up and he looked like he got his lip shocked on the microphone or something and then he just stood there. The rest of the band played the show and Syd kind of just stood there with his guitar.

So, there was this wonderful album we knew, the first one, *Piper at the Gates of Dawn*. The Alice Cooper group dove in and we knew every tiny nuance of it and loved it. Then we see them perform it live without the main ingredient. But it still sounded great. All of those sound effects that they do on the album, those weren't necessarily overdubs, they did all those *boom*, *shhh*, *whoop* sounds live. That was the guys making the various sounds with their vocals, vocalizing.

But moving into *A Saucerful of Secrets*, you're talking about a group that came up in England as a very poppy group, very happy and innocent, and then all of a sudden they quickly psychedelic-ized [*laughs*]. I assume they brought their audience with them, but they certainly went through some fast changes. It's such a shame that Syd was unable to participate; it's just tragic, what happened to him.

POPOFF: Speak a little more to this idea of *Saucerful* being darker than *Piper*. Build that argument for me.

BAILEY: I guess you've got to look at some of the individual tracks. *Piper*, to my ears, is just a much happier-sounding album. "Let There Be More Light," the first track on *Saucerful*, is kind of menacing, foreboding. You have these whispered vocals on top of the other vocals, and it's about aliens making contact on planet Earth. "Set the Controls for the Heart of the Sun," also kind of spooky.

"Corporal Clegg" is the first song Roger Waters wrote about war. Cynical, really, if you listen to the words. Corporal Clegg got a medal—he found it at the zoo. He didn't get a medal from the war, but he "won" a wooden leg. He was given a medal by the Queen, but that was in his dream. It's pretty dark and also indicative of what Roger would spend the rest of his career writing about, essentially.

There are probably two tracks on *Saucerful* that might be more similar to *Piper*. "Remember a Day" is a Rick Wright song, but interestingly a song that talks about the loss of childhood. Why can't we stay that way? In a sense, it's almost acknowledging that they've moved away from *Piper at the Gates of Dawn*. "See-Saw" is also maybe similar to *Piper*, although, in my opinion, probably one of the lower points of the album, not a particularly interesting song. In fact, the story goes that there was some sort of recording sheet where they were logging the songs and they called that one "The Most Boring Song I've Ever Heard Bar Two." I don't know what the other two were, but . . .

A 1968 US promotional edition of "Let There Be More Light," b/w "Remember a Day."

POPOFF: And Dennis, did you get a sense of darkness from Roger or David? Did you see anything in their personalities that would result in this kind of melancholic psych music?
DUNAWAY: They were all very polite, but they're not extroverts like the Alice Cooper group characters were [*laughs*]. I was very introverted at the time, so I could relate. But if you talked to any of them, they were quite friendly. But it wasn't so much that they would strike up a conversation. Roger Waters went over to our refrigerator and opened it to see what to eat, and all we had was a gigantic bag of carrots [*laughs*], and we were all joking around about that, so it wasn't like they were above having fun and stuff. But they were preoccupied with what they were going to do. Because here they were, the first time to America, and Syd wasn't functioning like he needed to in order to do a tour. There was a lot on their minds.

Another time, we're sitting there, Neal is there and Syd is just kind of stationary at the table while other conversations are going on. Then all of a sudden, for no other reason, Syd gets up abruptly and walks through the kitchen, through everybody. And he goes into the living room, where the lights were dimmed. I don't know why, but we just hardly ever used that living room. It was more like a place where somebody would sleep on the couch once in a while. So, Neal and I walked in there to see where he was going, and he had gone all the way across the room until he got to the corner, and he just stopped there, with his face to the corner, just stood there by himself. Les Braden came over and said, "This is what we're dealing with now."

POPOFF: This sort of cast a pall over your potential enjoyment of *A Saucerful of Secrets*, I imagine. How did you receive that record in light of the situation?
DUNAWAY: After seeing Syd's condition, when *Saucerful* came out it had a very emotional impact on me, because it's very sad for me to hear the change in style. As I mentioned, on *Piper* you had the feeling on some of those songs, like "Chapter 24" and "The Gnome," that you were very close, that Syd was right in front of you singing and you could almost hear his thoughts.

The new boy: Dave Gilmour onstage at the Paradiso, Amsterdam, the Netherlands, May 1968.

But then on *Saucerful*, everything is far away; the vocals are far away, almost timid. Even though it got more spacey, it got more relaxed. It was more like you were traveling through space, but it didn't have that erratic urgency that *Piper* had. Therefore, one of the elements I liked the most was now missing. When you get all the way to the end of the album, here is Syd again, and you go, "Oh great, now it sounds like Pink Floyd again."

But the lyrics to "Jugband Blues" kind of spell out the situation. It's not clear that I'm here, and who's writing this song if I'm not here? You get this biting insight into his feelings on the situation. But somehow this song jumps out like an old friend, as if maybe that happy chorus is telling us it's going to be relatively okay. Syd says, "I don't care if the sun don't shine," while there's this psychedelic marching parade going on. Then everything screeches to a stop and Syd is asking what exactly is a joke? Very odd. Anyway, it's great that Pink Floyd included that, and it's great that they would go back on later albums like *Wish You Were Here* and do a whole album with all these references to Syd.

As far as me missing the urgency that was on *Piper*, when *Saucerful* came out, it took a long time for me to let go of that, and then I could enjoy what they had done. It's also important to keep in mind that bands couldn't change a member and get away with it. The Stones did, but most bands, if they changed one member they lost their fanbase. Pink Floyd were still underground, but there were a lot of Syd Barrett fans who had to jump the shark to keep on board with them. Without the guys really explaining what happened, people had to put two and two together. The band didn't go out and say, "Well, Syd's not functioning anymore."

POPOFF: Would you say, perhaps, that *Saucerful* isn't particularly more radical, but that maybe it reflected more closely than *Piper* what the band was like live?

BAILEY: Yes, I'd align with that. They've always had this odd duality. They would write and record and perform these, I hate to say the word "cute," but little pop ditties, right? Like "See Emily Play." At the same time, they would launch into this twenty-minute, bizarre, freaked-out instrumental. They always had two sides to the coin that might rub one or the other person the wrong way. You would be glad to see this new band called the Pink Floyd with this great hit single, and after three minutes of hearing the hit single, it's "Interstellar Overdrive" for twenty minutes. So, it's not so crazy on *A Saucerful of Secrets* that they took this darker turn and had these long, drawn-out instrumentals. That was always part of their DNA.

POPOFF: What are some other points of interest worth mentioning on the record, if you were to take someone on a tour of the album?

BAILEY: Back to "Corporal Clegg," the words and the way they are sung, it's sneering and quite angry. You've got the wah-wah guitar, and then the kazoos come in, and that's one of the better tracks on the album. I get a kick out of it. My favorite part, actually, is when all hell breaks loose for much of the back end of it, and if you listen carefully they're all singing the chorus and somebody is laughing. Somebody just peals out a wicked laugh, and I smile every time I hear that. It sounds like they're having a great time.

And we talked about "Jugband Blues," but I like that Syd has his thing where things can be childlike and frivolous, and in the middle of this song it sort of falls apart. The Salvation Army band was brought in to play here and they wanted to know what Syd wanted them to play, and he said play anything [*laughs*]. I think someone else kind of stepped in and said, well, here's what we

Poster advertising Pink Floyd's appearance—alongside Cream, Traffic, and the Small Faces—at the Houtrusthallen.

think you should do. But it's a little more whimsical and fairy tale–ish, like "The Gnome" on *Piper*, at least musically.

POPOFF: The track with the greatest longevity here is probably "Set the Controls for the Heart of the Sun." But it's pretty radical. Are you surprised the label let them put songs like this on the album?
DUNAWAY: I'm surprised the label let them do a lot of stuff. They were innovative and out there, but they had proven themselves with their singles in England and I'm sure that gave them license to do more. EMI also had the Beatles, so being experimental—that road was paved by the Beatles. EMI was very strict in the early days—short sleeves, tie, ballpoint pen in your pocket—and the Beatles got more and more experimental and more and more successful to the point where nobody could say no to them when they wanted to do something crazy in the studio.

Well, Pink Floyd came along right after the Beatles had already proven that's how EMI is going to make money. But if you were a record executive, you're going, "Where's the single?" [*laughs*]. But as far as the length of songs, back then AM radio was singles, but FM, that's where you were allowed long, drawn-out, sprawling songs. So, the record company probably thought that's okay, because with FM radio, you got the chance to get that kind of play, and that sold albums too, just like AM play.

But "Set the Controls" live . . . as I mentioned earlier, when you first heard these albums, you would think there were a lot of overdubs but there weren't. When they played live, it sounded very much like the record. But when I saw "Set the Controls" it was Roger and that bass line that grabbed me. It was so persistent and mesmerizing. Roger's voice sounded like he was whispering even though he wasn't. The feeling was, to me, you're in outer space with this guy [*laughs*]. And he's thinking thoughts to himself. That bass part was so nonvarying, just coming at you and it would go forever. In German film, they have a concept called stimmüng where they would have a scene where somebody would be sitting on the bed, usually some heavy thing where they were crying or whatever, and the camera was just on them forever [*laughs*]. Today, you wouldn't do that, but back then, sure. The idea was that they would force you to start thinking about what the person was thinking. That's what this was like. You were forced to really be drawn into this thing. They didn't give you anywhere to escape.

On a lot of these, like "Let There Be More Light" and "Set the Controls," there are bass parts that are very repetitive. The Alice Cooper group would do that if we were jamming and looking for some kind of pocket that we could build a song around, but we would not stay on any groove very long; Pink Floyd would find a groove and stay on it longer than anybody at that time.

And that's what gave them that appeal where fans could sit back and absorb the entire album. Nowadays it's hard to find a kid that will even play a full song. So, *Saucerful* is very spacey, and the fact that Roger favors those high notes on the bass gives it this airy feeling. If he was playing the same part but much lower, it wouldn't have that flying-through-space feel.

POPOFF: Of course, way crazier than these is the title track, a twelve-minute instrumental.
BAILEY: It's your classic early Floyd instrumental with multiple movements. Roger told *Rolling Stone* that the concept was the depiction of a battle where you have the lead-up, the actual battle, and then the aftermath and the mourning for the dead. Apparently, he and Nick, both architecture majors, mapped this thing out, not in musical notes, but in their own shorthand. They drew this graph with peaks and valleys and stuff.

I like it. There's a part where we hear a repeating drum loop, over and over, and it becomes mesmerizing. On top of that, you've got all this crazy stuff going on with guitar where it just kind of ploughs you away. After that it gets all quiet. Then you have this church-like organ. They take you on this incredible trip, and then they gently, carefully, put you back down on planet Earth and now you're safe again [*laughs*].
DUNAWAY: This is more like electronic music composition with an emphasis on melding sound textures rather than notes and scales. Those drums of Nick's swell up and pull you deep into the mix while there's all this experimental

Wright, Gilmour, Waters, and Mason in Stockholm, September 15, 1968.

whining and squealing and scraping. Again, there's a spacey feeling, although there's also kind of an eerie angels-in-a-cathedral effect.

POPOFF: To wrap up, what do the more studious Pink Floyd fans out there think of *A Saucerful of Secrets*? It's certainly of a pairing with *Piper*, no?

BAILEY: What's important is that Pink Floyd was able to transition—right here, but also moving forward. You couldn't continue to do music like *The Piper at the Gates of Dawn* in the '70s. I don't want to say it was a fad, but it was indicative of the time. We had all moved on from that. If you didn't have the talent, ability, or willingness to move on from that, you didn't continue, probably. *The Piper at the Gates of Dawn* is now seen as the quintessential British pop psychedelic album . . . it's almost the stereotype, but Floyd invented the stereotype.

As for *Saucerful*, it's funny. Just last night I was digging around and I read the original *Rolling Stone* review—you can find it online—and they crapped on it. I don't think they had anything nice to say. I would be willing to bet if you asked *Rolling Stone* today, "What about *A Saucerful of Secrets*?" they would be much kinder. When you see the whole picture and you see where things headed and where things ended up, it's much easier to be kind.

As far as fans go, the type of people that I deal with—having done my Floyd radio show for about thirty years—they're pretty diehard, and *Saucerful* certainly is a pretty well-liked album by the diehard fan. Certainly as much as *The Division Bell* and *A Momentary Lapse of Reason*, but then again, these two camps rarely see eye to eye.

CHAPTER 3

MORE

WITH PAUL KEHAYAS AND JEFF WAGNER

SIDE 1

1. Cirrus Minor   5:13
   (Waters)
2. The Nile Song   3:21
   (Waters)
3. Crying Song   3:25
   (Waters)
4. Up the Khyber   2:08
   (Mason, Wright)
5. Green Is the Colour   2:54
   (Waters)
6. Cymbaline   4:45
   (Waters)
7. Party Sequence   1:05
   (Waters, Wright, Gilmour, Mason)

SIDE 2

1. Main Theme   5:24
   (Waters, Wright, Gilmour, Mason)
2. Ibiza Bar   3:14
   (Waters, Wright, Gilmour, Mason)
3. More Blues   2:47
   (Waters, Wright, Gilmour, Mason)
4. Quicksilver   6:27
   (Waters, Wright, Gilmour, Mason)
5. A Spanish Piece   1:00
   (Gilmour)
6. Dramatic Theme   2:20
   (Waters, Wright, Gilmour, Mason)

Recorded at Pye Studios, Marble Arch, London

PERSONNEL: Roger Waters—bass guitar, tape effects, percussion; Richard Wright—organ, piano, vibraphone, backing vocals; David Gilmour—guitar, percussion, lead vocals; Nick Mason—drums, percussion

Produced by Pink Floyd

Released June 15, 1969

Against the cosmic dust storm of "Interstellar Overdrive," "A Saucerful of Secrets," and *Ummagumma* yet to come, the sum total of the soundtrack *More*, despite its filmy cover (Hipgnosis's fifth ever) and equally filmy backstory, is as relevant as any other pre–*Dark Side* record in the band's confounding canon.

A fairly professional hippie film produced by Jean-Luc Godard protégé Barbet Schroeder, *More* tells the story of a German boy, Stefan, who hitchhikes to Paris and from there follows an American temptress named Estelle to sunny, free, and fun Ibiza, where she turns him on to naked sunbathing and hard drugs. Stefan overdoses on heroin and dies, providing cautionary overtones that made the project okay

in the band's book. In addition, Roger and Rick could relate to the Ibiza locale of the tale, having vacationed there in 1967 and been greeted as freakbeat heroes by the British expat hippies hanging about.

Floyd's involvement in the project—the money was pretty good, the guys intent on breaking into film—would prove a boon for the band's stature in France, where the movie became a youth culture favorite. The attendant soundtrack is a cogent fit for the many moods of the film—checking off boxes, but in the process, given its jagging dynamics, also emerging as an independent experimental rock album.

On the instrumental tack, we get Nick Mason pounding away like a caveman, hustling to keep up with an avant-jazz premise. We also get a rare bit of Spanish guitar from David, as well as typical soundtrack bits that, in retrospect, represent a slab of bedrock with respect to the cinematic devices that would soon make Floyd famed.

An odd happenstance is that all the vocals on the album (across essentially six songs proper) are performed by Gilmour, one in a near-falsetto, two as regular folk færie, and two with uncommon aggression. Forsooth, "The Nile Song" and its loud bang of an echo track "Ibiza Bar" are no more than past-their-due-date metal à la Hendrix, MC5, and Blue Cheer, due in part to Gilmour's completely uncharacteristic roar.

ABOVE: An undated portrait of Pink Floyd taken around the time the band made *More*.

BELOW: Label from the 1969 Italian release of the *More* soundtrack, along with a Japanese pressing on red vinyl from the following year.

"Cirrus Minor," "Crying Song," "Green is the Colour," and Cymbaline," all written by a Roger Waters still vibrating to the tune and tone of Syd Barrett, represent dark and contemplative mellow music—from bad trip to pastoral England—that the band address from *Piper* through *Obscured by Clouds*. These songs are the bridge, poetically so, given that *More* is the first album from the classic Floyd lineup, who produced the ragged collection themselves (of note—two songs heard in the film, "Seagulls" and "Hollywood," are not included on the album). As for the strength of the material, the band sufficiently appreciated "Green is the Colour" and "Cymbaline" enough to include them in their live set for a couple years.

Ergo, *More* is a record in three parts, and although the number of parts may vary, this compartmentalization mechanism would be applied to the band's next four records.

More saw wide international issue, including in the US, where, upon its reissue in 1973, it crept onto the charts at #153. On home turf, upon release in the summer of '69, the album managed a respectable #9. Its fortunes hinged on release of "The Nile Song" as a single (backed with "Ibiza Bar"), as well as a ramp-up clutch of standalone sides that kept the band in the entertainment papers. The band would capitalize on the situation, working with Schroeder again on *La Vallée*, which resulted in a second soundtrack album: *Obscured by Clouds*.

A French pressing of the soundtrack to Michelangelo Antonioni's *Zabriskie Point*, to which Pink Floyd contributed, and a poster advertising the film's release in early 1970.

POPOFF: This is a soundtrack to a movie called *More*. What are your thoughts on the film?

KEHAYAS: I thought the movie was typical hippie fare from the '60s. It's about a guy who falls in love with a woman who's a junkie—played by Mimsy Farmer—and they wind up in Spain. It's got a real sinister overtone to it. The music worked really well with it, but I don't think it's a wholly successful movie. It's effective but it's not a masterpiece of cinema.

I think the album works as a soundtrack to anything. That's just the whole point. Good soundtrack music or impressionist music—which is what I consider this to be—can work with your own pictures. When I first listened to it, I didn't know what the music was about, which was fine.

WAGNER: This was an era when Floyd were doing several soundtracks. Anybody who is into Floyd from this era can hear why. They just had a very cinematic, theatrical sound. It's not your basic pop stuff, so it does lend itself well to movies. There was a short film called *The Committee* back in 1968. Hardly anybody knows about that—one of their first bits of soundtrack work. You had *Zabriskie Point*, of course. They weren't the sole soundtrack, but they were a key part of

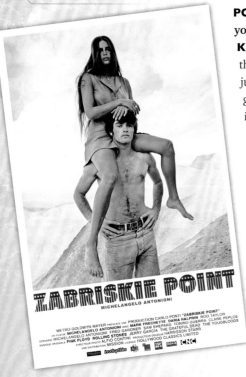

it. Later, you get *Obscured by Clouds*, which was also a soundtrack. But yeah, they got in with movie people who started giving them work. I saw the movie *More* a long time ago when I first got into Floyd, just out of curiosity. I didn't love the movie, which is a typical '60s drug abandon sort of movie. But the Floyd songs done for it just kind of run as an album; you don't need any reference to the movie to enjoy it. It's a pretty strong piece of work, generally.

POPOFF: Would you agree, Paul? Is *More* a valid Pink Floyd album?
KEHAYAS: I think it is. I know that they probably don't assume it is. It's the third record they made. But there are also a couple of non-LP singles that happen around this time, just before they start the soundtrack to *More*. And this indicates the need to divorce from the whimsical that they had been in. In particular, there's a piece of tripe known as "It Would Be So Nice," which, granted, comes out before *Saucerful*, April of '68. Awful, awful, awful. This is what happens when you get the architecture students and their new recruit to try to write a song in the style of the whimsical Barrett. It is possibly the worst song of any notoriety that that band ever came up with. It's so wrongheaded for them. It's trying to be a pop single. It's so saccharine it's ridiculous.

And there was another single that came out after, in December of '68, just before they started recording *More*, called "Point Me at the Sky," which was slightly better. But at this moment a soundtrack is requested of them. They go into, interestingly, not EMI, but Pye Studios and are using various other low-budget studios, or other studios that are not necessarily associated with EMI's main studio. They go in to work on this rather impressionistic batch of songs. And you can tell that there's a lot of freedom, because they are experimenting with, effectively, having no song structure (although some songs do have structure). They also allow themselves to sound different than they used to. There are some really, really wonderful songs on this thing. And one curious fact: their lead singer on every song is David Gilmour, even if he didn't write them. This is the only album that Roger didn't sing any of them on, including his songs. Indeed, the first three songs—"Cirrus Minor," "The Nile Song," "Crying Song"—they're all Roger's. The only song that David writes by himself is "A Spanish Piece," which is a slight Spanish guitar thing and not really a song.

POPOFF: I guess it's no surprise that when *More* is remembered at all, it's for the fleshed-out songs. But it's funny, the fact that "The Nile Song" is pretty much everyone's pick for highlight—and it was even issued as a single—shows somewhat of a thirst for Pink Floyd to rock out of their shell almost, no?
WAGNER: Sure, I'd buy that idea. That's just a heavy, sludged-out bludgeon of a track. Voivod covered "The Nile Song" on *The Outer Limits*, and I don't think

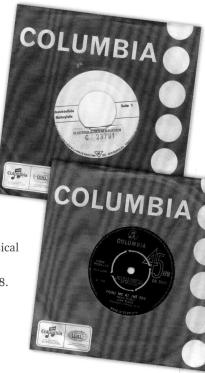

Two non-album singles. "It Would Be So Nice" was released shortly before *A Saucerful of Secrets* and is pictured here in a German test pressing. "Point Me at the Sky" was released in December 1968, just prior to the recording of *More*.

The only single drawn from *More* was "The Nile Song," pictured here in its Japanese release b/w "Main Theme."

it's nearly as good as the original. The original Floyd version of "The Nile Song" is just unbeatable. It's real heavy metal, and kind of like their "Helter Skelter."

It's got this thunderous, almost Bill Ward–esque type of drumming from Mason. But it's Floyd, so it's got certain nuances. I like the tortured, yearning vocals, that are just on the edge of breaking out in screaming, but then there are very covert, stealthy bass lines by Waters.

It's kind of reprised later on the album. I don't know if this is intentional or not, but with "Ibiza Bar," kind of like one rhythmic beat is changed up in that riff, where you go, well, it's not like "The Nile Song," it's a different thing. But it's clearly like the stepbrother of "The Nile Song." Not quite as heavy, but together the two create a theme, so that's a strong point.

KEHAYAS: That's a rocker, and I'd say it's the heaviest song they ever did. It's the one I always like to cover. I can never get anybody to do it solidly. But I love that song. It's the heaviest dumb-headed song they did, and was probably constructed in the studio in no time. But it's incredibly effective. Jeff is right, it's an incredibly close relative of "Ibiza Bar," which gets a four-person writing credit. So, I figure "Nile Song" came first, and then what's likely is the band jammed on it and came up with "Ibiza Bar" afterward. But these are two great pieces that sum up the main differences as to how they would play as a band, that they would be more muscular with David Gilmour in this group than with Syd Barrett. And it's the moment, I'd say, where they start to experiment with different styles. In other words, they could've been a great boneheaded band. But that's not going to happen.

POPOFF: At the far end of the spectrum is something like the opening track, "Cirrus Minor," pretty long and very, very quiet.
WAGNER: Yes, and maybe not the best choice for an opener for that reason. It's very spacey and mellow, on the longer side for an opener of this sort. Heavily sedated vocals, some really creepy organ; it's ambient. I don't recall there being any drums in there. There's birdsong; they seem to like birdsong a lot. And the end is a total drug trip thing, which dovetails nicely into the plot of the movie, which is an excursion into the world of heroin. So, as a piece for the movie it works well. The song itself is on the nice side of Floyd's mellower trip. I just don't know if it works that well as an album opener.
KEHAYAS: It's the moment where they start to sound like that intermediate period of Pink Floyd. It has atmosphere and it has creepiness, and it's definitely a different animal than previous recordings, signaling a great turnaround from the awfulness of "Point Me at the Sky" and attempts to sound like a hit band. They've given up trying to sound like they're writing singles, that's the main thing. The freeing thing is, we don't have to write a single, therefore we're not. So, I'd

disagree and say "Cirrus Minor" is a wonderful way to start the record, beginning with birdsong sounds and ending with atonal organ—just really atmospheric. And, of course, it crashes into the next piece, "The Nile Song."

POPOFF: Where do we get the clearest glimpses of a future Floyd? After all, this is the record that marks a clear break with Syd, even though there's the complicating premise of it being side work, so to speak.
WAGNER: "Cymbaline" is kind of classic Floyd. To me, if I'm comparing it to things that came later, it's always reminded me of a mixture of like "Planet Caravan" by Sabbath and "Then Came the Last Days of May" by Blue Öyster Cult. It's a little more optimistic and brighter than those, but it's got that kind of sway and momentum to it, kind of easy, but a little bit like you're looking over your shoulder in paranoia.

There's also a reference to the music business, which is interesting because they later did "Have a Cigar." It's curious to hear them mention that stuff in lyrics this early. I love the lyrical reference to Doctor Strange. I'm not sure what the actual context is there, but it always gives me chills and I don't know why. I just think it's a well-placed line, a nice bit of poetry. But I just love the vibe and the atmosphere of "Cymbaline"; it's all about the emotion.
KEHAYAS: "Cymbaline," yes, wonderful track about a nightmare, if I'm not mistaken, that Waters had. Plus, a bit about the manager and agent. They would use this live. This is the point where they would do the quadraphonic sound that they were working on and had used in the original group. But now they would start to do all sorts of creepy things, like stop for minutes and people would just be sitting there listening to somebody walking around the perimeter of the hall to come back to the stage. They had something they called an azimuth coordinator; on the DVD portion of the box set, they have somebody explaining it and you get to see it. I never even knew what it looked like. It's these two total 360-degree joysticks—amazing.

POPOFF: And "Green is the Colour" is interesting, with the almost falsetto-type singing, along with some, I guess they class it as tin whistle, provided by Nick's wife Lindy.
WAGNER: Yeah, and I wonder if it was written much earlier. Because it harkens back to those earlier pop singles that the Floyd—*the* Pink Floyd—would put out, right? It's just got that mood. It's wistful, it's dreamy, there's some sweetness to it, there's those piccolo or recorder sounds in there. At the end it kind of fades out. As you say, the vocal is kind of interesting. So, this one sticks out to me. Not in a bad way; it adds depth to the album, in that you get a little glimpse of maybe earlier Floyd.
KEHAYAS: I like it; it's effective. Again, they'll try out anything. This one's an experimental song. "Green is the Colour" depicts their version of England that we see across the first two records, emerging in that sort of childhood-steeped *Wind in the Willows* kind of way. I get the impression it's a young man's version of a "getting it together in the country" kind of vibe, a slightly more mature look at what a retreat to a smaller place would look like, what "not London" would feel like [*laughs*].

Then they do other songs on the record like "Crying Song," which is lovely, and where we start to see the interaction of these vocalists. It's probably Rick Wright and David Gilmour singing together, one of these spots where the harmonies start to emerge between those two; pretty sure that's them.

POPOFF: Is "Up the Khyber" one of the more memorable bits from the instrumental or soundtrack end of things? After all, it's nice to see Nick get some room to blow.

WAGNER: Yeah, I like "Up the Khyber." That's one of the more successful bits of instrumental. I don't know if you would call it improv, but there is certainly jazz piano with semirandom strikes and accents. It's kind of a swirling, twisting track.

KEHAYAS: That's cool. It's not something you run to play at a party, like, "Hey everyone, listen to this wonderful piece." But it has a texture and it's interesting enough that when it's playing, you're like, oh, okay, something interesting is happening there.

POPOFF: I always thought "More Blues" didn't fit the spirit of the album *or* the movie, or even the band for that matter. All three were about fearless exploration, and this is as traditional as it gets.

WAGNER: Yeah, I've always called "More Blues" "Less Blues" because I wish it wasn't on the album at all. It's kind of a throwaway. It's short, inconsequential. I'm not sure it works. As you're listening through the album, it seems like this is the time to get up and get a coffee or a beer.

Record producer Norman Smith worked with Pink Floyd through the period 1967–1969.

KEHAYAS: I like the way "More Blues" is recorded. I don't think it's particularly inspiring, but I'm always sucked into how deep the thing sounds. It represents for me the first element of the classic Pink Floyd idea of slowing . . . down . . . everything. And that's an interesting thing to note—Pink Floyd would start to slow stuff down. That's the secret for them to be able to put sound effects all over things. Because if it's too fast, you can't do that. So, "More Blues" has that very languid beat, but it's not particularly the most wonderful composition.

To me this album is more about color and shading rather than actual writing. Whereas the earlier works, the majority are about the songwriting—of one member. These guys hadn't really gotten the knack of writing amazing songs yet. Some of them are great, and I may like "The Nile Song," and I might say that if I was a DJ at a party, I would throw that one on. But even that's not a meisterwork of songwriting. That will come later.

POPOFF: Any other spots of magic among the instrumental material?

WAGNER: "Main Theme" is really good. Very soundtrack-y and has a similar drone and bass line as "Careful with That Axe, Eugene." It also reminds me of that Italian band Goblin, who were a soundtrack band for the most part. But it's got that dark wizardry to it.

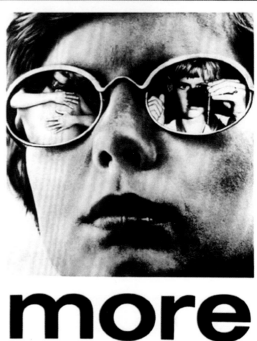

Two posters advertising Barbet Schroeder's *More*, a tale of drug addiction on the Spanish island of Ibiza.

"A Spanish Piece" is short, just a bit of Spanish guitar with some spiteful drunken gibberish over the top of it, which makes it kind of interesting.

But I really think "Quicksilver" is worth talking about, because it foreshadows the wackier experiments to come on *Ummagumma*. You know, manipulated sounds of what to me always sounds like a piano being systematically destroyed. I know it's not that, but that's the imagery I see—it's pretty jarring. So, that's the first part, and then you get a bit of a silence, and then the second part is just this various fussing about with soundscaping and cosmic atmosphere that again, they really pushed to the fore on *Ummagumma* and parts of *Meddle* and the *Live at Pompeii* performance. "Quicksilver" is pretty important in the realm of their sound experiments.

KEHAYAS: Influence-wise, they were listening to things that came into their orbit, just like you and I might do. It's not all necessarily great. There are some embarrassing moments later. In "A Spanish Piece," there's some really horrible stereotypical Spanish, somebody talking, obviously somebody in the group trying to sound Spanish.

"Dramatic Theme" is their version of jazz. Their version of cod jazz, as I like to call it. But in a sense it's still very much Pink Floyd–sounding. It's something that they were already doing; there were live segments with Syd Barrett where they did jazzy things.

POPOFF: What are they bringing to the table as far as interest, inspiration, influence? Psych music was growing up in the midst of what they called the British blues boom. And this is right at the point where psych is giving way to prog.

WAGNER: Most rock is based primarily on the blues, at its very root, so it's not very surprising. It's more interesting what they do with it. Like I said, on "Up the Khyber" you have this freeform critical mass, with piano tinkling and stabbing, basically intuitive or improv, not hard-written into sheet music or anything. They didn't map things out and that comes from the jazz world.

As for classical, I don't know. We hear the first real signs of classical on *Atom Heart Mother*, but that was largely due to Ron Geesin's influence, the guy who helped write and orchestrate that piece. I don't hear a ton of classical prior to that. Although you could argue things like Gustav Holst's "Planets" would probably have been very inspirational on these guys. In fact, having said that, I would put money on it.

Prog has its nexus, arguably, in the year *More* comes out—1969—because I've heard people say, "Well, Floyd weren't truly a prog rock band, because they didn't have the virtuosity of an ELP or a Yes" (although everybody knows Gilmour's

From left: Louise Wink, Klaus Grunberg, Mimsy Farmer in a still from *More*.

Ron Geesin, who first worked with Pink Floyd on the band's soundtrack to *More*, at his home studio in Ladbroke Grove, London, 1967.

a great guitarist). I guess what's true about that is, sure, maybe they weren't virtuoso level, or maybe they weren't putting it out there the way that those other bands did.

But people forget that with prog rock, it's just as important that the imagination is large and wide. And Floyd had massive imagination and massive creativity. Were they progressive rock? Absolutely. And, of course, a key characteristic of prog is a synthesis of genres, and Floyd absolutely took disparate musics and put them through their own filter. They have all the makings of a progressive rock band. Not that we need to label, but I don't like when people drop them out of that conversation just because they weren't virtuosos. Because again, the imagination is almost infinite.

KEHAYAS: Yes, I'd agree, and the way they do that right here on *More* . . . it's a difficult but pivotal record. It's more important than anybody wants to give it credit for. And if you look at the old *Rolling Stone* record review guides and the like, it'll get a one star—completely pigheaded. It's a record in need of reappraisal.

CHAPTER 4

UMMAGUMMA

WITH CRAIG BAILEY AND JEFF WAGNER

SIDE 1
1. Astronomy Domine   8:25
(Barrett)
2. Careful with That Axe, Eugene   8:47
(Waters, Wright, Mason, Gilmour)

SIDE 2
1. Set the Controls for the Heart of the Sun
(Waters)   9:21
2. A Saucerful of Secrets   12:51
(Waters, Wright, Mason, Gilmour)

SIDE 3
1. Sysyphus—Part 1; Part 2; Part 3; Part 4
(Wright)   13:28
2. Grantchester Meadows   7:23
(Waters)
3. Several Species of Small Furry Animals
Gathered Together in a Cave and
Grooving with a Pict   4:47
(Waters)

SIDE 4
1. The Narrow Way—Part 1; Part 2; Part 3
(Gilmour)   12:14
2. The Grand Vizier's Garden Party:
Part 1—Entrance; Part 2—Entertainment;
Part 3—Exit   8:55
(Mason)

Recorded at Mothers, Birmingham, UK;
Manchester College of Commerce,
Manchester, UK; EMI Recording Studios, St.
John's Wood, London

PERSONNEL: Roger Waters—bass
guitar, vocals, all instruments and vocals
on "Grantchester Meadows" and "Several
Species of Small Furry Animals Gathered
Together in a Cave and Grooving with a
Pict"; David Gilmour—lead guitar, vocals,
all instruments and vocals on "The Narrow
Way"; Richard Wright—organ, piano,
Mellotron, vocals, all instruments and vocals
on "Sysyphus"; Nick Mason—percussion, all
instruments (except flutes) on "The Grand
Vizier's Garden Party"

Produced by Pink Floyd (Sides 1 and 2) and
Norman Smith (Sides 3 and 4)

Released October 25, 1969

While *More* and *Obscured by Clouds* are often debated as illegitimate Pink Floyd albums due to their soundtrack status, *Ummagumma*—a double album of four live tracks and five new studio tracks—somehow escapes that argument.

First, the live record of what was originally a gatefold two-LP set. Typical of the era, in what is essentially a crease in the fabric of time between the convalescence of psych and the birth of prog—'69 to '70—we get a defiantly anticommercial set of four songs, and not one under a tripping eight minutes. Contrary to the original credits, these space jams were recorded on April 27, 1969, at Mothers in Birmingham, famed birth club of

Black Sabbath, and May 2 at the Manchester College of Commerce on "The Man and The Journey" tour, named for the rambling series of pieces played on the tour, some of which morphed into the studio material loitering onto the set—"Cut!"—here.

Variously considered superior, more intense, and more in the spirit of extrapolation and jazz than their original versions are "Astronomy Domine," "Set the Controls for the Heart of the Sun," and "A Saucerful of Secrets." But of most value is the non-LP track "Careful with That Axe, Eugene." (Most *significant*, perhaps, is that fans wouldn't see a fully live album out of Pink Floyd until *Delicate Sound of Thunder* in 1988.)

TOP: A portrait of the band in 1969, during the period in which they made *More* and *Ummagumma*.

INSET: Label from the UK mono edition of *Ummagumma*.

The studio LP is equally challenging, opening with Richard Wright's "Sysyphus." It was Wright's idea to do this album in the first place, to make some "real music." He would soon regret the exercise as much as the others. It's always the ivory-tinkler, isn't it? Keith Emerson's extravagances are what fans remember about ELP and *Pictures at an Exhibition*, while it was Jon Lord who drove the process behind Deep Purple's bombing classical album. (And Rick Wakeman gave us a hundred Rick Wakeman albums.)

Meanwhile, Roger channels his functioning Syd (meets Donovan) for "Grantchester Meadows" and then his gone Syd for "Grooving with a Pict." David fluffs his way through what ironically became the most substantive piece on the album, "The Narrow Way," tentatively penning lyrics for it when Roger refused (learning his lesson, he would refuse no more). Finally, "The Grand Vizier's Garden Party," loosely attributed to Nick, combines all the bad habits of what came before, adding flute from his wife to the dog's breakfast.

If a brave face can be painted on *Ummagumma*, it is that Pink Floyd were obviously unafraid to be grimly avant-garde and wildly uncommercial. Forget the Edgar Broughton Band or Hawkwind and the free concert concept. *Ummagumma* was a form of audio terrorism that should have necessitated the band paying any of the hairies dosed and deaf enough to show up.

I exaggerate, of course. Pink Floyd were, unbeknownst to us and them, gleaning valuable lessons as they went, honing their skills at sonic sculpture, tape manipulation, engineering, and production— it is important to note that the band wouldn't work with a big-name producer until *The Wall*—on their way to the mighty *The Dark Side of the Moon*. That album and everything that followed up to *The Final Cut* would wear a few of the faded but still discernable badges of honor earned in the battles fought on *Ummagumma*; that is, both those songs worked out live and those that were tried out and either kept or discarded on the wilderness of mirrors that was the exasperating second record.

POPOFF: To start, could you describe what we get with *Ummagumma*? It's not exactly a traditional Pink Floyd studio album, if there is such a thing.

BAILEY: Let me start with this. I interviewed Storm Thorgerson from design house Hipgnosis, who provided the artwork, and he pronounced it "oomagooma," so now I always pronounce it that way; most people think I'm wrong, but I think I'm right [*laughs*]. That aside, we're in a transitional period for the band, between dandies of the psychedelic world in Britain on their way to the concept album thing of the '70s.

And more than *Saucerful* and *More*, *Ummagumma* is indicative of a band searching for some direction. You could imagine, Syd was their primary songwriter, and most people would say that Floyd was Syd's band. He helped cofound it, he named it, and then he's gone. And members of the band have been pretty upfront saying as much, that they were a little lost and searching for a way to go forward.

In a sense, their solution with *Ummagumma* was to not be a band at all. They put together an album of live material plus four solo mini EPs. Rick Wright had the idea that maybe what they should do is take a disc and divide it into fourths, and each member of the band could essentially do their own thing. That's the main thing with *Ummagumma*—is the new material "Pink Floyd" or is it solo stuff from the different members?

WAGNER: Exactly. Of the fifteen Floyd records, maybe *Endless River* excepted, *Ummagumma* is not a true or pure Floyd record, right? It's a double album, it's got four live songs—three they'd done previously on other albums, one a B-side. And you've got basically solo works by each guy on the other set. So, it's quite different.

Early on in their career, it's a brave step to put an album out like that. But it's something that now the band doesn't look at very favorably, kind of a failed experiment. I know that from the things I've read, obviously more recently. But the solo thing was cool. ELP and Kiss would both do something similar years later. But it's not the kind of thing you listen to all the way through as a total experience. You either choose the live side or you choose the studio side.

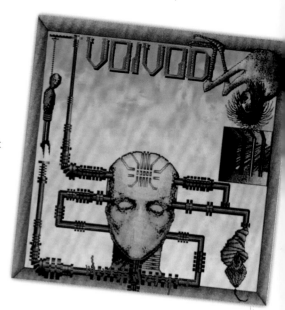

Nothingface by the metal band Voivod features a cover of Floyd's "Astronomy Domine."

POPOFF: Jeff, as a progressive metal authority, explain the significance of "Astronomy Domine" in the metal world and the merit of this live version?

WAGNER: First song on *Ummagumma*, the live side. That first appeared on the band's debut, and it's one of their earliest cosmic epics, very trance-inducing and hypnotic. And it does have a fairly heavy hand. I'll say this: I think everything on *Ummagumma* is improved from the previous versions. It shows the band gelling, getting heavier, getting darker, and that goes for "Astronomy" as well. I might be an outlier, but I think Voivod's version of "Astronomy" is actually better than the Pink Floyd one. I know that's unusual to say, because the original is the bedrock or foundation, but Voivod executed it in such a way that it became a Voivod song and it became a better song. And obviously they're progressive metal leaders, so it certainly has a lot of clout in that realm.

BAILEY: A lot of people would say that these are superior to the studio versions, but that's subjective or a flip of the coin. Any time a band gets in front of an audience, they're going to perform differently than when they're in the studio. If people say that the live tracks have more punch, more energy, more fury than those tracks done in the studio, it's arguably fair. They had never put out a live album before, so the live disc is significant in that sense, particularly for a band that had made so much of its name on their live performances.

It's amusing how quiet the crowd is mixed. When you record a concert, you can do it a million different ways. I've heard live albums that you would never know were live. Because they chose simply to mix it in a way that you would never really hear the audience. But just because the audience is fairly quiet on that live disc doesn't mean they weren't engaged.

WAGNER: I think there's no crowd because they intended to present this as more of a studio thing. They wanted the performances to sparkle and didn't really care to have the crowd that involved. Plus, the crowds back then were kind of chilling and listening. This was heady music—music for the head. It was something you kind of sat back and ingested. But I also think they kind of tried to

Pink Floyd at the Victoria Rooms at Bristol University, England, March 4, 1969.

bury it. I think the mastering on the original is kind of low. So, not only is the music a bit tamped down, but the vibe of the audience may be as well.

POPOFF: I suppose the most substantive piece for Floyd fans on the live disc is "Careful with That Axe, Eugene," given that it's not on any of their studio albums and is extended as well.
WAGNER: Right, it's the B-side to "Point Me at the Sky" from December 1968, and in the original form, it was not quite as menacing as it would become. It's fairly sedate, a little bit trancey, has that kind of hypnotic bass line. But it really grew over the next year or so. I think the ultimate versions of all these *Ummagumma* songs are from *Live at Pompeii*, which, sadly, they haven't put out as an album proper. They should, because that's Floyd at a certain peak.

But even here, "Careful with That Axe, Eugene" is astoundingly good. And everybody knows that this song is so totally great for one single moment, and that's that bloodcurdling scream Waters lets out. It's even more like a horrid screech. That's certainly a protometal vocal moment in the most extreme sense. Until that moment, until that horrible scream—and I mean horrible in the best sense of the word—it just builds from this soft, quiet tension, that kind of creepy little bass line into that insane climax.

That's an example of a band taking the foundation of the original composition and building, seeing what they could do with it; it evolves through *Ummagumma* and then ultimately to *Live at Pompeii*. But it's a fascinating track for me because it got me into Floyd. I was coming more from a metal background, and I thought, wow, these guys can dig into the kind of raw, sick, frightening intensity that metal has, just with that one scream. Really, it's heavier than so much metal could ever be.

POPOFF: Any comment on this live version of "Saucerful"?
WAGNER: It's kind of like, "Careful with That Axe" because it shows this band taking the original version and expanding and maturing it. It's the logical and very psychedelic companion to "Set the Controls" because it also originally appeared on *Saucerful*. It gets into these damaging sound experiments of noise plus this 3/4 jamming for a while, so it demonstrates that early foreboding darkness that they had. But again, it's a moment that is even better in the *Pompeii* version.

POPOFF: What do you know about this idea that it was Richard who kind of drove this process with the solo studio material?
BAILEY: They were looking for a way forward. Rick's notion was, let's break out of the standard four-person rock band thing and try to make some real music [*laughs*]. The other guys went for it. I guess nobody had a better idea.

Rick is seen as the underrated member. Roger was out front after Syd left, and we hear all sorts of things about David and Roger back and forth, but Rick was the quiet one.

He brought a lot to the table, and David said as much in recent years when they put out *The Endless River*. Listening back to all those tapes, it reminded him of what Rick brought to the band. Rick, like David, is less triumphing over more. Not on this album, but listen to "Us and Them," which Rick wrote the music for, and it's fairly simple, but beautiful, extremely effective. And Rick was seen in the early years—and this is interesting, because we know what happened later—as the heir apparent, maybe, to Syd as far as songwriting.

Before Pink Floyd, Rick had written a song and sold it, and another band had recorded it. That was pretty hot stuff. And in the early years Rick had a lot more songwriting credits. Then in later years he would taper off. In fact, he would be kicked out of the band, essentially, by Roger, for lack of contributing during *The Wall*. But in the earlier stuff, we see more of his songwriting and more of his singing, even on "Astronomy Domine" and "Matilda Mother," which were Syd's. But he was never comfortable singing; he didn't feel he was a good singer.

POPOFF: It's Richard's "Sysyphus" that opens the studio record. What do you make of this one? Is it a creative success?

WAGNER: I like that comment from Rick about him wanting to make some "real" music—it sounds earnest to me. In later years he considered the exercise pretentious, so maybe he doesn't like it now, and that's fine. But it's good. It reminds me of how Floyd were ahead of their time, but they were also sort of *out* of time.

There's very little you can compare to "Sysyphus" other than maybe some avant-garde or modern classical music. For me, part two is particularly harrowing. It's a bit of evil noise. I keep bringing that darkness up, but they really had a lot of that back in the day. And it just helps explain why Floyd appealed to so many fans of noisy protopunk or heavy metal or modern extreme music. If Wright doesn't like it, then, oh well [*laughs*].

POPOFF: There's a lot of Mellotron in part four.

WAGNER: Yes, and Pink Floyd were not the key Mellotron band. They used it, but it was pioneered by the Beatles and Graham Bond two or three years earlier.

They always had an arsenal of sound and instruments, and Mellotron is fairly regular, but it's a sound I associate more with the Moody Blues and King Crimson. Rick is an organist, with his roots in Farfisa.

POPOFF: Moving on, Roger swings wildly from traditional song to the most abstract thing on the record.

BAILEY: Right, and they are both highlights for me [*laughs*], and for entirely different reasons. "Grantchester Meadows" is just a beautiful ballad, immersed in a pastoral setting that puts you in a very pleasant state of mind. A real high point of the album.

On the polar opposite end is his other track, "Several Species of Small Furry Animals Gathered Together in a Cave and Grooving with a Pict," which is this musique concrète kind of thing where apparently it's just him, his voice, and drumming his hands on things and varying the tape speed to make all these crazy sounds. And it's just this aural assault, nothing like the happy pastoral "Grantchester Meadows" but entirely on the other end of the spectrum.

The band was willing to try anything. I think most people agree that *Ummagumma* and, say, *Atom Heart Mother* are both kind of transitional, the band kind of poking around, and then in 1971 when *Meddle* came out, that's when the tires gripped the road, especially with "Echoes." That was indicative of what their direction would be.

WAGNER: "Grooving with a Pict," that's where Floyd got bonkers. It's a reason it's one of my two favorite eras of the band. But for people who don't know, Picts were people that lived in northern Britain, which is now Scotland. But this track is all very weird, basically an experiment in voice and tape manipulation.

I read that Picts had a very meat-heavy diet, and I sometimes have this unpleasant image now thanks to that knowledge, of the Picts spearing these furry cave animals for food. It's not a pleasant sound; it's not birdsong like you hear in "Grantchester Meadows." It doesn't sound like the animals are happy. It evolves into some nonsense and goes on perhaps a little long, but if you're up for the experimental stuff, it's a bit of a trip.

"Grantchester Meadows" is one of those beautiful, sedate songs that Waters would do in this era, which tempers the darker side of the band at that time. It still had that veil of mystery over it that typified this era of Floyd. It reminds me of "Cirrus Minor" on *More*, very much sounds like a companion to that, stylistically.

POPOFF: Any comment on the album cover? It seems a step forward in terms of sophistication.

BAILEY: It's Hipgnosis again and they used a technique called the Droste effect. The concept of a picture being within a picture of itself, which of course has a picture of itself in it and so on and so forth to infinity. It's the group sitting at a doorway, and there's a picture on the wall, which is in fact a picture of the cover

OPPOSITE: Rick Wright, the driving force behind much of the *Ummagumma* material, onstage in the Netherlands in April 1970.

of the album. It's actually not a Droste effect, if you want to get technical about it, because in each picture, they've changed positions, and they've rearranged the setting a little bit. And if you look carefully enough and go far enough into that repetition, eventually the picture on the wall is a picture of *A Saucerful of Secrets*.

WAGNER: *Ummagumma* was a slang term for sex from somebody that was close to the band, a crewmember or something. "I'm gonna go have a little ummagumma with the missus." As for the cover and the Droste effect, they did that a lot back in '60s and '70s comic books. And it's interesting, they had a Gigi album cover on the front that they whited out for certain American versions, likely because of copyright issues.

Dave Gilmour circa 1970 . . . fantastic at taking one note and making it sound like a conversation.

POPOFF: Okay, let's look at "The Narrow Way." But first, what kind of guitarist is David Gilmour? What did he do more or less of than other guitarists?

WAGNER: I think Gilmour was—and I'm not the first person to say this—but he was so fantastic at taking one note and making it sound like a conversation, almost. He told a story with very few notes, right? Very much an emotion guy, and he could bend a guitar string like no other. I'm sure some people might say Clapton could do the same, but he was that kind of player, and therefore you get a lot of these flowing, sustained sorts of atmospheres and aesthetics. That's a key part of Floyd's sound and it started to come out of this era.

As for "The Narrow Way," not to be a downer, but Gilmour doesn't really like this. He feels like he's phoning this in. But I just don't hear it that way. Maybe that's his thought, but as a fan, I really enjoy this, and it's probably the strongest solo piece on *Ummagumma*. I hear a prefacing of later material in terms of vibe and the mid-'70s sound. I see little nuggets of that in "The Narrow Way." It's a pretty engaging, rewarding listen.

I always felt that the heaviness from this band tended to originate with Nick Mason and Roger Waters, but in the second part of the song, here's Gilmour doing what I almost call doom. It's heavy and it's dark, but then in part three, you get into this George Harrison–esque thing, both vocally and musically, and it just makes a very well-rounded yet diverse piece. And it's too bad that Gilmour doesn't like it [laughs].

Gilmour has a personality, a stamp he puts on his compositions, and "The Narrow Way" is where that first really takes root. And to add to the Beatles comparison, it drones away at the end, much like several Beatles tunes would back in their more experimental era. It's kind of a cycling, repetitive fadeout. Yeah, I'm going to say "The Narrow Way" is great.

BAILEY: Yeah, David admits that he kind of fudged his way through that one. He took bits and pieces of this and that and kind of put this thing together. David has never been that keen on writing lyrics; he puts it off and he's just not a big fan of having to do it. And the story goes that he asked Roger for some help and Roger turned him down. It's funny . . . "The Narrow Way" is three parts, but there's only one part that has vocals in it. And the vocals are mixed so low you can't even tell what he's singing. Maybe that's indicative of the fact that he wasn't that confident with what he had come up with lyrics-wise.

POPOFF: I like that with "The Narrow Way" we get to see the full range of David's abilities as a guitarist, not to mention that he's penning the words and singing as well.

BAILEY: This song is a guitar showcase, isn't it? As a guitarist, David had a difficult task ahead of him, because he was replacing a different style of guitarist, and they obviously weren't going to play guitar together. David and Syd were school chums before Pink Floyd ever existed. He doesn't play in a style that Syd plays. He had to find his way in those early years and figure out how he was going to pull that off. Generally speaking, and I wouldn't say this is necessarily tied to this timeframe, but David is usually applauded for not overplaying, for not being afraid to let the song breathe and leave some spaces between the notes.

POPOFF: And Nick's thing, "The Grand Vizier's Garden Party"?

BAILEY: Not something that you would probably put on during, say, a dinner party [laughs].

WAGNER: No [laughs], I mean, there are a lot of drummers in great bands that also write great music and make great contributions songwriting-wise, and I don't think Nick Mason is one of them. Although Nick had a great role in Floyd. I would say he's almost underrated because he has this kind of Keith Moon/Bill Ward approach to drumming, which for me, is all about feel and vibe and texture, and he lays it down great on so many of these early Floyd songs. Not knocking Nick Mason there.

But "The Grand Vizier's Garden Party" makes it obvious that he wasn't a great writer. It's a bit wayward, with lots of percussive bluster as you might expect. His then wife plays flute on it. It's a nice attempt to make something interesting, adding some xylophone; it's somewhat dynamic. I do like the cutup nature of

Nick Mason, Roger Waters, and an unidentified figure (left) backstage in London, spring 1969.

the second part, "Entertainment," but it wears out its welcome; it's not arranged well. Not great, but not totally terrible either.

POPOFF: Closing comments on *Ummagumma* or the state of the band at this time?
BAILEY: I guess most people would agree that *Ummagumma* is not an album that has stood the test of time very well. As we've discussed, band members have been pretty disparaging about it.

As for the state of the band, a record like this wasn't going to make them big, but of course that was all going to change. From their roots as a psych band, history would say that Floyd is the winner. So many contemporaries of early psychedelic Floyd just never took off. The Pretty Things are a band you hear a lot about when you start researching Floyd. A lot of people say, "Man, the Pretty Things, they should've been as big as Pink Floyd," but they just weren't.

It's so complicated as far as who becomes popular and who stands the test of time and who doesn't, and it's not just because of talent. There are a hundred different factors, and probably at the top of the pile is luck [*laughs*]. What kind of label deals you get, was the label behind you, did they work hard enough? So many factors.

I'm not saying that Pink Floyd doesn't deserve the legacy it has—clearly, they do. But there were certainly other bands in the same experimental area back in the early days that simply didn't have the chance to be remembered fifty years later.

POPOFF: Do you ever wonder why the label would let the band put out a record like *Ummagumma*?
WAGNER: I guess they'd already gained enough clout. I don't think *More*, for instance, was all that successful, but the first two albums were looked at with some fondness. The band wasn't huge the way Floyd are now, but they were certainly a thing, an event, live.

And back in the day, record labels were more open to newness and experimentation. Essentially, late 1969 marks the start of the prog era, where things just went

crazy in terms of creativity. In that sense, Floyd were the right band at the right time, and the time was right for them to put out an album like *Ummagumma*.

OPPOSITE: Poster advertising Pink Floyd's show at Mothers in Birmingham, England, April 27, 1969.

POPOFF: Is it an honorary Krautrock album?

WAGNER: Sure, that's there too [*laughs*]. There's a similar impetus or inspiration in that anything goes. Through the braver efforts of the Beatles and Zappa and the Beach Boys, a band like Floyd is thinking, "Yeah, we can do our *Pet Sounds* too; we can do our *Sgt. Pepper's*." Of course, they already started weird; they were never that conventional to begin with. So, again, right band at the right time to produce this crazy material.

POPOFF: Are they even a rock 'n' roll band at this point?

WAGNER: They rarely rock! I mean, maybe here or there. There are parts of *Wish You Were Here* or *Animals* that rock, and perhaps more so even in the Syd era. It's amusing, on *Live at Pompeii*, Roger Waters is kind of referring to Floyd and he says something to the effect of "That's rock 'n' roll for you." Something like that. But *are* they rock 'n' roll? [*laughs*] It's an interesting debate.

Whatever it is, they did something pretty great with it. That's the thing about Floyd that speaks not to the virtuosity of the band, but to the creativity and imagination of the band. They took this slow-paced thing, made a career out of it, made all these completely different albums out of it that were so highly influential—it's magic.

It also speaks to the chemistry of the members. They're one of those fortunate case studies like Rush or Queen, where if those key members hadn't met, there would be nothing there. We wouldn't have these works. It's so fortunate that these four guys came together and were able to do all of this with, I'm not going to say very little, but they weren't Yes-level virtuosos. And yet they made this incredibly cerebral music for a very long time.

CHAPTER 5

ATOM HEART MOTHER

WITH RALPH CHAPMAN, LEWIS HALL, AND JEFF WAGNER

SIDE 1

1. Atom Heart Mother   23:38
   (a) Father's Shout
   (b) Breast Milky
   (c) Mother Fore
   (d) Funky Dung
   (e) Mind Your Throats Please
   (f) Remergence
   (Mason, Gilmour, Waters, Wright, Geesin)

SIDE 2

1. If   4:25
   (Waters)
2. Summer '68   5:29
   (Wright)
3. Fat Old Sun   5:19
   (Gilmour)
4. Alan's Psychedelic Breakfast   12:55
   (a) Rise and Shine
   (b) Sunny Side Up
   (c) Morning Glory
   (Gilmour, Mason, Waters, Wright)

Recorded at EMI Recording Studios, St. John's Wood, London

PERSONNEL: Roger Waters—bass guitar, acoustic guitar, vocals, tape effects; David Gilmour—guitars, vocals, bass, drums; Rick Wright—keyboards, vocals; Nick Mason—drums, percussion.

GUEST PERFORMANCES: EMI Pops Orchestra—brass and various other instrumentation; Haflidi Hallgrimsson—cello; The John Alldis Choir—vocals; Alan Styles—spoken vocals, sound effects

Produced by Pink Floyd; executive producer Norman Smith

Released October 2, 1970

The fifth record from Floyd, *Atom Heart Mother* is arguably the first, without any qualifications, from the classic lineup. In other words, not a soundtrack or a grab bag. But bless their Henry Cow Krautrock souls, that doesn't mean they stopped being audio terrorist Situationist performance artists. From the Warhol-inspired cow on the cover art on down, *Atom Heart Mother* is essentially *Ummagumma* without the live album—or rather, with a spooky new title track replacing the live material on this ostentatious and apocalyptic epic.

"Atom Heart Mother" grew organically, as these things must, becoming a twenty-four-minute behemoth with Python-esque names for its parts. It was the first performance to make use of Abbey Road's new eight-track system and, as a result, the band were told they could not do any tape splicing, resulting in Nick and Roger performing the bed tracks straight through in one go. The brilliant adjunct came with the idea to hand the pile over to Ron Geesin, who was tasked with orchestrating to the finished backing track. The EMI Pops Orchestra resented having to apply their talents to such absurd and avant-garde music and bucked Geesin all the way. It fell to conductor John Alldis to mediate, with Alldis helping orchestrate as well as navigate onto the dark and soundtrack-like terrain an even more harrowing death cult of a choir. The result is very much an equal collaboration between Floyd and the orchestra with their complex strings and brass.

Also similar to *Ummagumma*, side two of *Atom Heart Mother* found each but Mason turning in a somewhat solo piece. Opening the side is Roger's "If," which is so quiet and peaceful (yet tense) that it feels like a prototype of his preferred arrangement style across the likes of *The Final Cut* and beyond into *Amused to Death* or even *Is This the Life We Really Want?* Richard's "Summer '68" brings the most elegant, emotive, and memorable piano passages he ever wrote, along with, as a bonus, glints and gleams of tribute to the Beatles and the Beach Boys. David's stoned "Fat Old Sun" sees a similar amount of elbow grease and is the track most lauded and applauded on the record, even if it's "Summer '68" that deftly adds new color to Floyd's kaleidoscopic palette.

The album closes with "Alan's Psychedelic Breakfast," which, although it gets a full-band credit, is historically ascribed to Nick. The thirteen-minute journey is remembered mostly for side-trips into the oft-unadorned sounds of roadie Alan Styles preparing and chowing down on his breakfast. But in the main, it's meandering music similar to "Atom Heart Mother" but dominated by piano and organ instead of classical instruments.

The band looks back on *Atom Heart Mother* as a period bereft of ideas and full of pressure to come up with something, a recurring theme with the Floyd. But the record is testimony to the idea that when or how an artist plunks himself down and produces, the art will out. Nothing about the bulk of *Atom Heart Mother* sounds uninspired or less inspired than the material across the expanse of the band's numerous records before they hit it big with *The Dark Side of the Moon*. The album reached gold status in a number of territories, with French Floyd fans eventually buying over three hundred thousand copies. Then again, the French gave us Magma.

Label from the Italian stereo release of *Atom Heart Mother*.

POPOFF: To begin, can you break down what kind of record *Atom Heart Mother* is, specifically as it relates to its predecessor *Ummagumma*? What are the connection points and what are the divergence points between those two?

A view from behind the stage as Pink Floyd perform at the Holland Pop Festival in Rotterdam, June 28, 1970.

CHAPMAN: *Ummagumma* is kind of a bastard record because it's half live, half almost like *The Monkees Present*, where it's a showcase for individual members. I know what they were getting at. The band is presented by the live aspect, and each individual member is highlighted by things like "Sysyphus" and Waters's contributions "Grantchester Meadows" and "Grooving with a Pict," that dreadful, extraordinarily indulgent piece of shit.

Thirty years ago, I worked at a 24-hour gas station, and the night man would come in around ten o'clock. He was an *Ummagumma* fanatic, a guy named Rob Matthews, and just to torment me as I was trying to do what was known as "cashing off," he would play that at full volume and it would drive me insane. It permanently stained my attitude toward *Ummagumma*. It was only, as a matter of fact, weeks ago that I finally listened to the live side. When you're a Pink Floyd fan, there are certain records you buy out of obligation, and for me it was *Ummagumma*—that was the obligatory record.

Atom Heart Mother, in my mind, still has those elements, especially on side two where something like "Fat Old Sun" seems to be almost completely a Gilmour solo recording. Apparently, he plays bass, he plays drums, obviously does the vocals. There is some keyboard coloring that Rick adds, but for the most part, it's a solo experience.

HALL: Also, *Atom Heart Mother* is similar to *Ummagumma* in the sense that they've both got the long instrumental tracks and passages. The other stuff is sort of, send the individual musicians off and see what they come up with. One of the better tracks is "Fat Old Sun," which is all Dave Gilmour. "If" is just Roger Waters. He sat there with his guitar and came up with that. And "Summer '68" is Rick Wright singing about his groupies again. As for the title track, using the brass band, what a great sound. The first time I heard this, I assumed it was by the Beatles. That chorus has such a hooky Beatles-esque feel, and then bringing in the brass band, it's almost like *Sgt. Pepper*.

"Alan's Psychedelic Breakfast" is credited to the whole band and has really interesting sounds of somebody frying up some breakfast, followed by a quite good chord sequence. When the music comes in, there's some doubled-up piano and organ, and quite a triumphant end to it. You could say this is kind of a concept album, that the whole of the first half is virtually a classical piece, and then a couple little tracks, and then the finale, which takes us back to the beginning aesthetic again.

It's different than *Ummagumma* in that sense, because *Ummagumma* is part live album, but based around the four different musicians. You could say that those tracks are weaker because of that, but they're a bit more unique as well. They were lucky, and we were lucky, that they had the freedom and flexibility to have that studio time and to be able to go away and do that.

WAGNER: I'm not the biggest fan of this album. The stuff that came after was all pretty much brilliant up to and including *The Wall*. But *Atom Heart Mother* seems like a slip to me. I look at the cover art, and it's just like we're leaving cosmic stuff altogether and going to the most basic thing you can think of: a cow in a field. It's intriguing, but the album cover could also be taken like, "Well, we didn't really try that hard with the compositions, we're not going to really try that hard with the cover." Of course, I know that's not the original impulse and I'm sure some people think the cover's a fantastic work of art.

And the title track, at twenty-four minutes, I'm not going to say they didn't put work into that, but to me it's largely aimless. As a title track and an opener that long, it ought to be better. Of note, this is also a time when every rock producer and every rock band was putting horns on everything. Uriah Heep, *Salisbury*, you name it; there's a long list. Sometimes it works, sometimes it didn't. And here, horns just don't work for Floyd at this stage.

The problem is you get that long track and then you get three by Waters, Wright, and Gilmour, kind of repeating the *Ummagumma* pattern of, okay, this guy's gonna take this song, this guy's going to take this one, this guy's going to take this one. And none of those are classic Floyd. They're all pretty sedate and that's wonderful, but they just don't hit me hard.

Then you get "Alan's Psychedelic Breakfast" to end the album. Okay, what is this? This is either total genius or like a thirteen-minute failure made up of breakfast sounds mixed with some really noncommittal music. It just doesn't have that commanding sonic wizardry as the previous couple, or that compelling, dark psych element. And maybe you could argue they were going in a new direction, but if you look at what came right after with *Meddle* and *Obscured by Clouds*, those were clearly much more inspired albums than this one.

HALL: Jeff mentioned the cover art and I must respond. They're all done by the same company that did a lot of their albums, Hipgnosis. It was just this idea of taking a picture of a cow in a field and it's brilliant. In some ways, it's a better album cover than the next couple that came out, which are a bit hard to work out. Ultimately, it's almost as iconic as *The Dark Side of the Moon* and *Wish You Were Here* as far as recognizable album covers go. It's a funny one because it's not their most popular album, but it's important in the story of Pink Floyd and their development.

BELOW: Waters at the July 18, 1970, "Free Concert" in Hyde Park. The bill also featured future Pink Floyd collaborator Roy Harper.

OPPOSITE: Gilmour performs at the "Free Concert" in London's Hyde Park, July 18, 1970.

LEFT: September 1970, Waters performing at the Fête de l'Humanité at the Bois des Vincennes, Paris; the event was a yearly fundraiser for the French newspaper *L'Humanité*.

RIGHT: Gilmour at the same event.

POPOFF: Point out a few impressive spots among the shorter material on side two.

CHAPMAN: "If" is an interesting song in the sense that, first, it's got a very unusual construction. There's no chorus. It's just verse, guitar solo, verse, guitar solo with piano added, verse. It's an unusual piece of work musically. Second, in my opinion—and a lot of people would disagree— it's the true emergence of Roger Waters as a lyricist of the same caliber as Lennon and Dylan and Townshend. These guys who innately understand not just the human condition, but can hold the mirror to themselves.

In the opening stanza, he says, "If I were a good man, I'd talk with you more often than I do." Lines like that. "If I were a good man, I'd understand the spaces between friends." That's an extraordinary line for a twenty-six-year-old guy in a rock band to write. Understanding that if I offered myself, if I was a better guy, I'd be more available to my friends.

Which of course foreshadows the splintering of the band, first with Wright's departure and then the acrimonious split between Waters and Mason and Gilmour. Which, I don't care what anyone says, still exists . . . I know Mason and Waters have made up, but Gilmour and Waters, they will never be the same again. This was a guy who was basically saying, "I don't have the time for friendship." You could see that this was going to lead to the eventual self-destruction of a band that depends on camaraderie.

That's really significant, as well as just generally the maturity of his lyrics. It's not just the self-awareness. He also offers one of the most tender moments for me. "If" offers this line: "If I were alone, I would cry/And if I were with you, I'd be home and dry." Which really nails the importance of having a loving partner, that in the end all you want is to be home and dry and with someone who will take care of you. There's a fascinating juxtaposition between complete self-absorption and sudden tenderness. And vulnerability. Which will lead to why I love *Final Cut* so much.

HALL: I gravitate to the first side, partly because there are quite a few interesting sounds and technologies used, particularly in some of the sections with stranger names. There are various bits where they put different instruments through the Leslie speaker besides just the organ. That sound of somebody going "whoo-hoo" through the Leslie speaker, which sounds like a train going through a tunnel. You might've thought they just got really stoned and made some strange noises, but it's really interesting. *Atom Heart Mother* is one of those albums that crosses over from prog fans to people who are into classical music to those who like a bit of rock. The title track covers it all because of the classical elements with the choir and the band. But it has some great rocking, grooving moments as well. Plus, it works really well live with just a four-piece, but also when they had the orchestra and the choir.

As for Ron Geesin, it's somewhat hard to listen to in some respects because he's not just adding normal brass parts. It's very clever stuff, with lots of strange and different notes going on that create a somewhat discordant style of music that makes you feel a bit uneasy in places. But then he brings you around again. As I've said, I've heard them play it without any backing band at all and it sounds equally as good. So, it works on two levels.

POPOFF: Back to side two, any other songs that stand out?

CHAPMAN: What struck me about "Summer '68" is not that the lyrics are about banging a groupie and ultimately it doesn't mean anything. The thing about "Summer '68" that always takes me away is that it's a Rick Wright song. There's no question that historically his role in the band gradually became more and more diminished, so by the point of *The Wall* he's nonexistent, basically. So, every time I hear a Rick Wright song, with him singing, it brings me back to why he was this wonderful George Harrison–esque part of the band, the dark horse who could all of a sudden leave you in your tracks because of how he played or how he sang. It makes me value him when I hear that song.

Roger Waters at the Concertgebouw in Amsterdam, November 6, 1970.

The other thing about "Summer '68" is that on the chorus, which is kind of rudimentary, just the repetition of "How do you feel?" he brings Dave in. Their voices work so beautifully, which we'll see in full flourish on "Echoes" and "Time." And that's another asset of the band that was underutilized.

WAGNER: That's a really good point. As you say, you get that a lot with "Echoes." You also get that with the *ahh-ahhs* on "A Saucerful of Secrets," the wordless *ahhs* at the end of that one, at its peak. They mesh so well. That's something you don't hear talked about enough with Floyd—the strength of their three vocalists.

CHAPMAN: The other interesting thing about "Summer '68" is the horn solo, which I thought was an interesting touch. And going back to "If," you really start to see them paying attention to not just arrangements, but these subtle production touches. There's a great moment on "If" where he says, "If I were asleep, I could dream." And they put this hint of reverb on "dream," and it's, especially on headphones, a lovely, lovely moment. These guys may have felt short on song ideas, but they were really evolving quickly as producers.

WAGNER: "Summer '68" sounds like it could have been on *Saucerful*, which came out in '68. And yes, there are more horns on that one. It's okay, but to me it sounds like something that could've been left off the solo part of *Ummagumma*. It's kind of inconsequential. I hate to completely rip on it, but this album, *Atom Heart Mother*, is a big question mark for me. "Fat Old Sun" is folky, it's a bit melancholy, kind of sleepy. Gilmour does that kind of thing really well, so it's not surprising that he wrote and sang this. I just feel like he's done this kind of thing better before and after.

Something like "If," that's Waters in his more pastoral setting. And vocally he does very well. This is the guy who was screeching on "Careful with That Axe." It shows quite a bit of range emotionally. But Floyd, to me, is always more of a sculptural-meets-emotional experience. I'm not sitting down looking for the four-minute nugget with a great catchy chorus. It's truly an experience with them. And that's why I always think of sculpture when I think of Floyd. It's music that's created from a different angle.

POPOFF: Do you find Roger's early writing reflects an odd continuation of, or parallel with, the psychic and stylistic package that was Syd Barrett? He writes similarly to Syd in that gauzy, English pastoral style, even if it's something that is going to change very soon.

WAGNER: You're right, it was just a wonderful happenstance that they have Roger kind of in the wings and ready to take the lead when their leader could not take the mantle any longer. Roger Waters steps up, bassist, and he starts writing, and it seems to be an approximation of a logical continuation of what Syd Barrett was going after. If they hadn't had Roger Waters, I don't know that it would still be truly Pink Floyd, or something that would make sense going from the first album to the second and onward. Roger Waters provided the bridge to keep Floyd going in the spirit of their original intent, and then of course expanding greatly beyond that.

POPOFF: What do you make of "Alan's Psychedelic Breakfast?"
HALL: Very obscure in the catalog. I'm not sure if they actually played this track live. They did similar things early in the development of *The Dark Side of the Moon*, when instead of "On the

Rick Wright tunes Waters's bass during Floyd's show at the Falkoner Konserthuset in Copenhagen, November 12, 1970.

ABOVE: The *Relics* LP brought together "A Bizarre Collection of Antiques and Curios." It is pictured here in its black-and-white UK edition and the full-color Australian release.

BELOW: The *Big 4* EP, released in Japan in 1971, comprised four songs: "One of These Days," "Julia Dream," "Point Me to the Sky," and "See Emily Play."

Run," there was a scene where the band came on stage and maybe made a cup of tea. Not long before *Atom Heart Mother*, they had these long suites called "The Man" and "The Journey," a concept piece they performed live, and again there might've been five minutes of the band sitting around on stage drinking tea. So, the concept of doing more theatrical, visual things wasn't new to the band. It perhaps doesn't come across quite so well in audio on album, but on this record it fills a gap at the end and provides a really good ending.

As for pulling this kind of thing off live, they had the resources and the budget to invest in lots of gear and experiment with it and record it and we got some fantastic results. But it was hard for them to recreate a lot of that stuff live, because unless you bring on loads of tape machines, which I think they did in later years, it is impossible to do with the equipment they had then. I can see why more experienced, intellectual musicians would criticize them at the time, saying that they were just messing around with sounds. But it doesn't matter—they started it and it sounds great, and millions of people love it.

POPOFF: And they were the ones sticking their necks out daring to do this. Sure, they got some criticism for it, but if you're the only ones doing it, you're going to be remembered for doing it.

HALL: Of course, and so many people have done things like it since. There's nobody that you can say sounds exactly like Pink Floyd, but if it wasn't for Pink Floyd, you wouldn't have some of the more modern, dark drum and bass, underground dance music, which really uses a lot of the same techniques to create interesting intense atmospheres of mood-building. Which I suppose comes from classical music, but a lot of these young people making drum and bass wouldn't have heard classical music. But they have heard Pink Floyd; they've been at a student party and got stoned and listened to Pink Floyd and subsequently created their own version of it. I wouldn't say Pink Floyd is quite as influential as the Beatles, but they're not far off.

POPOFF: Any other comments on some of these specific tracks?

CHAPMAN: With "Fat Old Sun," I guess so much has been said about Dave's love for that song, and when I saw Dave a couple of years ago, that was the highlight of the show. It's a song that, legend has it, he was forced to write. He wasn't allowed to leave the studio until he came up with a song. There was some supposition that he had pinched elements of the Kinks' "Lazy Old Sun," but still the song stands on its own.

And regarding this idea that he apparently played drums on it, there's an interview where Dave says, "Oh, I played drums on the original recording and it's awful," or something. But I don't find it awful—it stays in time. It's very Nick Mason–esque in the sense that it's exploring. There's the song "Long, Long, Long" on *The White Album* that uses drums in the exact same way, sort of microdynamics within the song.

POPOFF: Where does *Atom Heart Mother* live within the Pink Floyd catalog?
WAGNER: It's a total stopgap. A spear stabbed right in the middle of the earliest version of Floyd, into what becomes kind of the classic middle period, starting with *Meddle*. I know *Atom Heart Mother* has its fans, and I appreciate it, but it just feels like it's not enough.

"The Whale" by composer John Tavener was released on a gatefold LP by Apple Records in 1970. Tavener's use of a choir recalls Ron Geesin's work with Pink Floyd.

CHAPMAN: I can answer that [*laughs*], but first I have to respond to this idea of yours of *Atom Heart Mother* being Krautrock or at least honorary Krautrock. I do like that idea, but I never saw them as Krautrock—because of Nick Mason. Because Nick Mason is no Jaki Liebezeit. Mason swings. I'm not able to hear Krautrock in Floyd because, me being a drummer, all I hear is Ringo. Nick has this subtle swing to him, and there's no swing in Krautrock.

You may find other people you talk to who say, "Oh, this is kind of British Krautrock," if such a thing could exist. But to me, it's just painting, sonic painting. I go to what at the time would be contemporary classical composers like John Tavener, who in '68 or '69, did a piece called "The Whale" that utilizes choir in a similar way with chanting and swoops and long-held vocal notes. That reminds me of Tavener, what Geesin does.

Why I love *Atom Heart Mother*, the album, is there's so much foreshadowing of what is to come. Obviously, taking up one side with the title track can't help but foreshadow "Echoes." And a lot of people say that "Echoes" is far more successful and band-driven. I'm sure you know the story that the band cut it and handed the tapes to Ron Geesin and he was forced to orchestrate it. But a lot of the mood and the colors, despite Geesin's contributions are, if you find them, they're there. Specifically around the ten-minute mark, where they just start jamming and Wright has that stabbing organ, and Gilmour's soloing over it and really sounding a bit like Paul Kossoff from Free. It's kind of uncharacteristic. But then it creeps into this eeriness around the twelve-and-a-half-minute mark and there's Mellotron.

As opposed to what they used on "Echoes," which is Gilmour creating this whale song, this very eerie cry of whales on "Atom Heart Mother," they use choir. This is Geesin. At one point the choir starts to chant and hiss and gurgle, and then the brass swells come in and I could see how that foreshadows their desire to create something extremely dramatic and ominous for "Echoes."

I would say, touching back on your question at the beginning concerning the difference between *Ummagumma* and *Atom Heart Mother*, *Ummagumma* was definitely, for the most part, complete indulgence. Conversely, *Atom Heart Mother* had its critics—certainly from inside the band, from Roger and Dave. It was called barrel-scraping and things like that. But there's no question that the songs themselves, the solo songs, that are aided and abetted by the members, are much more concise and powerful pieces of work that again look forward. Unlike what could be validly leveled at the band circa *Ummagumma*, *Atom Heart Mother* is not a band that is out of ideas.

Pink Floyd - Atom Heart Mother

CHAPTER 6

MEDDLE

SIDE I
1. One of These Days   5:50
   (Waters, Wright, Mason, Gilmour)
2. A Pillow of Winds   5:10
   (Waters, Gilmour)
3. Fearless; including "You'll Never Walk
   Alone" (Rodgers, Hammerstein II)   6:03
   (Waters, Gilmour)
4. San Tropez   3:42
   (Waters)
5. Seamus   2:09
   (Waters, Wright, Mason, Gilmour)

SIDE 2:
1. Echoes   23:31
   (Waters, Wright, Mason, Gilmour)

Recorded at AIR Studios, Oxford Street, London, UK; Abbey Road Studios, St. John's Wood, London, UK; Morgan Studios, Willesden, London, UK

PERSONNEL: Roger Waters—bass guitar, vocals; Dave Gilmour—guitars, vocals; Rick Wright—keyboards, vocals; Nick Mason—percussion

Produced by Pink Floyd

Released November 13, 1971 (UK); October 30, 1971 (US)

WITH ROBERT CORICH, LEWIS HALL, AND PAUL KEHAYAS

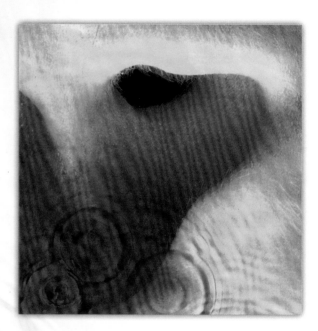

The last of the albums strong-willed by Waters, *Meddle* can also be framed as the first among Pink Floyd's deliberate and self-assured mid-period, in a sense more so even than *Obscured by Clouds* (which will forever be viewed as suspect due to it being a soundtrack album as well as its short and accessible songs).

Meddle suffers none of these qualifiers while benefitting from healthy distro, a strong gatefold presentation, and the clear intention and delineation of the individual tracks in terms of their personality and provocatively prog purposes. On the visual front, if the cover art was the work of Hipgnosis—Storm Thorgerson and Aubrey Powell—still finding its footing (both are dismissive of it), fans still got

an image that made sense. The outer wrap is both spacey and liquid, cosmic and submersible, depicting an ear (that looks like a nose) underwater; inside the gate we see a handsome lot depicted just as plain as can be and shot in black and white. Once the listener is inside of the music, the confidence depicted in the eyes of the band members takes flight. "One of These Days" marks a victory for instrumental music generally and Pink Floyd instrumental music specifically—arguably, this is the most charged, exciting, and memorable song on this record or any Floyd record before it. Where technology was merely tinkered with before, fumbled even, here the band manhandle it to create museum-grade sculpture.

"A Pillow of Winds" is similarly top-shelf Floyd of a type—again, fey turned to flourish. Then there's "Fearless," a second Floyd classic on the side, and a gorgeous ascending chord sequence dovetailing with a thoughtful and world-beating vocal melody. The Frankensteining of field music to the end of the track marks another milestone—Floyd locating the third eye, the symmetry, two disparate pieces crashing to add a third emotional wave, an effect to be used a half-dozen times on *Dark Side*. And if "San Tropez" and

TOP: Gilmour and Waters backstage at the Ahoy, Rotterdam, April 3, 1971.

INSET: The alternate artwork for the US edition of *Meddle*.

Period advert for *Meddle*.

"Seamus" find the band up to old habits that aren't going to get them anywhere, using spare rooms for storage, the three intriguing tracks of Floyd-ness on side one raise eyebrows.

With side two the band deliver an escapist classic. "Echoes" is what happens when a band is forced to write and record cut while fulfilling touring commitments. Fragments of music were named, variously, "Nothing" and "Son of Nothing." Then "Echoes," in early performance form, was called "The Return of the Son of Nothing." Band members tried playing in isolation with only vague directional rules and then overlapped the disparate parts. The song took six months to build, and three studios were used in the process. Alas, "Echoes" emerged as a twenty-three-minute epic serving as a metaphor for the unglamorous elbow grease necessary for mortals to make music.

In the victorious spirit of side one, "Echoes," despite being the longest Pink Floyd song ever that is not broken into parts, quickly became a Floyd classic. Hugely preferred over previous interminable epics, it served as an improbable highlight of *Live at Pompeii* and even as the opening selection during early shows on the band's *A Momentary Lapse of Reason* tour.

Floyd fans have recognized the quality of the record, with *Meddle* going double platinum in the US, where no other pre–*Dark Side of the Moon* album has ever gotten past gold. Little wonder *Meddle* has been deemed the first record of the band's renowned second chapter.

POPOFF: Set up what kind of band Pink Floyd is in 1971. They begin recording what will become *Meddle* in January and work on it on and off for the next seven months or so. How are they doing?
HALL: They were very busy, working really hard and just experimenting with different things. I think they were trying to be quite successful, although they weren't hugely so at that time. They'd had a bit of success with their earlier stuff, but of course it would all change a few years later. But they were just working really hard, doing as much as their manager told them to do [*laughs*], and we've got the results in front of us.

Meddle, as it turns out, would be sort of "up there" because it's got "Echoes" on it, as well as "One of These Days," which was featured a lot live in the years to follow. A lot of the other stuff is probably skipped over on people's iPods, but it's some of their best work. I'd say *Meddle* is very well respected and quite important in the Floyd catalog.

CORICH: Growing up in New Zealand, I was ten or eleven when I heard *Meddle*, and it was actually the first Pink Floyd album that I listened to in its entirety. I had singles and heard the singles occasionally on the radio, and one of my brothers had the first couple of albums in his collection, but they kind of passed me by. It's still one of my favorite albums of any band. And it's not just the music, it's the cover—brilliant—which I was enthralled by. It had the band members inside, but the piece of art on the outside was great. I lapped it up, not realizing at that age that drugs would've enhanced the experience of the cover.

POPOFF: I suppose Floyd does get accused of being a stoner band decades before there was an actual genre called stoner rock.

HALL: I certainly think there's an element of them being a stoner band. They definitely took full advantage of the development of stereo and improvements in hi-fi equipment to where people could sit at home and listen to something in stereo, either on headphones or on a nice speaker system, and I'm sure that various drugs could enhance the enjoyment of the music. People do ask me this all the time: What would you describe Pink Floyd as? Like Led Zeppelin, it's hard to put a label on them because there's just such diversity across pretty much every album, and *Meddle* is a prime example of this. It's got some really heavy rocking stuff, it's got some beautiful melodic stuff, acoustic, folky stuff. It's quite an eclectic mix. So, it's hard to put any label on it other than "Pink Floyd." They're kind of their own genre, really.

KEHAYAS: As the album after *Atom Heart Mother* and before *Obscured by Clouds*, *Meddle*'s the first full-length record of what I would consider to be the new Floyd sound, and yet it's the last record of what I would consider to be the old Floyd sound. *Obscured by Clouds* straddles the line as well. I would consider *Obscured by Clouds* to be an extension of side one of *Meddle*.

It comes from things recorded when they were playing a lot of shows and they had no material for them, as evidenced by the fact that "Echoes" was called "Return of the Son of Nothing." And they basically would do all sorts of weird experiments, like have each member try to record separately without hearing each other with just basic direction, and

Italian pressing of "One of These Days," the sole single from *Meddle*.

that just didn't work. They were wasting a lot of studio time trying to make these experiments work, like recording household objects, things found around the kitchen or house. This is the first instance where they would try experiments like this; they would try it again later in the *Wish You Were Here* sessions. Again, it shows that they didn't have many songs. But for going into a studio situation with barely anything except some spark ideas, it turned out pretty good.

INSET: Advertisement for Pink Floyd's performance at what was billed as a "Garden Party" in London's Crystal Palace Bowl, May 15, 1971.

TOP: Gilmour surveys the scene backstage at the Crystal Palace.

POPOFF: This is also evidenced by the opening track, "One of These Days," which finds the band presenting one of their famous sound collages rather than a song with verses and choruses.

CORICH: Sure, but "One of These Days" is, to this day, the best song based around bass I've ever heard by a rock band. I can't think of any other song that goes nearly as far in showing the simplicity of the bass guitar but also the power of the bass guitar. Very clever. Yet the bass playing is pretty standard, while David Gilmour's guitar work, with the swooping and the slide, is just absolutely stunning.

David's the king of less is more. He's not a busy player, generally, although on "One of These Days" he's quite rough and raucous and in-your-face when he gets going. Usually he's very gentle and laid-back, but at the same time, he has a beautiful substance to his playing. Absolutely wonderful player. I saw him in October 2016, at Royal Albert Hall, and everyone who was at that gig was absolutely blown away. He played "One of These Days" as well, which was as good as it ever was. Having said that, when Roger Waters does it solo, it's good too. Great song and very unusual.

HALL: The song is completely driven by the bass. I think it's the only time that Pink Floyd double-tracked the bass. Even though I'm the bass player in a Pink Floyd tribute band, I'm not 100 percent sure if it's Roger Waters or David Gilmour playing the bass on it. It could be both, or it could just be Gilmour, because he's by far the better bass player of the two. At least in the beginning it's both, each through one of the two stereo channels—Gilmour's bass is louder and Waters's more muted.

But it's essentially two bass guitars playing at the same part. One's pretty much panned over to the left side, one is pretty much panned over to the right side, both with like a timed delay. So, it's by pressing . . . by playing one beat each bar, the delay gives it kind of a triplet, shuffle effect, and there are two of those going on. Apparently, one of them is using newer strings than the other, so you kind of get a clear sound and a not-so-clear sound. That creates a pumping, driving beat, which I don't think there was much of back then. There's certainly a lot of dance tracks and other rock tracks that have taken an influence from it since then, but I think at that time, there wasn't much else that sounded like that.

There's also a lot of studio trickery of cymbals and pianos recorded and played backward, guitars slowed down. Of course, there's the one vocal line, which is Nick Mason saying, "One of these days I'm gonna cut you into little pieces," and that's been slowed right down to create this almost demonic sound. Which, again, they're just trying out new techniques and it becomes this fantastic instrumental piece.

The story of that quote, Roger Waters was particularly not a big fan of a British DJ on Radio 2 called Jimmy Young, previously a sort of British crooner. He became a radio DJ and was renowned for rambling and babbling quite a lot. Roger Waters particularly hated him. There's a bootleg recording, an early version of "Sheep" called "Raving and Drooling," where basically they'd recorded various parts of this guy's radio show and chopped them up using 1970s tape-editing equipment to create this whole track of him literally rambling, with all his words mixed up and sped up.

POPOFF: That's interesting that ardent Floyd heads aren't even quite sure who is playing the bass on there.

HALL: Yeah, and that goes for a lot of Floyd stuff. Recording myself, sometimes you just need to get the job done and it's not about, "Oh, he played bass live so he should play it here" or "He plays guitar there." Quite often Roger Waters is playing acoustic guitar and Gilmour's playing the bass just to get it down, or to get the right sound or vibe for what's needed. I don't think any of them were that precious that they needed to only play their own instruments.

As I've been playing the music myself for so many years and studied it, I can now pretty much work out when it's Roger Waters playing the bass or the acoustic guitar, or when it's Dave Gilmour, because Waters has got a certain energy, whereas Gilmour is certainly a much more accomplished

ABOVE AND OPPOSITE: On June 15, 1971, Pink Floyd performed at the Abbaye de Royaumont on the outskirts of Paris at the invitation of its owners.

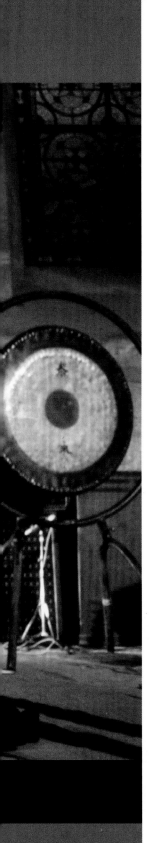

and precise player. On some of the later tracks, where there are bass solos, slide, or fretless bass, stuff like that, that's generally Gilmour playing.

KEHAYAS: Beside the bass, I would say "One of These Days" is important as the first time you hear major sound effects being front and center, hitting you right in the brain. The grand gestures begin to hit at a really big success rate. Not saying that they don't work on *Atom Heart Mother*, but this is where they really start to work. Because *Atom Heart Mother* is the whole experiment with the orchestra, these other elements seem like a little sideline. On *Meddle* it's heavily integrated into their writing.

That bass is done through a . . . they didn't call it an Echoplex; it was a Binson Echorec, which is an Italian echo box, tape delay, that they'd been using since the early days. And you've got lots of the soaring guitar, lots of slide guitars, that David will do a lot more of. There's the texture that Pink Floyd will develop over the next few records. There are lots of piano and the new way that Nick Mason is starting to drum. It's probably the last song that will be fast. Otherwise, all Floyd is taken at a slow pace. That's just one thing that happens.

The chord changes are another thing that work interestingly well for that. Because unlike the rhythm, they move at a glacial pace. There's a lot of room within each chord progression for contribution, particularly from the guitar. Everything is really memorable. It's one of these rare occasions when they realize they can do a rock song, and then they really, really just decide to pummel the heck out of it. It's always a thrilling thing to hear that, and to hear Nick Mason start pounding his floor toms when he's doing his vocal line there.

A Binson Echorec II, as used by Pink Floyd on *Meddle*.

That's one of my favorite moments, when he's just starting to bang the hell out of his drums. I turn up the speaker [*laughs*]. Wonderful, wonderful piece.

POPOFF: I always saw "A Pillow of Winds" as one of the best of that pure David Gilmour style from *Saucerful* through *Obscured*.
KEHAYAS: "Pillow of Winds" is a lovely track. It's introduced with the wind noises that end the first track; they set the whole thing up and it's like a really calm breath of sea air [*laughs*]. It really is amazing. I keep using the word "glacial," but let's just use "smooth." That texture of David Gilmour's voice has really started to be explored, the resonant baritone, and it's double-tracked. He's not lost it, either. He still sings like that, with a beautiful resonance.
HALL: There's certainly a couple of acoustic guitars that are played in an open tuning, and there's slide guitar played by Gilmour, and then fretless bass, which, like I say, I'm pretty sure is Gilmour. Again, his lovely vocals—this is an early example of Gilmour double-tracking his vocals and creating this nice, smooth vocal sound, which wasn't really used on any of the earlier albums but is used greatly on the next album and on *The Dark Side of the Moon*. It's something that really becomes part of the iconic Pink Floyd sound.
CORICH: There've been rumors forever about who plays bass where. Early on the band definitely got on very well, so it would appear to me that if they did play something different, they wouldn't worry about the crediting. But I love "Pillow of Winds." It has a gentle substance to it.

POPOFF: And "Fearless," a memorable tune, is one that is instantly likable. I'm surprised it wasn't issued as a single because it sounds like a hit to me.
HALL: It was a B-side to "One of These Days." Perhaps, if they had released it as a single itself, it would've been a hit. That's another played with open tuning, written by Roger and David, both strumming along, playing acoustic guitar together, with Waters writing lyrics and Gilmour singing them. Apparently, it's written about Syd Barrett, like so many of their tracks. They put a nice slow groove on it to go with the acoustic feel, and then at the end they added this sample of Liverpool football fans singing "You'll Never Walk Alone," which is really bizarre, because I don't think any of the band were fans of Liverpool.
KEHAYAS: Again, perfect mix of acoustic and electric guitars. There might even be a twelve-string on it; sure sounds like it. If it isn't, it's six-strings multilayered to sound like a twelve-string, or thirty-six strings. It's really crisply produced with a fantastic lead vocal from David. I wonder if Rick is in there with harmony or whether it's just David tracked twice. There's a lot of usage of David and Rick as a close harmony team. I know it's David on lead vocals—it might even be Roger

kicking in occasionally—but Rick's got that certain voice that lends itself to harmonies. They're the ones doing the harmonies on "Echoes" on side two. And there's the Liverpool Kop doing the "You'll Never Walk Alone" football club chant at the end. I don't know why it's there but it works. It's a further exploration of found sounds that drives the song into a different context. The feel is radically changed; suddenly it doesn't make sense.

POPOFF: Side one sort of drifts to an end with "San Tropez" and "Seamus," which both seem somewhat inconsequential, wouldn't you say?
KEHAYAS: "Seamus," obviously that's just an excuse for them to get Steve Marriott's dog to howl, right? They ran in the same circles as Humble Pie, and Steve Marriott had this dog. That's the thing that he was well known for, as you'd start playing the blues, he would just start howling in the background. On *Live at Pompeii*, they have the dog there doing it; you can see that actually happen live. Not really much of a song, but it's cute.

Now "San Tropez," maybe you could call that jazz, but with maybe a Beatle influence, because the guitar solo sounds uniquely "Honey Pie"–esque. But it's obviously trying to be jazz, although it's slightly stiff.

Fans of Liverpool FC sing in support of their team from the famous Kop end during a match in the early 1970s. At the end of "Fearless," Pink Floyd famously sampled Liverpool fans singing Rodgers and Hammerstein's "You'll Never Walk Alone."

Pink Floyd backstage at the Hakone Aphrodite Open Air Festival in Kanagawa, Japan, August 6, 1971.

POPOFF: Is it dance hall?

KEHAYAS: I can't say that, because dance hall for these guys is R&B. It's kind of music hall—I'll go there. It's cocktail jazz as filtered through Roger Waters's version of what that might be. It's a lovely song, but it's not one of the most memorable things they ever came up with. Side one's songs are great, but they work more so as half of an entire album to be listened to as a whole. It's not something you turn off. In fact, you kind of need these to brace yourself for what will happen on side two.

HALL: I'm surprised they didn't release "San Tropez" as a single, because you could almost think they were trying to appeal to a certain radio audience at the time. It's quirky and not like anything else on the album. Apparently, that's the only one that Roger Waters wrote on his own and brought to the studio all finished, and he's playing acoustic guitar on that, and bass as well. But then Gilmour comes in and brings in some sort of reluctant slide solos over the top [*laughs*]. Perhaps he wasn't that happy about not having a hand in writing it, and I can see that as one of the early examples of them starting to have a few problems with who was going to become the main creative energy. Although Waters was kind of the de facto leader, they had done most of their stuff together. This is one of the first times where that wasn't the case.

Style-wise, it's got a bit of gypsy jazz, swing feel to it. Unusual but it works. It's easy on the ear, and both musically and lyrically you can sit back and listen and imagine that you're in the south of France, enjoying yourself. But it's one of those tracks that a lot of casual Floyd fans would just skip past and not really think of, on their way to the next more rock track. But as part of their eclectic catalog, I think it stands up.

CORICH: To me, "San Tropez" and "Seamus" are filler. "Seamus," I can tell you, when you're heavily stoned and you hear the barking dog, it's kind of funny. But to me, they are throwaways, six minutes that could've been so much better. But the first three songs, excellent. But they certainly weren't afraid of trying different styles early on. All those things they did, you can pick them apart and analyze them, and in most cases they are very clever. I admire a band like that, that does try different stuff even if it's not always going to work.

POPOFF: Paul, are you an "Echoes" fan?

KEHAYAS: Definitely, from day one. First time I ever heard it, I went, "What the hell is this!" Because I was ripe for the picking. I was probably about thirteen years old when I heard that.

"Echoes" is slow and groovy—it unfolds. And the first verse is about deep-sea life. Maybe this is the reason that they wanted the cover of the album to be an ear underwater. I know that the people that made the cover, Hipgnosis, thought it was a shit cover. But then again, their suggestion of a baboon's anus close up—was that any better? I don't think so.

The Leslie effects on Rick Wright's organ—brilliant, absolutely. I know for a fact that they were pissed off with EMI, about the studio in particular. It's shades of *The White Album*, where when the Beatles were recording they still only had four tracks. And they heard about eight tracks, and even sixteen tracks in the States, and now comes an eight-track unit, but of course the bosses at EMI had to disassemble and find out how it works and put it back together again. "It needs rigorous testing, boys—it won't be available." They got all pissed off with them because they're staring at this thing in the room. So, they liberated it one night and brought it into the studio, completely getting people in trouble. But, whatever, they needed to use it.

The soundman and a small child take in Pink Floyd's performance at the K.B. Hallen in Copenhagen, September 23, 1971.

Pink Floyd weren't as rogue as that, but what they did was they started copying the initial sessions that they had made, and they transferred it so they could take it to different studios. Morgan Studios was one, and AIR, I believe. But they wanted sixteen tracks, so they definitely wanted to work outside of EMI because they were pushing stuff. EMI probably woke up soon thereafter, because Floyd were back at EMI working on the next few records. By the time of *The Dark Side of the Moon*, they probably had their sixteen-track, but they were always apparently well behind. But it probably contributed to the sounds of the records. They needed flexibility. There's only so much you can do with four tracks, especially with this kind of music, to layer down all that extraneous noise among all the core music.

But *Meddle*'s a really wonderfully done record. One of my favorite moments on "Echoes"—and it's a beautiful trick, very atmospheric and probably an edit—is the moment at about seven minutes where they go into their little funk bit, followed by David with the whale noises on his guitar. But that jam, it's always the moment where I go, "Yeah, turn it up." It's just beautiful. But it has a great melody, great harmonies, and it goes on but it never seems long. I really love the ending of it where, at 19:10, they do this orchestral swoop that goes up and into the last verse. I'm always amazed at how inventive that is.

CORICH: Absolutely epic, "Echoes." Simply superb, from the opening sonar effects to the end of the track. When I first heard it, I was already blown away by "One of These Days," but I must've played "Echoes" twice a week for months. Absolutely captivated me and it still does.

When it was played live, sometimes they'd do it in two parts or sometimes three. But generally, it would be a part one, and they'd tuck into a few other songs in the set, and then they'd come back to part two, which is essentially the second half. And they often followed it along pretty much as the album did, but they had other effects in there. Yeah, I've loved "Echoes" all my musical listening life.

There are some excellent live versions of this. There is a bootleg called *Meddled*, recorded at the Paris Cinema in London on September 30, 1971, and on *Meddled*, you've got a sixteen-minute version of "Fat Old Sun," you have

Pink Floyd, flanked by stage lighting at the Roman Amphitheater in Pompeii, Italy, October 1971.

More than a movie! An explosive cinema concert!

'PINK FLOYD' is making motion picture history with record-breaking engagements in Cincinnati, Indianapolis, Detroit and Milwaukee.

NOW WATCH FOR IT AT A THEATRE NEAR YOU:

NEW YORK: August 14
LOS ANGELES: August 28
CHICAGO: August 2
BOSTON: August 14
SAN FRANCISCO: August 7
ST. LOUIS: August 7
SPOKANE/SEATTLE: August 14
DENVER: August 14
HOUSTON: August 28
NEW HAVEN: August 21

PINK FLOYD

An overwhelming full-volume Pink Floyd color experience!

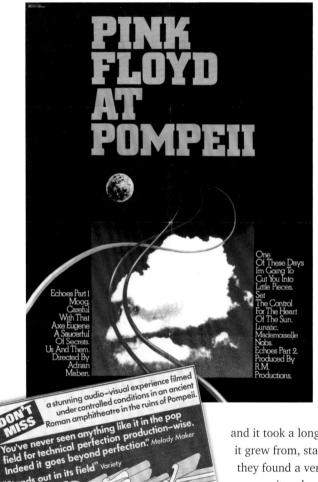

Poster and advert for Pink Floyd's concert film *Live at Pompeii*.

a seven-and-a-half-minute version of "One of These Days," you have a nearly twenty-seven-minute version of "Echoes," and then you've got an over-ten-minute version of "Embryo," and then some blues. It's a very well-put-together bootleg, and "Echoes" is fantastic—in all states of mind.

HALL: "Echoes" is actually not that well known, although it was featured heavily in the *Live at Pompeii* film and in later tours. But it's the definitive Pink Floyd track for me, because it encompasses everything one wants to hear in Pink Floyd. It's got great guitar solos, it's got some interesting lyrics, nice melodic verses, some really unusual experimental sounds in the middle, a nice long introduction. It's a pure, epic track that covers so many different styles and sounds.

I'd say there are some Beatles influences here. There are even a couple or three lines similar to lines in "Across the Universe," particularly "inviting and inciting me to rise," where the Beatles song goes "inciting and inviting me." But it's such an interesting track, and it took a long time to work on. There are various versions that it grew from, starting with an instrumental piece, and then perhaps they found a verse somewhere and decided to fit that in there. It was quite a long process, creating the final piece.

From the point of view of myself and the band playing it live, "Echoes" is always an interesting one, because it's in an unusual key for a guitarist. I think it's in C sharp minor; most guitars like to play things in E and in A. And Roger Waters is playing it really high up the neck. You can almost imagine that it's someone playing a bass for the first time, who knows how to play other instruments but not necessarily a bass. Because it's got some interesting lines and passing notes that are almost wrong that go between the chords. They almost shouldn't be there, if you're talking about strict music rules. But somehow, like with all these things in Pink Floyd, they just fit together. And sometimes they're so perfectly in time with what Nick Mason is playing on the drums, I can't believe it's all deliberate. I think a lot of it is happy accidents, where they just happen to do a fill at the same time and it just works.

As for some of the trademark effects, the main one is the ping that you hear at the beginning, which is a piano played through a Leslie speaker. Leslie speakers were created to work with Hammond organs. The Beatles were one of the early pioneers using these with other instruments, mainly guitars. But it's like a rotating speaker cabinet. You can change the speed, from it going very slowly to suddenly going really fast, which, with an organ, makes a soft-sounding chord suddenly sound really intense. People tried putting guitar through it and, in this instance, Floyd put piano through it. It's just one note played on a piano, but the effect of the speaker spinning around gives it this strange, almost alien sound that people wouldn't have heard back in those days. Some of the vocals are put through it too, which is used to much great effect later on with *The Dark Side of the Moon*. But in this instance, it's the final verse, the vocals are sent through a Leslie, which just blends the two harmonies together beautifully.

Also of note, there's this strange screeching sound in the middle, which is an accident where Gilmour—I think it was a wah pedal—plugged in the wrong way around; rather than going in through the in jack and coming out into the amp, they did it the wrong way around. We've experimented with this ourselves and it's bizarre, the sound it makes. If you let your foot off it, it creates this unusual, howling, screeching sound, which they exploited to great use in this track by adding reverb and delay to it.

Related, there's a track called "Embryo," which was never released properly, but Floyd used to play it live, not too long, maybe only the year before, and the whole middle section of that was very much like the middle section of "Echoes," with the same screeching and other unusual sounds. You can hear the development from that song to what comes very soon after.

Finally, lyrically, "Echoes" is very poetic and beautiful, hopeful and uplifting. I really enjoy listening to it and playing it. The *Live at Pompeii* version is more exciting than the original album version because they had a few more months to work on it. But it's just such a dynamic song and in some ways I'd argue it's the essential or quintessential Pink Floyd track.

CHAPTER 7

OBSCURED BY CLOUDS

WITH RALPH CHAPMAN AND LEWIS HALL

SIDE 1
1. Obscured by Clouds   3:02
   (Waters, Gilmour)
2. When You're In   2:22
   (Waters, Gilmour, Mason, Wright)
3. Burning Bridges   3:24
   (Wright, Waters)
4. The Gold It's in the ...   4:16
   (Waters, Gilmour)
5. Wot's ... Uh the Deal   5:03
   (Waters, Gilmour)
6. Mudmen   4:16
   (Wright, Gilmour)

SIDE 2
1. Childhood's End   4:27
   (Gilmour)
2. Free Four   4:07
   (Waters)
3. Stay   3:58
   (Wright, Waters)
4. Absolutely Curtains   5:49
   (Waters, Gilmour, Wright, Mason)

Recorded at Strawberry Studios, Château d'Hérouville, Hérouville, Pontoise, France

PERSONNEL: Roger Waters—bass guitar, vocals; David Gilmour—guitars, pedal steel guitar, synthesizer, vocals; Richard Wright—keyboards, vocals; Nick Mason—drums, percussion

Produced by Pink Floyd

Released June 2, 1972

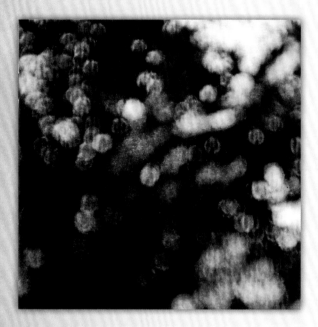

Back on the soundtrack trail for Barbet Schroeder, Pink Floyd slammed together a batch of songs at the famed but drafty and isolated Château d'Hérouville in France while watching clips of *La Vallée*, earnestly timing segments, and oscillating between instrumental music and quite fresh, uncharacteristic fully fleshed songs. The band worked efficiently over the space of just two sessions, broken up by a Japanese tour, with the record mixed back at Morgan Studios over a couple of days into the beginning of April 1972. However, relations with the film company went south, and the band disassociated themselves from the film, instead packaging the results as a standalone Pink Floyd album.

92

Still, we mustn't forget that the music was written and recorded with the film in mind. *La Vallée* is the story of a woman named Viviane, played by Bulle Ogier (the film also featured Miquette Giraudy from prog band Gong), who goes to the wilds of New Guinea in search of the feathers from a rare bird, but instead gets in touch with her own sense of humanity.

Given the plot and setting, the ragged urban rock that Floyd created makes little sense, though the hypnotic "Burning Bridges" addresses the film lyrically, while "Absolutely Curtains," after some instrumental space travel that nicely links the band's old psych with the more disciplined passages from the breakthrough album to come, ends with some singing from the Mapuga tribe seen in the film. In a sense, this field recording presages future Floyd much like the Liverpool Kop added to *Meddle*'s "Fearless"—both suggest how found voices can affect the listener when parachuted into the context of a rock performance.

Elsewhere, Rick's and Roger's "Stay" is standard early-period soft rock from Floyd, vaguely in the Eagles camp, distinguished, however, by one of the most forthright Rick Wright vocals, where one hears a sweet spot similar to that of Chris Squire. "Free Four" amusingly marries a brutally pessimistic "Time"-like lyric to (surprisingly) T. Rex glam, while "The Gold It's in the . . ." evokes heavy Neil Young. The opening title track serves the same painted purpose in the catalog as "One of These Days," proposing a place for instrumental synthesizer rock to come.

ABOVE: A posed portrait of the band at a Japanese garden in Tokyo, March 1972.

BELOW: Inner label from an original German pressing of *Obscured by Clouds*, which lists the album's subtitle as "Music from the Film 'The Valley.'"

93

Here Rick makes use of the EMS VCS 3 he had purchased from the effects people at the BBC Radiophonic Workshop, while Nick provides electronic drums.

But it is "Childhood's End" that serves as a microcosm for an album forever framed two ways: amusingly but regularly forgotten as part of the catalog, and also the album just before everything changed. In this latter light, "Childhood's End," with its well-reasoned intro, its muscular Jethro Tull–like authority, its *Dark Side* metronome, and its upfront Gilmour vocal, demands attention like golden-era Floyd. Something about the kick and clarity of this song foreshadows a future for Floyd that casts everything else on the album as fragile, defensive, and of a period and a direction to be shed.

POPOFF: How does Pink Floyd come to be commissioned for another soundtrack album?

CHAPMAN: Floyd struck me as a band who had a manager in Steve O'Rourke who was very aggressive in keeping them working. There are songs on *Atom*

Pink Floyd manager Steve O'Rourke backstage in Birmingham, England, December 4, 1974.

Heart Mother that reference it, certainly "Summer '68," and on *Obscured by Clouds*, "Free Four" references this idea of "all aboard for the American tour." So, you get a sense that this band is thinking about playing all the time. But they've done multiple soundtracks at this point, including *More* and *Zabriskie Point*. They have this sideline that almost operates outside the progression of the band. And they do use some of the music—"Us and Them" came out of *Zabriskie Point*. So, they're doing these projects, presumably because (a) they're interesting, but more probably interesting in the sense that they get to collaborate with different artists. Pink Floyd, if anything, were artists, so they were attracted to that sense of collaboration. But I think also (b) they wanted to make money, and (c) they were encouraged to be constantly working. Also, *Obscured by Clouds* is from a band that still hasn't hit it, so I'm sure they feel obliged to make the time to score this film.

HALL: Yes, this is at the height of Pink Floyd's busy period. They've just released *Meddle*, in October 1971, and that month they went to Pompeii to film various tracks for their forthcoming movie. They also are trying to get some sessions in for what would be *The Dark Side of the Moon*. Meanwhile they get saddled with this job recording a soundtrack for this French film. I've seen an interview with Waters from around that time, saying, essentially, "We're just doing too much at the moment. Our manager's taking on too much work, and we're kind of forced to do it."

Poster advertising *The Valley*, for which Pink Floyd provided the soundtrack. It marked their second collaboration with director Barbet Schroeder.

POPOFF: And as we asked of *More*, do you consider *Obscured by Clouds*, in light of all this, to be an authentic Pink Floyd album?

CHAPMAN: It was recorded real quickly, in about two weeks, and mixed in a couple of days. Contrast that with *The Dark Side of the Moon*, which they were concurrently writing and which was a much more involved affair. It's true that the album often slips through the cracks and is perceived as kind of a throwaway record. But I don't consider it a throwaway record—it's about these opportunities to bring out something else in the band, or things that you would never hear again.

There are elements of *Obscured by Clouds* that I adore, simply because they rock and are downright garage-y at times. You get to hear Nick play drum fills that were slowly squashed out of his mandate. Things became more autocratic, though not less, necessarily, creative, because you can't think of the opening to "Time" on *The Dark Side of the Moon* and say suddenly he's not being allowed to be creative. But there's just a ramshackle nature to a song like "When You're In." There are these great fills where he plays the snare off of the cymbals, and it's indicative of a band that seems to be blowing a bit.

Another example of that is "Burning Bridges." I believe "Burning Bridges" does what "Summer '68" does and what "Echoes" does, which again, utilizes both Rick and Dave as lead singers. And it's interesting, because they don't do harmony. They just present their voices, almost like a dialog. With "Echoes," they sing together, and "Time" is another one, where Gilmour takes a bit and Wright takes a bit. I'm always fascinated by how they used that, and again it's something I miss, because I could be wrong, but I don't believe they do it after *The Dark Side of the Moon*. They shed that, almost as if to say we need an identity now, and that just muddies the waters.

There's a great quote from Elton John that reminds me of *Obscured by Clouds*. Because the same year *Obscured by Clouds* was recorded, Elton recorded *Honky Château*, at the same studio in France. I remember reading an interview with him about the records he did there, and he talks about them fondly in the sense that he hadn't established an identity yet, so he could do whatever he wanted vocally. He could sound like Van Morrison one minute, he could try to emulate Jackie Wilson or whomever.

And that's what *Obscured by Clouds* feels like. It's a band that hasn't found their identity yet in the best possible sense. They're willing to do things that three years later they'd say, "No, we need this to be a tighter, more singular vision." And it manifests itself, not just in those choices vocally, but also the arrangements and, like I said, the way Nick plays. Technique and strategy doesn't yet trump the sheer power and fun of playing.

HALL: If you didn't know that it was a soundtrack album, you could listen to it and generally feel that it's an album that stands alone by itself. Compared to *More*, where there may be some complete tracks and the rest is little incidental bits that were written purely to fit what was happening with the film, here, of course, they were written for what was happening with the film, but they are standalone pieces. The first two tracks, "Obscured by Clouds" and "When You're In," I think of as one track, because they do fit together perfectly and that's how Floyd played them live. But they're short, catchy, instrumental things. They set the scene perfectly for the album with this new synth-rock sound. And the opening, the first time you hear the music, it sets the scene perfectly for what goes on at this strange island in New Guinea.

POPOFF: Drilling down to some of the tracks, "Free Four" is an instant charmer, almost a bit of a Marc Bolan or David Bowie thing. Tell me about that one.

HALL: I suppose it's a bit like "San Tropez" in the sense that it's a Roger Waters–composed song and sounds a bit different. It was released as a single in the US, and even though it didn't chart, I can imagine it being played on AM radio, with the label trying to find a new audience. You could argue that Pink Floyd were doing a lot to be commercial. Maybe *The Dark Side of the Moon* was a bit more commercial, and I suppose there are clues on this album that make you think they were trying to be more accessible. They proved on this album that they could write a three- or four-minute pop song that still has a good solo and some provocative musical and lyrical things going on.

"Free Four" is a bit of a tongue-in-cheek thing like a lot of Roger Waters things were. It's poking fun at the managers and all the things they made the band do. And the title itself . . . Pink Floyd were quite well-spoken by British standards. They were from quite well-to-do families, so they'd never say, "One, two, free, four!" I see it as a bit of a tongue-in-cheek poke at some of the more common people that they worked with, maybe their roadies and management team that were getting them to do things they don't want to be doing.

CHAPMAN: If "If" was the beginning of Roger proving his lyrical genius, then "Free Four" is the next step. As far as I know, it's the first time he specifically references the loss of his father. But more importantly, what always got me about "Free Four"—and again, it always comes back to why Roger, in my mind, is one of the greatest lyricists ever—is his ability in a few simple lines to nail the fear that runs through almost all of us.

And right off the top he draws a parallel between a man's deeds and his memories and then says, "You shuffle in gloom of the sick room/ And talk to yourself as you die." What a harrowing image that is, of an inevitability—eighty years if we're lucky, he goes on to say. The human condition—the dread and the fear and the yearning and the expectations and the gift of life, and the agony and terror of death, he dispatches in eight lines. Beautifully.

Musically, it wasn't until you referenced glam that I heard it, because what I noticed most was this use of synthesizer, where before it was for the most part analog keyboards, some Mellotron. And on *Obscured by Clouds*, right out of the gate, you get that bubbling, gurgling synthesizer. So, back to "Free Four." It starts with that low bass, which sounds like glam to you, but to me that conjures Taurus pedals, although they're not Taurus pedals—it's VCS 3. But it conjures Rush; it conjures progressive rock. And that's why I was taken aback by your glam comment, because obviously it's used in glam too; they use those pulsating synths.

But the other thing about "Free Four," musically, is Dave's guitar work, especially the final solo. And Roger does what he does in "If," where he takes the first verse and then goes somewhere else lyrically, but then on the last

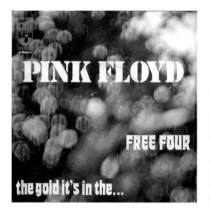

Italian and German pressings of Pink Floyd's "Free Four" single, which featured "The Gold It's in the . . ." as the B-side.

TOP: Château d'Hérouville on the outskirts of Paris, circa 1973. In addition to *Obscured by Clouds*, several landmark LPs of the 1970s were recorded here, including David Bowie's *Low*.

INSET: An EMS VCS 3 portable analog synthesizer, with which Pink Floyd first experimented on *Obscured by Clouds*.

verse he returns to the sentiment of the first verse, or he simply repeats it, as if to say, "Don't forget, this is what this song is actually about: 'Death is a long cold rest.'" Then there's this extraordinary, unrestrained guitar solo.

I get the sense that it's Dave saying, "Because this is a soundtrack, because there's no overhanging vision or restriction, I can let loose." There's a wonderful moment right at the tail end of "Free Four" where either Roger or Dave does this lovely little bass run that tells you that they're trying, that they're interested. This is not just by rote. They are still having fun as musicians.

POPOFF: "Burning Bridges" is a typical, very mellow Floyd original that one could picture on the likes of *More* or *Atom Heart Mother* or *Meddle*. Would you agree with that?

HALL: Sure, and this is one where it's mostly Rick Wright, who has come up with the organ melody and the chords, taking it to the rest of the band, mainly Waters, who'd come up with the lyrics. We're hearing more of Gilmour's multitracked vocals, which create this lovely, smooth sound, and then Rick Wright is doing the harmonies in the chorus. It's a similar sound to "Echoes," where you've got this really nice vocal sound, which I don't think, until *Meddle*, we've really heard from them. It's all over *The Dark Side of the Moon* and things after, so they'd found this approach to melodic vocals and subtle harmonies, which creates quite a nice, easy-listening track.

"Mudmen" is a variation of "Burning Bridges," a sort of sister track. It's
the same chords, but it's in a different time signature, a slow 4/4 rather than
6/4, which gives it a different feel. But there are some really great dynamics,
specifically a soaring guitar solo that comes in and lifts it. The more unusual
synth sounds from the VCS 3, which was a new purchase for them and used quite
a lot on this album. And that ends the first half. We forget these days what it was
like to listen to an album in two halves, and with this album the first half ends
pretty dramatically and the second half begins somewhere completely different.
CHAPMAN: "Burning Bridges" deftly summarizes the plot of the movie, where
this woman decides to leave everything behind and go find not just freedom but
enlightenment in New Guinea. It's a song that's just doing its job. I'm imagining
Barbet said just write some songs that are basically about what the story is and
then they watched rushes of the film and did that. It's a collaboration between
Rick and Roger, with Rick doing the music and Roger penning the lyrics.

Gilmour and Mason onstage
at the Winter Gardens in
Bournemouth, England,
January 22, 1972.

This is going to sound like a real love-in with Roger, but even when he just has to write songs or a set of lyrics that reflect a film, a task so straightforward, he still manages such wonderful poetry. And the last verse of "Burning Bridges," which begins, "The doorway stands ajar/The walls that once were high"—it's just so vivid. Even if you haven't seen the movie and haven't even heard that it was a soundtrack, you're riveted to the story of this character. The magic of Roger is he can sing about himself but he can also write character songs. He doesn't do it a lot, but in that sense, he can sometimes pull the best of Lennon and the best of McCartney.

And, yes, the associated track, "Mudmen," is one of these pretty much forgotten tracks unless you're a real Floyd head. But it has this wonderful synth break on it. Again, even if these guys are just fooling around, at this point they're so creative and so enthralled with the tools they're using that they can't help but create interesting sounds. The interesting thing about Pink Floyd with regards to synths is that their approach was never like, say, Pete Townshend. It was never that transcendental. It was always seemingly about color and pulse and drive. It wasn't about architecture, like Townshend, who would create whole songs around synth lines. They seemed to instinctively know that it was simply a tool to add another color.

POPOFF: Lewis, odd question, but are there *Obscured by Clouds* songs that your band, Think Floyd, find cool enough to include live in your set?
HALL: Yeah, at the moment, we open the show with the first two tracks, "Obscured by Clouds" going to "When You're In." I found a bootleg recording of them playing it, because they used to open the show with it when they were touring *The Dark Side of the Moon* in '73. It's got a great vibe live; they would play the two tracks and they would go into a bit of a jam session and then go back into the riff of "When You're In."

We're also currently working on "Childhood's End," which is the perfect opener for side two. It's got such a great opening sound, which arguably presages what would come with "Shine On You Crazy Diamond"—with the long chords, the mixture of organs and synths slowly building into something completely different, something they'd not done previously.

POPOFF: Is "Childhood's End" the song most indicative of where the band would go, perhaps across the next three albums?
HALL: Yeah, I'd say that is fair enough. It's got a good long introduction, a great groove to it like "Have a Cigar" and "Pigs (Three Different Ones)," and it's not a particularly complicated song as far as the production goes—guitar and bass and drums and a bit of organ. But it sounds great and it doesn't need any more. It's a rare lyric from Gilmour as well; he's based that on the sci-fi book of the same name. After this, Gilmour doesn't get a writing credit until about fifteen years later with *A Momentary Lapse of Reason*. Roger sort takes over in that department.

OPPOSITE: Waters at Winter Gardens in Bournemouth. The January 22, 1972, show featured one of the first full performances of *The Dark Side of the Moon*.

CHAPMAN: Yes, he does [*laughs*]. Rumor and legend have it that at this point, Waters says, "I write the lyrics from now on. I'm the only one that can write good lyrics." And I don't necessarily agree with that, but certainly it worked. But I like "Childhood's End"; it has that chugging rhythm from Mason that reminds me of "Time."

POPOFF: Along those lines, would you agree that the use of the tribe sample feels like future Floyd as well?
CHAPMAN: No, you see, that to me was more about finishing the album with something that was distinctly rooted in the film, as opposed to an artistic statement. When that song reaches a climax, it reminds me a bit of "Let's Get Metaphysical" on Gilmour's solo album, *About Face*—like the sun rising, or this explosion sound—but I don't really necessarily see a specific connection of that moment to *Dark Side*. I really see *Obscured by Clouds*, for the most part, sonically, as a parallel narrative, where they were developing the VCS 3 for use on *The Dark Side of the Moon*.

Poster advertising Pink Floyd's February 1972 residency at the Rainbow in London.

HALL: I'd agree with you, plus you could say the future of music, really. It's there because it's part of the film soundtrack, but how many albums have we heard in more recent years that use the same idea of finding old blues recordings or tribal recordings and adding more modern sounds to produce a new unusual sound? Maybe Pink Floyd were the first to do that, by doing this. But it fits so nicely among the layers of synths and organs. Suddenly, you hear this remarkable ancient recording, dug up from the depths of somewhere, that ends the album perfectly.

POPOFF: I'd like to get a comment on "The Gold It's in the . . . ," which is like a rousing, stomping, hard rock song for them.
HALL: Yeah, it is, and they're helped by the fact that they are writing a soundtrack. They don't need to have songs that logically lead from one to another, so they are able to transition suddenly from something really nice to something more rocky. But it's a great track. It's short—only about three minutes long—as are a lot of the songs on here. But it's got a good beat, some great guitar solos and tones, and it's very much a song of its time. You mention that it sounds a bit like a Neil Young track and it does; it certainly has a West Coast post-psych thing to it.

POPOFF: Any comment on "Stay"? This has both a lot of piano and a lot of Rick Wright for a Pink Floyd song. Not to mention wah-wah pedal out of the Jerry Garcia songbook.

HALL: It's another Rick Wright song; seems to be written about his groupies, like "Summer '68" on *Atom Heart Mother*. The first time I heard this, I didn't believe it was Pink Floyd, because it sounds like a ballad you would hear on easy-listening radio from the time. You could imagine Barry Manilow or Andy Williams or someone like that singing it. So, it does seem out of place on a Floyd album. But it's got connections to similar songs like "Burning Bridges" and "Summer '68," so we'll accept it. Nice track.

POPOFF: Ralph, you bring up an interesting point. I wonder how the band could be so disciplined as to not cough up some of their *Dark Side* material for this project. I mean, how many bands could conceive of two records at once and keep them straight?

CHAPMAN: I'd say because it was a soundtrack. They were given parameters. I imagine why someone like Nick Mason allegedly loves *Obscured by Clouds* so much is it was freeing just to be a band and knock out these songs, and yes, use some of the elements that they were using much more perhaps consciously or creatively, on their other project. But it was like a vacation for them; that's my feeling. Also, the actual time spent on it kind of betrays that. Plus, the thing about that album is—and this isn't a pejorative about the record—if you removed *Obscured by Clouds*, if it never existed in the catalog, it would be a seamless transition from *Meddle* to *The Dark Side of the Moon*. I think that's one of the subconscious reasons why it's been shunted aside.

Let's not forget that they were touring around the recording of *Obscured by Clouds*. They were on this nonstop treadmill. And *Obscured by Clouds* was just a job that I imagine they saw as a musical adventure at some level, but it wasn't about their progression. It was just a piece of work.

Early summer of '72, they really start recording *Dark Side*. So, they're going on tour, they're working up material that they know is going to go into *Dark Side*, they're also pulling on stuff from *Zabriskie Point*, chiefly "Us and Them." But they figure, okay, we're in the middle of writing for *Dark Side*, but we haven't started recording yet. But we've got this job to do. So, let's get some songs together quickly that aren't about our progression, but are simply about the task at hand. And the magic of *Obscured by Clouds* is that, even though that was the process, they still couldn't help but create a progressive record that foreshadowed, specifically in a song like "Free Four," much of the band's future direction, certainly lyrically.

HALL: They first performed a version of *The Dark Side of the Moon* quite early in 1972, January 20, in Brighton. They were then recording *Obscured by Clouds* in February, and it was released June 2. February 17, they did a performance of early *Dark Side*, which was called *A Piece for Assorted Lunatics*, and then the next week they were in recording *Obscured by Clouds*.

I've heard a really interesting bootleg of it and a lot of it's there: "Breathe" is there, "Time" is there, "Money," "Brain Damage," "Us and Them," "Eclipse." But the stuff that links the tracks isn't there. So, "On the Run" and "Great Gig in the Sky" and "Any Colour You Like," they're not there.

And it's those bits which are perhaps more similar to *Obscured by Clouds*. Because "On the Run" is just experimenting with the synthesizers and all the different sounds. "Any Colour You Like" is a synth-based track as well. *The Dark Side of the Moon* turned out so differently because it's the first time that it is just a complete album that you've got to listen to from start to finish.

A candid moment during the band's performance at the Amsterdam Rock Circus, May 22, 1972.

There's no way of dropping in halfway through; you've kind of got to listen to it all.

Obscured by Clouds really does set the scene perfectly for that. To reiterate, the band had this version of *The Dark Side of the Moon* ready to perform, and then after they performed it a few times, they then went into the studio and created the new bits, which became the final album.

POPOFF: Last question on this album: What do the deep fans, friends, and associates of yours think of *Obscured by Clouds* after all these years?

HALL: I'd say it depends on the age of the fan and when and where they came to it. For people who only got into Pink Floyd after hearing *The Dark Side of the Moon* at the time, this is probably missed, because they got *Dark Side* and thought they'd look into the back catalog, and they would find *Meddle* and they would find *Atom Heart Mother*. Maybe they would find the Syd Barrett stuff and not like it. But for somebody more of my age, born after it all, it stands out as just as important as any of the others, really. Sure, it was just a soundtrack and it was just thrown together relatively quickly and relatively cheaply, but it really is the perfect steppingstone—with the production, the sonics, the smooth vocals of Gilmour, the synths—from what they were doing before with *Meddle* to what came after with *The Dark Side of the Moon*.

CHAPTER 8

THE DARK SIDE OF THE MOON

WITH STEVE HACKETT, JORDAN RUDESS, AND KYLE SHUTT

SIDE 1

1. Speak to Me   1:30
   (Mason)
2. Breathe   2:43
   (Music: Waters, Gilmour, Wright;
   lyrics: Waters)
3. On the Run   3:30
   (Gilmour, Waters)
4. Time   6:53
   (Music: Mason, Waters, Wright,
   Gilmour; lyrics: Waters)
5. The Great Gig in the Sky   4:15
   (Wright, Torry)

SIDE 2

1. Money   6:30
   (Waters)
2. Us and Them   7:51
   (Music: Waters, Wright; lyrics: Waters)
3. Any Colour You Like   3:24
   (Gilmour, Mason, Wright)
4. Brain Damage   3:50
   (Waters)
5. Eclipse   2:03
   (Waters)

Recorded at Abbey Road Studios, St. John's Wood, London

PERSONNEL: Roger Waters—bass guitar, vocals, synthesizer, tape effects; David Gilmour—vocals, guitars, synthesizer; Richard Wright—keyboards, synthesizer, vocals; Nick Mason—percussion, tape effects

GUEST PERFORMANCES: Clare Torry—vocals; Dick Parry—saxophone; Doris Troy—backing vocals; Lesley Duncan—backing vocals; Liza Strike—backing vocals; Barry St. John—backing vocals

Produced by Pink Floyd

Released March 1, 1973

Forty-five million copies sold worldwide. On the *Billboard* charts for 741 weeks. Every last song a cozy, filmy classic rock radio excursion. *The Dark Side of the Moon* is woven into the fabric of pop culture as deeply as any album in history. And this was accomplished while the band somehow retained the essence of its outlaw cult status so laboriously earned on the seven records before *Dark Side*, records left in the dust as Floyd arrived and held court in the upper echelons, not departing until the 1980s, undone by their own hand.

As a perhaps crude but simple statement, but one that seems to hold up, *The Dark Side of the Moon* makes the suddenly dark-period Pink Floyd albums sound like a mass tangle of demos for *The Dark Side of the Moon*—as if a checklist of the band's top-ten character traits had been taken to the lab by doctorate candidate versions of Waters, Gilmour, Wright, and Mason, and there perfected through a combination of science and forbidden knowledge.

What were once creepy choirs become Clare Torry and a shockingly soulful set of backing vocalists; the surveillance miking of "Alan's Psychedelic Breakfast" morphs into what are the top half-dozen found-sound bits to date; the Vertigo Records rock of "Childhood's End" transforms into FM-smasher "Money"; cryptic and occasional musings about Syd are now the devastating lyric to "Brain Damage" (as good as the purported best ode to Syd, namely "Shine On You Crazy Diamond"); and the somewhat nostalgic technology of "One of These Days" alchemizes into the warp-speed flash of "On the Run" and the provocative "Any Colour You Like."

More fundamentally, the now responsible citizens populating the band discipline themselves away from the sidelong tests of patience, even if the most recent dog's breakfast, "Echoes," received positive coos and murmurs from the all-too-faithful. *The Dark Side of the Moon* would contain approximately only six conventional songs, about the same as average. But the sleight-of-hand genius of the album's pacing and sequencing convince the listener that there are more, or that six are enough, or even that the whole sweet ride is comprised entirely of effortlessly accessible songs, given (a) the trim strength of the instrumental bits and (b) their placement as intros.

Also pointing to their perfection of character traits, the likes of "Breathe," "Us and Them," and "Eclipse" are examples of what Pink Floyd had been doing all along: owning the world of languid, slow songwriting wholly lacking in ego. There's no rise to impress with progressive rock flash, just the methodical construction of a narrative unique to them, all the while artfully daring their listeners to be bored (Nick and his drumming as good a metaphor for that as anything).

Adding to this pile of evidence refracting light through a prism on why we should not be surprised the record sold superlatively, *The Dark Side of the Moon* was an industry-changing milestone of production and hi-fidelity. Indeed, the author has spent his whole life arguing that there's Before 1973 and After 1973.

By March of that year, Pink Floyd had achieved perfection—all that any ear could want, or any stereo system could deconstruct. From here forward, (a) bad sound simply had not learned the lessons taught by Floyd, and (b) now that

ABOVE: Gig poster from Tokyo dates in early 1972.

BELOW: Label from the US edition of *The Dark Side of the Moon.*

ECLIPSE
(A Piece For Assorted Lunatics)

By
PINK FLOYD

perfection had been achieved, anything one heard as bad, even if not bad due to lack of budget or lack of skill, now came down to taste, deliberate choice. In other words, this album is my go-to old-analog metaphor for today's record-making on laptops: you can now do anything, sample and repeat any sound, so that music has become a series of artistic choices without technological limitation.

That is perhaps as important a distinction as any inside the inscrutable and austere gatefold of *The Dark Side of the Moon*— the inspired crafting of the ultimate audio test record. The fact that the lyrical and musical grist of it represented a laser-focused distillation of a collective and fearless psych and prog persona forged across seven wacky records . . . well, that's simply a bonus.

POPOFF: To start, why do we consider *The Dark Side of the Moon* such a huge album in rock history? What is the magic of that record?
HACKETT: You have to understand when it was conceived, and the audience that it targeted. Lifestyle's got its part to play in this. In a way, lyrically, it addresses the walking wounded. I think within the ranks they had the perfect example in Syd Barrett, who was largely what a lot of their songs are all about. There's a process of grieving that goes through a number of very inventive lyrics.

You know, someone who embraces drugs, goes mad, and loses their marbles; someone very young, very creative, very handsome. When you've got youth, confidence, creativity, and good looks, and when it happens within the ranks, you've got a very rich seam to mine later on. Now I realize that the later example, "Shine On You Crazy Diamond," to a greater degree addresses that, but it ran deep with them, including here on "Brain Damage."

In a way, Syd handed the band to them on a plate so they would carry on the legacy. I suspect with Floyd, as guys who came from privileged backgrounds, save for Roger, and went through the public school system—which means private in England—being carted off to boarding school often creates very successful people. I saw that with my own experience in Genesis. Having been subjected to the same school system that was unchanged for a long time, with the idea of fragging, which meant that you could have a younger boy do everything—polish your boots, run around, be your own personal slave—it's not very healthy. You're kind of brutalized and then suddenly you're in a position to be the slave master, and what are you going to do with that? And you've got to learn to be a bastard and not be afraid to wield power. That kind of school system is designed to produce captains of industry and people in the military

BOTTOM: Onstage at Olympisch Stadion, Amsterdam, May 22, 1972.

INSET: A US *Dark Side* promo EP featuring different edits of "Time," "Breathe," "Us and Them," and "Money."

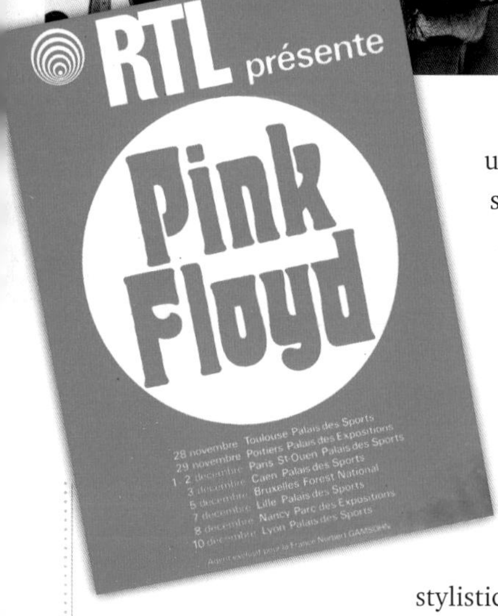

TOP: The band departs for a twelve-day tour of Japan, March 3, 1972.

INSET: Advert for a string of dates after the band's engagement with French choreographer Roland Petit's Le Ballet de Marseille in late November 1972.

capable of leading a charge in the Crimea without flinching, or certainly they need to order one around without having their orders questioned. It'll produce a Churchill, it'll produce a Genesis, it'll produce a Pink Floyd.

But it creates two types of people. It creates people who are very successful and people who are very wounded. And perhaps you had both with Syd: initially very successful and then unfortunately no longer with us to tell the tale. Perhaps in the same way that Lennon and McCartney were addressing their discarnate mothers, I think there was always a sense that this album was aimed at Syd, that this was about him . . . they had such reverence for Syd and his ideas.

On one level, I think they felt that they should lead their life like him. On the other level, it's the idea of pulling back from the brink and becoming these obviously intelligent people who ended up, as I say, writing songs for the walking wounded. There's this slightly somnambulant aspect with the preference for slow rhythms in Floyd and indeed all over *Dark Side*. This is just my own personal take on it. With *Dark Side*, it addresses madness, isolation, dissociation. And overarching that, they've always been about, not necessarily unity, but divisions, the things that separate people, if there's ever been a theme that seems to have run through most of the songs post–Syd Barrett involvement.

POPOFF: Lyrical themes aside, musically and sonically, the album was a milestone.

RUDESS: Yes, at that point they were kind of merging their known stylistic elements with the production coming together like that, making, perhaps for the first time, a package that was exceptionally powerful—it was very much the fact that it just sounded so good. Any band takes time to come into focus, and although to me all the Pink Floyd albums are special in their own way, I just feel like with *Dark Side* they really came into focus on all levels. It's like everything all of a sudden went, *Ding ding ding!* and they came up with an amazing score.

There are certain albums in my life that I would basically stack up next to my turntable so I could put them on at a moment's notice, the ones that really, really made a difference in my life, things like *Electric Ladyland* and *Close to the Edge*. And *The Dark Side of the Moon* is one of those where it's like, okay, I'm always

A promotional portrait of the band, taken just prior to the release of *Dark Side*.

in the mood to hear this. Whereas other records, it's more like I have to be in a certain frame of mind or headspace. Somehow *The Dark Side of the Moon* is part of my DNA, if you will. It's that powerful of a statement.

POPOFF: Of course, millions of people feel that way about the record. It's one of these that is truly talismanic or at least iconic, comfortably iconic, without hyperbole. Kyle, you've created a whole side band to perform a doom metal tribute to the album. Why this record?
SHUTT: I grew up in a small town in west Texas, the Midland-Odessa area. If you ever heard of *Friday Night Lights*, I grew up there; basically, it's a real thing [*laughs*]. But to find old stuff was really hard. There weren't really any cool kids to learn anything from, so reading magazines like *Hit Parader* or *Guitar World*, that's how I found out about a lot of classic rock.

Pink Floyd was one of those bands. You saw *The Dark Side of the Moon* everywhere. And twelve years old, any head shop you'd go into, any record store, there's a fucking prism on the wall, this super-iconic thing. I'd be staring at this prism with the rainbow shooting out of it, and I have to know what that is, it

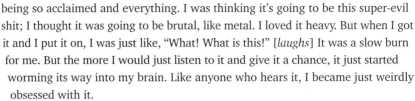

being so acclaimed and everything. I was thinking it's going to be this super-evil shit; I thought it was going to be brutal, like metal. I loved it heavy. But when I got it and I put it on, I was just like, "What! What is this!" [*laughs*] It was a slow burn for me. But the more I would just listen to it and give it a chance, it just started worming its way into my brain. Like anyone who hears it, I became just weirdly obsessed with it.

POPOFF: Why do you think it has such an exalted place in pop culture history?

SHUTT: That's a really good question, because it's not really accessible at all, if you think about it. It kind of meanders here and there, there's only really like five songs on it, if you break it down into arrangements and stuff. It's really unlikely and hard to explain and I'm sure people have been trying to dissect it forever. But you can't argue with the fact that everyone has a *Dark Side of the Moon* story. Like the first time they smoked a dirt-weed joint and they put it on, or going to see the band or even going to see the laser show at the planetarium. You can't really predict what's going to cause ripples in society like that. They just knocked it out of the park. Personally, when I heard it, for the first time I could envision myself in a band. Pink Floyd is one of those early bands that made me think I could do this if I really applied myself.

As for the draw of it, there's just something about those songs, something about the chord progressions and the melodies that probably goes to a deeper level of human subconscious. That combination of waves you're hearing coming out of the speakers just does something to your brain. You're just along for the ride and watching it happen.

And these massive, culturally spanning world-changing albums, like *Thriller* or *Sgt. Pepper*, I don't think that's ever going to happen again. I say that, but then who knows? Someone could come out and totally do it. But something like *Dark Side* was a product of time and place, and it turned out to be the perfect record for them to take over the world.

POPOFF: Digging into the record, *The Dark Side of the Moon* is one where every member of the band shines. Jordan, from a keyboard standpoint, what are a couple of your favorite tracks and Rick Wright moments?

RUDESS: It's hard to pick favorites on that album, because it's so classic. Certainly "Us and Them" is a real favorite. Did you know that Dream Theater covered the entire *Dark Side of the Moon* live? We did the whole thing. I also like "Brain Damage" a lot. "Time," I love the whole introduction to that song; it's very, very powerful, and then finally when it kicks into the tune, it's like, yes! It kind of slams down and that's it.

Just a pair of singles was released from *The Dark Side of The Moon*: "Money" b/w "Any Colour You Like" and "Us and Them" b/w "Time."

But thinking about Rick, "On the Run" is the coolest, because to me Rick Wright was an expert at being—and this sounds academic and boring, but in an apologetic way—he is like the perfect functional keyboardist. He would always play just the right thing. He would be holding a nice organ chord and having the patience, like on "Us and Them," to just lay on the chord and not play too much, just hold it and for the right amount of time [*laughs*]. It takes a lot of patience to do that. Even things like the accompaniment to the whole gospel bit; it's just incredible how patient he could be. He wasn't necessarily somebody who had a terrific keyboard technique, but he would just kind of be in the style and know what would work and what wouldn't.

On that album, there was a real spirit of experimentation. Everybody was just immersed in their tools and discovering new things and trying different things. From a keyboard point of view, they were getting into pretty advanced synthesizers. The famous EMS VCS 3 synthesizer was used. The "On the Run" thing, that was so cutting edge and new at that point. Nobody had heard anything like it unless they were really deep into electronic music and listening to unusual, hard-to-find stuff. For a rock band to do that was kind of brave, but they went for it.

But then in some ways, the way that they would use keyboards was kind of leaning toward the older stuff. I know Rick Wright would always use his Farfisa organ, which is this classic, really old sound. But it seemed to work, along with things like a Wurlitzer, like a piano, that are kind of like standard and quite vintage. I don't know if that was the first time they used a Moog synthesizer, but they used a Minimoog on *The Dark Side of the Moon*, and that was very cutting edge at that time as well.

SHUTT: They were working at the height of their ability and of technology at the time. You had to make your own tape loops back then and then record it. There was so much legwork in making such a simple concept, a synthesizer loop. When we were trying to recreate "On the Run" in the studio, I needed to have that loop, and the machine that we had that could do that wouldn't do it on a click. You couldn't time it perfectly. It was like a millisecond off every loop, unless you plugged a MIDI cable into it and told the computer to make it go at a certain bpm, and then it would do it on a click. But these guys had to do that with a tape machine running and all this shit [*laughs*]. It's mind-blowing to me how a song like "On the Run" sounds so simple. Those songs, it sounds like there's nothing to them but they're just so intricate.

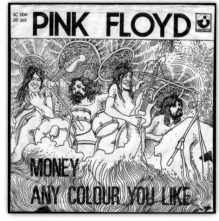

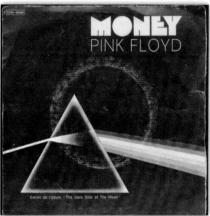

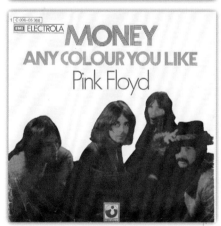

"Money" featured an odd time signature that Pink Floyd made seem normal. Danish, Belgian, and German pressings.

A Minimoog synthesizer, as used extensively on *The Dark Side of the Moon*.

POPOFF: And Steve, where do you think the grand statements are on this record?

HACKETT: For me, the songs that stand out are "Us and Them," the idea of the divide, and then "Eclipse," which is a kind of resolution, but it's a kind of . . . an *acceptance*—a kind of resignation that runs throughout it. I wouldn't say that any of it was particularly cheerful, which is also part of Floyd's appeal. They weren't writing happy, chirpy, chappy things. It's the complete opposite. It's about the things that fuck us up.

Both of these are very slow of tempo. Somebody described their effects as, perhaps, somnambulism set to music. There's a sense of sleepwalking through a lot of these things. There's something of the slow suicide in here, isn't there? There's an awful lot of guilt that seems to run through it. But the guiltier their songs become, the more successful they become. And it seems even now Floyd can do no wrong; having had two of their number pass on, people are still talking about them. But you do get the sense of closing doors. And, of course, that is their story. It's a dying of the light, but they do continue to rage at it.

POPOFF: Kyle, I find this idea of Floyd being accepted by heavy metal guys interesting. Because it's so true. Why do metal fans love *The Dark Side of the Moon* so much?

SHUTT: When "Breathe" comes in, you wouldn't think it's really heavy, but there's something about the vocals, just the delivery of them along with the instrumentation, that's heavy. There's something about the quality of the vocals on that album in general that is heavy. It's like a really nontraditionally heavy album. Everything is done with such authority that it's a similar effect as when you listen to *Master of Puppets*. Even though it's not as fast or sonically intense, it's deceptively heavy.

If you look at something like "Time"; the lyrics can sometimes be so poignant that it's scary. And sometimes you're like, that's what you decided to write about there? [*laughs*] It's like amateurish at the same time as being totally genius. But "Time," the second verse, when it comes in, it's just evil, so I can understand metal fans getting Floyd.

It's hard to critique them. Me being a dude in a rock band in this day and age . . . those guys, they came from such a difficult time to be in a progressive band like that. There were bands like Yes at the same time as them, but Floyd were really pushing the envelope as far as what can be accepted as music or performance. In the early days, they were trying to sue club owners for not paying them because the club owners said that they weren't even playing music. And a judge upheld that decision! [*laughs*] It must be so hard to be a band and

A wide shot of the expanded *Dark Side* touring band, featuring backing vocalists Black Grass and sax player Dick Parry.

a fucking judge is actually ruling that you're not playing what can be considered music. I don't know, it's just hard for a guy like me to want to sit around and critique them. They're fucking visionaries.

POPOFF: Any comment on Clare Torry and her vocal on "Great Gig in the Sky?"
RUDESS: What a voice. What's interesting about that is, applied to a basic rock band, that vocalization that she did is a soulful, gospel-type thing, and it's not part of the normal vocabulary of a rock band. That performance really took it out of context to the point where the band was taking a chance. To ask fans to embrace that. But she was just so powerful and emotional that it was hard to avoid. It's almost as if it was a master plan to include that style amid other things, to bring people into something that they wouldn't have normally listened to.

POPOFF: Any other favorites anyone wants to mention?

SHUTT: A particularly intense one is "Brain Damage," about Roger Waters trying to deal with the loss of Syd, and that decline into a mental delusion. It's really sad, the whole thing, because he started this thing that those four guys were able to turn into something crazy, but then he was just left in the dust. I remember when he died. It was one of those things like, where were you when Syd Barrett died? I was working at a photocopy center getting ready for our band's first album to come out.

Also "Us and Them" is just a phenomenal song; it's so simple that it's deceiving. And there's no solo in it. For a song that's almost eight minutes long, there's only one little tiny piano lick that can even be considered a solo. Usually when a prog band has an eight-minute song, it's just chock-full of keyboard solos and guitar trickery and vocal trickery, but "Us and Them" is so simple. And that's what it's about: us and them. And the chorus, the way the vocal harmonies work, that vocal melody in the chorus, it's just so haunting.

POPOFF: An anomaly on the album, perhaps, is "Money." "Time" is fairly angular and rocky, but this is much more rhythmic, almost funky.

HACKETT: Yes, "Money" is just a very good rock song, about greed, and it functions in a strange time signature. I can't remember if it was a seven or nine.

POPOFF: It's kind of a 7/4, but it deviates.

HACKETT: And then it goes into a shuffle, so you've got a 6/8 as well. I remember seeing them opening with "Money," with the sound of the cash registers, or the sounds of the bags of change, perhaps, of walking around the wall—Floydian slip—walking around the room. I saw them at London's Rainbow Theatre, which is a place where Genesis played once or twice too. I thought this early version of what I guess you could call surround sound was very impressive. This placing of the sound that way turned out to be important.

Reality has caught up to Floyd where, doing surround sound mixes now, addresses that; it's become the norm rather than the exception. I remember doing an album and mixing it Ambisonically, which I think Floyd were using at one point. I know that they were using quad before that. I believe they moved to Ambisonic. Now, of course, that is an industry standard. They were at the forefront of that type of thing also.

RUDESS: I like "Money" as well. It's one of the more commercial songs. I love the fact that it's a great example—especially if you're a prog musician—of playing in an odd time signature but not having it in your face. Because a lot of times we musicians will go at an odd time signature in kind of an academic way. But "Money" is a song that flows. People don't even realize that it's in an odd time. It's come up for me many times in various bands along the years: Let's do something weird where it's, like, in seven, but it's not in-your-face kind of seven. "Money" manages to do that but keep it smooth. That kind of smooth quality, that's a big part of what Floyd represents.

POPOFF: And "Money" has got a great guitar solo, one of the livelier ones from Dave, to match the swing of the track, I imagine. Tell me about Dave as a guitarist.

RUDESS: A lot of it is just his tone, which is just so beautiful. It's interesting to look at David Gilmour through the lens of kind of years later, and seeing how much guitar playing has evolved in terms of playing and technique. We have these guys playing a million miles an hour, which is just so incredible. But not many of them will have the soul and the emotion that David Gilmour is able to bring to his playing.

What's interesting to me about an instrument like the guitar, unlike a piano, the expression really comes from the pitch bending and the speed and the depth of the vibrato. There are two things, speed and depth, when you're playing a lead. And those are things that allow you to tell who's who. If you listen to Steve Morse or Jeff Beck or David Gilmour, you very much can tell who's who. And it's by the way they use the vibrato and how wide the vibrato is. David Gilmour has his emotional, almost perfect vibrato—not too fast, not too slow; it just really sits well. Plus that great tone.

SHUTT: David Gilmour is one of the most minimal guitar players you'll ever hear. But every note he plays seems pored over. He really pours his soul into every little tiny lick he does. Because the guitar in Pink Floyd isn't really at the forefront. It's just as important as the keyboards or anything else going on, the background vocals. And the way that Roger Waters plays bass, it's almost like the guitar part is being played on the bass, where David Gilmour gets to noodle here and there. Almost like a call and response to the vocals sometimes.

But yes, as a guitar player, he put so much thought into his little tiny parts. It's inspiring to me because I'm usually drawn to guitar

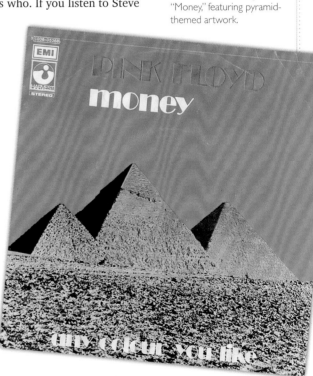

Italian seven-inch single of "Money," featuring pyramid-themed artwork.

Radio City Music Hall
Midnight Performance
Sat. March 17th, 1973

1260 Avenue Of The Americas,
New York, NY 10020
Admission $4.00

Pink Floyd

The Dark Side of the Moon

1973 U.S. Tour

Gilmour and Waters flank Mason's drum kit during a show on the final US
leg of the *The Dark Side of the Moon* tour, June 1973.

players who do things that I would never think to do. When I was younger, I was really into Randy Rhoads, Dimebag Darrell, supreme metal shredder dudes. But the older I got, the more I got into things I can't do. And David Gilmour is the king of that. He's taking an instrument like a Stratocaster and doing things with it that shouldn't be able to be done [*laughs*].

HACKETT: With David, there's more of a blues approach. Funny enough, whenever I work with my brother and do guitar for him on the occasional thing, he always wants me to play in a bluesy style. And it's because of all of the sonic developments that happened with electric guitar, the really important things, like a guitar learning to sustain and scream and truly emulate the human voice, as opposed to just sounding like Duane Eddy or some of the guitarists who sounded like they were playing *Bonanza* theme stuff, Hank Marvin and all the rest—and I'm not disparaging those guys—the stuff for spy movies and cowboy movies and all the rest. But that was a different era.

Now guitar starts to change, the sound starts to change, and it happens within blues. It happens with Eric Clapton, the Stones, Hendrix, Jeff Beck. I suspect it's happening in Britain before it's happening in America. But perhaps there's that idea of the guitar sounding most authentic when it's played in blues phrases.

I think there's a certain amount of Eric Clapton in Floyd. Also there's a kind of Stratocaster sound, isn't there? The hollowness at the root of that. The deliberately single-coil pickups type of thing. I find his playing interesting, but for me it's the lyrical strength that is more so the calling card of Floyd.

POPOFF: Anything you want to say about the front cover?
SHUTT: It's one of those record covers you can just stare at. It's so simple and stark that you wouldn't think there's much to look at, but it's just so classic. It makes you want to know more—that's what I love about it.
HACKETT: It's minimalist, but it could've been better, to be honest. Maybe there was some kind of justification. I'm not sure there's a complete marriage of title and image. But then people who are taken with it probably ascribe an awful lot of justification after the fact.

A closeup of the gong on fire during the first of two benefit shows for the homeless charity Shelter, which took place at Earls Court, London, May 18, 1973.

That's the other thing Genesis had in common with Pink Floyd: the fact that we used Hipgnosis, who were providing album covers for Pink Floyd, Led Zeppelin. And sometimes they would try to sell us the same ideas, and if we didn't take them, they would just crop up on a Led Zeppelin album. Literally—I'm not kidding you. Genesis always preferred to have something pictorial rather than graphic. And it wasn't until I left the band that they were eventually talked into having something fairly graphic, like *Dark Side* or *The Wall*.

POPOFF: In the final analysis, does all of this add up to what we would consider a progressive rock band? Is *The Dark Side of the Moon* a prog album?
RUDESS: There's a legitimate argument whether Pink Floyd is really prog or not. I think they are because they were so cutting edge. Basically, progressive rock refers to the kind of bands that are pushing the boundaries, opening new channels, trying things that haven't been done before. Whether it's with harmony or rhythm or sounds or production techniques. Pink Floyd, with their spirit of experimentation and invention, on that level they're very much prog. It just so happens that they're one of the more mellow prog bands.

And with their pretty unique use of spoken word and sound effects, they obviously got inspiration from a lot of other things, and it's always challenging to call on these elements. But they came up with that formula, and with perfect timing it turned out to be a twist on the idea of prog and rock that basically had a huge impact on the world.

HACKETT: The true decision-makers are not the perpetrators. It's not the writers and performers, it's the audience that will get together and will say, "Oh, remember that moment and that moment?" They'll all agree what that moment was all about, and there'll be some sort of concurrence, a kind of quorum, among the supporters and critics, and people will understand in time after something has being digested over decades. I think we all can agree now that an album like *Dark Side* created an industry standard.

CHAPTER 9

WISH YOU WERE HERE

WITH HEATHER FINDLAY, STEVE ROTHERY, AND KYLE SHUTT

SIDE 1
1. Shine On You Crazy Diamond (1–5) 13:32
   (Lyrics: Waters)
   Part 1
   (Music: Wright, Waters, Gilmour)
   Part 2
   (Music: Gilmour, Waters, Wright)
   Part 3
   (Music: Waters, Gilmour, Wright)
   Part 4
   (Music: Gilmour, Wright, Waters)
   Part 5
   (Music: Waters, Gilmour, Wright)
2. Welcome to the Machine   7:32
   (Waters)

SIDE 2
1. Have a Cigar   5:24
   (Waters)
2. Wish You Were Here   5:40
   (Music: Waters, Gilmour; lyrics: Waters)
3. Shine On You Crazy Diamond (6-9) 12:29
   (Lyrics: Waters)
   Part 6
   (Music: Wright, Waters, Gilmour)
   Part 7
   (Music: Waters, Gilmour, Wright)
   Part 8
   (Music: Gilmour, Wright, Waters)
   Part 9
   (Music: Wright)

Recorded at Abbey Road Studios, St. John's Wood, London

PERSONNEL: Roger Waters—vocals, bass guitar, synthesizer, guitar, tape effects; David Gilmour—vocals, guitars, lap steel guitar, synthesizer, keyboards, tape effects; Richard Wright—organs, synthesizers, piano, backing vocals; Nick Mason—drums, percussion, tape effects

GUEST PERFORMANCES: Roy Harper—vocals; Dick Parry—tenor saxophone, baritone saxophone; Carlena Williams—backing vocals; Venetta Fields—backing vocals

Produced by Pink Floyd

Released September 15, 1975 (UK); September 12, 1975 (US)

A painter paints, a writer writes, and writing is rewriting. These lessons inform the making of *Wish You Were Here* as well as the finished record, quite possibly the band's crowning achievement. Its effortless success reminds the blocked artist that if he or she follows the above dictums, good things happen.

Floyd began the album with the enviable challenge of having nothing left to prove and sacks of money too heavy to carry. They were also beginning to get on each other's nerves and had lost the loving feeling of playing live as well. They were beginning to attract a massive and diverse crowd, many of whom were seemingly ignorant of the band's purpose and its hard-hoed path to the top.

The machine demanded, however, that they make another record (and they almost said no, forgetting that they were artists). Journalist Nick Kent wrote that they had lost it and the band almost believe him, in the process demonstrating their thin skins. But they also had the bones of some new music that they floated live. Almost sleepwalking, they took these tracks into the studio and began acting like a recording band, doing what they were told. "Shine On You Crazy Diamond" is one of those songs. And despite a dearth of material, two others, "You Gotta Be Crazy" and "Raving and Drooling," were tossed in the save pile to emerge later on *Animals*.

Working at Abbey Road from mid-afternoon to late into the night for most of the first half of 1975, the band apparently did a lot of nothing for long stretches—playing darts, getting drunk, trying to get Nick Mason to care while he was consumed with divorcing his wife. Writing and rewriting, thinking, doing those things mortal artists do, second-guessing and strategizing—all became replacements for lightning bolts of inspiration. Roger set upon the idea of absence as a theme for the record, thereby ascribing a concept to a Floyd album for the first time.

PINK FLOYD

TOP: Wright, Mason, and Gilmour prepare for a game of pre-gig football in Colmar, France, June 22, 1974.

INSET: Yugoslavian pressing of *Wish You Were Here* featuring alternate artwork issued by the Jugoton label.

Waters onstage in France, June 1974.

But the concept of *Wish You Were Here*, as it finally wound to completion, was loose, and those are often the best kind of concepts. "Shine On You Crazy Diamond" succeeds brilliantly in telling the intense tale of Syd Barrett's flameout—a sort of reportage that paints a positive where there was none to be had. Roger wishes Syd was there for Syd's own sake.

"Wish You Were Here" on the other hand, is the receptacle of most of the empathy for Syd, but its genius and status as many a fan's favorite cherished Floyd moment lies in its multiple refracted meanings. It's a tragic lament of a love song; it's also a howl of pain at the hollowing out of the four souls in Roger's band, each scarred in its own way by burnout, summed up in the concept of the thousand-yard stare to which so many spent rockers quietly admit.

Waters underscores the idea of concept by nestling "Wish You Were Here" between two thirteen-minute chunks of "Shine On You Crazy Diamond," one that opens the album about as tentatively and Ninja-like as an album was ever opened, one that closes the album as grandly as "Eclipse" closed *The Dark Side of the Moon*.

Also wrapped in this truckload of gauze are two songs that relate to Syd only in a contrived manner, but nonetheless relate strongly to the concept of absence—the band being absent from each other, absent of ideas, absentmindedly going through the motions on stage, absent from normal life, absent in the studio. Both "Welcome to the Machine" and "Have a Cigar" are acidic diatribes aimed at the industry, the first set to flourishes of machine-stamping synths, the second to a welcome bit of workingman's rock, guest vocalist Roy Harper uttering the immortal line, "By the way, which one's Pink?"

In the end, *Wish You Were Here*, despite its challenging status as arguably the world's longest four-track E.P., notched sales of six-times platinum in the United States and is estimated to have sold over thirteen million copies worldwide. As well, the album hit #1 on the *Billboard* charts. Every last song on it is a regular-rotation classic rock staple—"Shine On You Crazy Diamond" is spun mostly in its four-minute single edit form—and deep Floyd fans have mostly deemed the record flawless. Darkening the experience, however, is this deflating thought: *Wish You Were Here* is the last record for Pink Floyd as anything resembling a democracy.

POPOFF: To start, can you give me a bit of a summary of the conceptual theme or themes addressed on *Wish You Were Here*?
FINDLAY: It's quite diverse, really. It's nice that it's bookended with the "Crazy Diamond" theme but in the middle it's an attempt to bite the hand that feeds in a few ways, addressing how they felt about their record company at the time. Obviously, they thought they weren't getting fed as

ABOVE: Rick Wright at the Birmingham Hippodrome—one of nine stops on the British Winter Tour '74.

BELOW: The comic book–style program for the band's 1974 tour.

much as they should be and they were dissatisfied with the returns that they were getting. So, there's a little angst in there, and obviously it's reflective as well, given the theme of Syd Barrett, and the band lamenting his not being around with them anymore.

POPOFF: But for a brief moment, Syd was there! What do you know about that story of Syd showing up at the studio?
FINDLAY: Very peculiar. There are variations on what happened, but Rick Wright seems to have the most informative account. He states that it was definitely just as the vocal sessions for "Crazy Diamond" were about to begin, and given the lyrics were about Syd, it was most peculiar. In more recent years both Nick Mason and Roger Waters have said that they don't know if it was actually that particular song that they were about to record when he walked in. But the fact remains that Syd just showed up that day, and it was quite traumatic for them to see that there was this guy who was acting weird, hanging about, and then after almost an hour they realize it's Syd Barrett. And that, coupled with the poignancy that it was "Crazy Diamond" that they were

beginning a vocal session for . . . quite spooky, really. Who knows how his intuition led him there that day?

ROTHERY: Yes, so Syd shows up at Abbey Road, and it's ostensibly to record his parts. Nobody recognized him, which is a terribly sad thing in every way possible, really. But I agree, "Shine On You Crazy Diamond" is incredibly powerful and a quite poignant acknowledgement of how special Syd was in those early days and how he'd basically lost it.

As for the secondary theme, this disdain for the industry, there was the alienation Roger felt after the success of *The Dark Side of the Moon*, and he was looking to experiment. In fact, at the beginning there was the experiment of making music without any musical instruments. Or was that after? Part of the pad sound on "Shine On You Crazy Diamond" is from that session, where they rubbed the edge of a glass to sustain a note and then actually mixed that in with the string synth at the beginning of "Shine On You Crazy Diamond."

A 1980s twelve-inch pressing of Syd Barrett's "Wouldn't You Miss Me (Dark Globe)," a song he originally released in 1969. According to several accounts, Barrett showed up at the studio as the band prepared to record vocals for "Shine On You Crazy Diamond."

So that spirit of experimentation is obviously still with them, and they essentially started off doing something that was very much a direct rebellion against the success that they'd had with *The Dark Side of the Moon*. For me, *Wish You Were Here* is as close to a perfect Floyd album as you could find. To give you an idea of what it means to me, I was fifteen when it came out, and I remember listening to it on a portable cassette recorder on the beach at night in Whitby where I was living, and looking at the stars and thinking, this is it, this is what I want to do with my life. There can be no better thing to do with your existence. It was such a strong influence on me, not only as a musician, but as a signpost to what it's possible to achieve.

It kind of transcends; there are certain artists and certain albums throughout time that stand head and shoulders above others, and for me, *Wish You Were Here* is one of those. From Dave Gilmour's guitar playing, which is so sublime, to the way that the different themes worked together. Far and away, it's my favorite Pink Floyd album.

SHUTT: It's personally my favorite Floyd album as well. I came in about the time they did the *Obscured by Clouds* soundtrack and *Meddle*, and I feel that *Wish You Were Here* was their shining peak. "Shine On You Crazy Diamond" is a great bookend to the album, but the three songs in the middle just really resonate with me, having been through the music industry wringer of seeing all the suits and the people that don't know how to make music trying to tell you how to make music.

Lyrically, more so than *The Dark Side of the Moon*, *Wish You Were Here* is just fantastic. There's really nothing wrong with it at all. "Wish You Were Here," the song, is the best song ever written. From a band that is known for doing these crazy long prog jams, it's this little ditty that has two verses and one chorus. If you ask me, the chorus to "Wish You Were Here" is so good, I'd like to think they heard it and played it and recorded it, and were like, "Yeah, let's just do it one time—it's perfect." Like why beat it into the ground? [*laughs*]

Growing up hearing "Wish You Were Here" on the radio, I loved it but I didn't really understand it. He only sings the hook once in that whole song and it's super effective, just a really different arrangement for them. It's the best song ever written.

The band I've put together to perform our *Doom Side of the Moon* tribute album is covering it. And approaching that one is like, how do I approach covering the best song ever written? Like, what the hell? But for my money, *Wish You Were Here* is hands down their best record.

POPOFF: Before we get too far into the songs, what do you make of the album cover? How does it relate to what the listener is about to experience?
FINDLAY: The way I've always interpreted it is this relationship between them and their record company, and possibly this sense that record contracts have a tendency to be doomed or ill-fated, and there's always this darkness that lingers underneath them. What's the point of contracts in the first place? They go up in flames—the thing that you signed in the first place—because there's not much truth to it. And that goes along with their philosophical, truth-seeking approach to earlier Floyd albums.
ROTHERY: I always thought that Storm Thorgerson's forte was to create something that asks more questions than anything else. Like, "What's happening there? Why is this guy on fire? Where are they meeting?" It posed all these questions. I didn't really ascribe any direct reference to the cover other than it's a stunning visual that pulls you in and makes you ask questions.
SHUTT: It's a lot like a cover for one of my other favorite bands, the Replacements, the cover of *Pleased to Meet Me*, where there are two total opposites shaking hands, meeting in the middle. The *Pleased to Meet Me* cover was a take on an old Elvis cover, where it was a big-suited, ringed-up, Rolexed hand shaking hands with a blue-collar, covered-in-grease kind of hand.

And the cover of *Wish You Were Here* has a dude in a suit, all prim and proper, shaking hands with somebody who is literally on fire [*laughs*], which sums up the music industry versus the artist. Because the industry works on a nine-to-five basis, just like any other job. These record label guys, they clock in in the morning and they leave Friday at five p.m. and they don't think about anything. But the dudes in the bands, we have to constantly make more songs, be in the studio, we have to tour more than ever these days to make a living.

Back then, too, the labels dictated a lot more of the band's touring schedule. It wasn't as much of an independent venture as it is today with bands. Being on tour for nine months out of the year and having to go write another record and make it and keep up with all the fans who track you down and then do interviews—you really do feel like you're on fire sometimes.

The band performs in France under the watchful gaze of the Chairman, 1974.

I like the little touches that you wouldn't normally notice, like how the edge of the photograph that's on fire is bleeding out of the frame instead of going into it. On the back of the record, you can't see the person inside the suit. That's a really cool image; it's a guy holding a record, but the record is not gold, it's clear, and the person isn't even in the clothing. And they're in a desert, devoid of any life, and if you look below it, the white border is slashed and some of the sand from the desert's pouring out. It's a really depressing but honest depiction of what it's like being in a successful band that has to tour constantly. You're constantly drained and you just feel like you're on fire. Sometimes you feel trapped and there's nothing you can do to get out of it.

POPOFF: Looking at the album itself, I suppose the anchor is "Shine On You Crazy Diamond." How would you characterize the way the guys look at Syd in that song or song suite?
FINDLAY: It shows a lot of compassion for him. They obviously missed him and they obviously thought he was a genius. They were all childhood friends with Syd, and the fact that he wasn't around anymore was something that saddened them all greatly. And along with any fans of Syd's music at the time, everybody lamented the fact that he wasn't able to be there, and they wanted him to be able to shine as he once did.

Unfortunately, substances and mental health issues got the best of him, and that reflects well in the lyrics. What better tribute than a twelve-and-a-half-minute tune? It says a lot about how much they cared for him, and missed him being around. When Syd was placed aside, the new dynamic became Waters versus Gilmour. Those two then had to battle things out between themselves, and sometimes that disrupts the creative flow. But I quite enjoyed the contrast between Gilmour and Waters. They're kind of like the fire and the ice, aren't they? But when a band member is removed, the structure has to be rebuilt and this is what we got, and arguably this is the very last album on which it would ever work without dysfunction.

SHUTT: Yes, and it's weird, but the pressure of being so big was getting to them and beginning to tear them apart. *The Dark Side of the Moon* was such a massively successful album and they were basically on tour for two years supporting it. And the thing was on the charts for fifteen years. But as far as the interpersonal relationships in the band, success had started to drive them apart, and Nick Mason was going through a divorce, which kind of made him withdraw from giving a crap about the day-to-day operations. Essentially, the record just fell on Gilmour and Waters.

POPOFF: Back to "Shine On You Crazy Diamond," another thing I was wondering, what does this idea of breaking it up into two sections accomplish?

SHUTT: It makes for a good live show. Once you start playing part one of "Shine On You Crazy Diamond," the crowd already knows what they're in for, and it kind of whets the appetite of everyone watching. But as far as listening to it on the record, I miss albums that were meant to be listened to as albums.

Yes is another one of my favorite bands, and they're known for doing these entire sides with one twenty-minute song, just like Floyd earlier in the '70s. But breaking it up is a smart device because generally those songs are noodly and meandering; if you create a two-part framing structure, it brings some kind of cohesion so the prog people can actually sit there and, with help from the record sleeve, try to figure out where all the different parts start and stop. So, it provides another level, something extra to think about, and it makes you think of the album as a cohesive narrative, even if it's loose or not one at all.

FINDLAY: "Crazy Diamond" is almost an album in itself. Not many people have succeeded in a nine-part epic at twelve-and-a-half minutes. Then you add to that its counterpart, its bookend. I like the idea, but I feel that the songs in between seem a little ungrounded. And were they really meant to fit in with Syd's story? "Wish You Were Here" fits well, but then you've got "Welcome to the Machine" and "Have a Cigar" that are clearly about how they're feeling about the music industry.

That's where you get this slightly disjointed feel. But I think they serve as glue. This was a difficult album for them to put together in the studio, but it worked musically despite this lyrical disconnect. Everything seemed to gel sonically, and somehow this feels like a family of songs. But I still think, lyrically, they're slightly farther apart than you would guess at first listen, and that's something that is helped by framing the album with the two sections of the same song.

I particularly like the combination of synthesizers in the long intro of "Crazy Diamond," and all the frequencies that come through on headphones, from these classy synthesizer tricks weaving in and out intermittently. Plus, I'm a sucker for David Gilmour's voice. He's got a voice that puts me in quite a meditative zone. Whatever it is about the frequencies in his voice, whenever he starts

Pink Floyd—including sax player Dick Parry—during the US leg of the *Wish You Were Here* tour.

To coincide with Pink Floyd's 1975 US tour, Capitol Records put out a seven-track promo LP, *Tour/'75*.

singing, that's always a great thing for me. I love Rick Wright and his wonderful jazz-influenced keys playing and the interplay between him and Gilmour.

As a female prog singer, I appreciate these backing vocals. Venetta Lee Fields was a session singer at the time. She was a musical theater actress and was part of this group loosely called the Blackberries. She sang with the Stones and Ike & Tina Turner and some other soul artists and was a busy session artist at the time, and this is her and Carlena Williams.

POPOFF: And as you say, the song that relates thematically most closely to "Shine On You Crazy Diamond" is the title track. That intro to "Wish You Were Here" is a classic Floyd moment. What might that say about the Syd story, it being off in the distance, and then the acoustic guitar coming in crystal-clear? Does that have any resonance for you as a metaphor for the Syd situation?

FINDLAY: Maybe. The fact that there's this very English-sounding radio broadcast, and something off in the distance. Is it that they have difficulty tuning him in and, in any event, he's at home? Wherever they are, they're always thinking of Syd and they wished they were with him. It does offer a sense of distance. But then there's closeness at the same time, because that stunning acoustic guitar intro offers intimacy, and with a lamenting feel. Something about that acoustic part and the arrangement feels so tribute-like as well.

ROTHERY: "Wish You Were Here" is one of the few Floyd songs you can sit down with an acoustic guitar and play [*laughs*]. One of the things we do sometimes is our Marillion weekends, these three-day concerts. We did one in 2003 and we did "Wish You Were Here," so I got to be David Gilmour for a day. A friend of mine, Bonnie Tyler's guitarist, Matt Prior, played acoustic guitar and it's up on YouTube and it's one of our most popular videos, at around a million views. And the funny thing is, Steve Hogarth, our singer, didn't really know it, but the audience sang it; quite an interesting thing to watch. I remember first hearing it, with the radio being tuned in and the guy playing along to the radio. It seemed like such a cool way to introduce a song.

SHUTT: Favorite song on the album, hands down. It starts out with the tinny little radio going between stations, which I believe they recorded out in Nick Mason's car. It then goes into that little twelve-string electric melody, kind of in the background, and then when that acoustic solo comes in over that, right there at the beginning of that song, that's one of the best guitar solos ever written.

And I love the solos and everything that are on top of the synth runs in "Have a Cigar"; those are great, but there's something about "Wish You Were Here." It's the best damn song ever written. I don't care who you are. If you can find a better song than "Wish You Were Here," good luck to you.

POPOFF: And as we've touched upon, "Welcome to the Machine" and "Have a Cigar" are closely related. Can you flesh those two out a bit more?

FINDLAY: It certainly seems that there's a sense of dissatisfaction, that they're maybe a bit jaded with the amount of work and time and effort that they're putting in. And "Have a Cigar" is about when they enter a meeting with the record company, and the record company has a complete polar-opposite view that it's all about them.

And maybe this is also about Roger Waters and his need to be in control and to have everything as it should be and know everything down to the finer details. It echoes how many artists feel they're pushed around, and how the greed and hypocrisy of the record company can wear you down. We become farmed like ants, and there are one or two people at the top reaping the rewards.

It was brave of Roger at the time to make this unprecedented move of biting the hand that feeds. To strike out against the record company, there must've been a risk and a gamble involved, although contracts were probably in place to protect them to a degree. But the way it's been handled in the music is very creative. And it's quite a menacing backdrop we have in "Welcome to the Machine."

ROTHERY: That whole pulsing aspect in that song was interesting, although it's not one of my favorite tracks. Something doesn't quite satisfy. But very visual and cinematic, with the synths sounding like a machine throughout and turning it off at the end. It's a great way to encapsulate that feeling of the machinery.

We had moments in our career where we had just a glimpse of that sort of success, in the mid-'80s, when our album *Misplaced Childhood* and "Kayleigh" did really well and we sold several million copies. And it does become a machine. Unless you have very strong management, you can't help but feel exploited. We toured for nearly a year and a half for that record, several times around the world, and by the end you're pretty dysfunctional as a human being.

I can only imagine what it must've been like for those guys, the amount of success they were having. It's a coldly impersonal machine that's designed to exploit the artist and make as much money for everyone involved—record companies, management, promoter—with no thought to the costs it takes out on the musicians.

I can completely relate. We've been signed to a major label, we've done seventeen albums, and we've had all those faxes from the label saying that they're going to take no prisoners to make sure that this record is a success. The usual kind of music bullshit. I can see exactly where they're coming from in terms of their frustrations and disillusionment.

POPOFF: Can you also relate to the idea of "Which one's Pink?" Not knowing who the guys in the band are sort of thing?

ROTHERY: Absolutely. When Fish left Marillion and Steve Hogarth joined, the first tour we did in America with Steve, Capitol was still turning out promo

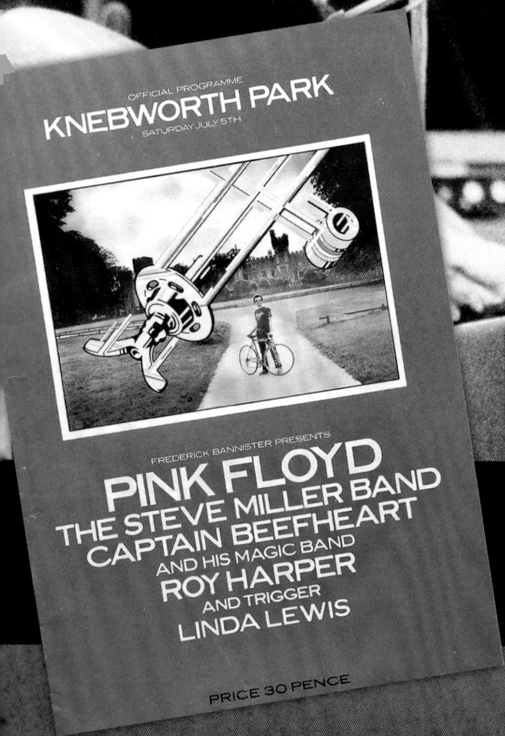

OFFICIAL PROGRAMME

KNEBWORTH PARK
SATURDAY JULY 5TH

FREDERICK BANNISTER PRESENTS

PINK FLOYD
THE STEVE MILLER BAND
CAPTAIN BEEFHEART
AND HIS MAGIC BAND
ROY HARPER
AND TRIGGER
LINDA LEWIS

PRICE 30 PENCE

ABOVE: Roger Waters leads the way during Pink Floyd's headlining performance at the Knebworth Festival, July 5, 1975.

INSET: A program for the event, which was attended by more than one hundred thousand fans.

photos with Fish in them. Absolutely they have no idea. And they don't really care—they could be selling beans, really.

POPOFF: I can really see that happening with Pink Floyd because they famously were the faceless band.
ROTHERY: Absolutely; what they came to represent was the show. And that continued throughout Floyd's career. Roger is, on the whole, the main songwriter and Dave Gilmour is that visual focus when he's playing. But, ultimately, the Pink Floyd show is that—it's a show. It's not about the individuals. Which is the reason there are so many successful Pink Floyd tribute acts out there. Because they put together something that very much looks like the live show that the Floyd had maybe during the *Momentary Lapse of Reason* time. And it becomes almost theater. They'll wear the same clothes and it's almost like a choreographed approach to recreating the albums. That's why it works, because it wasn't so much about their personalities, it was about the visual impact of their shows.
SHUTT: It depends on your personality; everybody is different. Sometimes you can write amazing songs but you really don't want to be in front of a microphone with thousands of people staring at you. Maynard Keenan from Tool is a good example of that—a frontman who takes a back seat to the imagery—and Roger Waters is the same. He was an unfortunate frontman. He never wanted to be the frontman or anything, but when you're a musician of a certain caliber, certain things aren't a choice. You have to play the show and you have to make the album, and when things that go along with that conflict with your own personality, that's when it can get weird. Sometimes it works and sometimes it doesn't. With Pink Floyd it worked, because they were able to take that frustration and pour it into their art, which was a marriage of visuals and musical compositions. And they were just so original that I can't imagine anybody else coming along that would even come close to doing what they have been able to accomplish.

POPOFF: Kyle, what are your thoughts on this pairing of songs, "Welcome to the Machine" and "Have a Cigar"?
SHUTT: "Welcome to the Machine" is such a strange song. Despite loads of synthesizers, it's such a simple concept. It's almost like a nonconcept. Look, if you took the vocals off that song, it would be little more than like a sci-fi soundtrack. But whenever the vocals come in, you realize that there is a song underneath all this sparse noise. With our band the Sword going further and

further, we're starting to recognize that songs are more than just a collection of riffs. Floyd has taught me that, to kind of step back and hear the song for what it is.

As for "Have a Cigar," Roy Harper did a great job on the vocals. I've read that Roger Waters wished that he had done it himself. It's one of their most traditional song arrangements, because it's verse-chorus-verse-chorus. The chorus isn't even really like an entire refrain. It's almost like a pre-chorus, getting ready for the guitar solos that come in. It's such a good song, but it does things only one time. They do this one cool little descending guitar lick in the intro, and you think that would be a hook normally, but they did it one time and then went on to other things. That's what I love about Floyd.

POPOFF: Heather, what do you think of the guys bringing in Harper to play the record company bigshot on "Have a Cigar"?

FINDLAY: I love Roy Harper, so it's really cool that he got the break to do that tune. There are various stories. But this is probably where we start to see the competitive element between Gilmour and Waters, reading between the lines. I've heard one story where Waters just said, "Hey, I've been thinking we should get Roy Harper in to do the vocal on 'Have a Cigar.'" I think he was calling their bluff a little, and they went, "Yeah, that's a brilliant idea. We love Roy Harper!"

And I think he was a bit disappointed that everybody else agreed. Because when you hear that vocal, it's so similar to his vocal on "Sheep" on *Animals*, that it must've been a very fine line as to what Waters and Gilmour seemingly put down before and decided that they didn't like. What you have with Roy Harper's final delivery is something in between the essence of Gilmour and Waters, that they tried before.

But was it really a case of they couldn't decide who had done the best take in the end and maybe they just decided to get somebody else in? Because possibly there was friction over deciding who should take the lead vocal on that one. But you never know band politics. The scenario could have easily been something slightly more band politics–related than just Roy happened to be in Studio 3.

French and Japanese pressings of Pink Floyd's "Have a Cigar" single, b/w "Shine on You Crazy Diamond (Part 1)" and "Welcome to the Machine" on their respective B-sides.

POPOFF: Could you just elaborate a bit more on Roger's personality and how it dominates the band dynamic? Because his position in the band is a big part of the narrative moving past *Wish You Were Here*.

SHUTT: Roger's a harsh critic of the modern world [*laughs*]. Success seemed to affect all of them in different ways, and maybe he started to feel that he was more important than the rest. I know once it all blew up they didn't talk for a very long time.

You can't be in a band with somebody for twenty years and not simultaneously hate their guts and defend them to the death. It's hard to work these interpersonal relationships into a business that's thriving over decades. It's just impossible. I'm slowly learning how to do it as the Sword is kind of nearing the end of our second decade. We've been around longer than we haven't, as far as our ages go.

With Floyd, when it's on such a massive scale, it can't be easy to maintain those interpersonal relationships. I'm sure egos had to get wildly out of control, especially when money and drugs are involved, and especially if you surround yourself with people who are just yes men and friends with motives other than your best interests. It's got to do crazy things to your point of view.

Gilmour and Paul McCartney backstage at Knebworth House.

FINDLAY: I agree, and compared to David, Roger is naturally the more fiery character. Roger seems to be very much an alpha male. I know he's been described as a megalomaniac, and he likes to be very much in control of things. Gilmour has always sounded very much like the opposite of that, very laid-back and would go with the flow. But he's somebody that doesn't like to be pushed around as well.

Creatively, David's always admitted that he's not so much a lyricist, and that he tends to be a collaborator lyrically. Whereas Roger Waters seems to have a very clear idea of where he wants a song and an idea to go. Roger says what he thinks, whereas Gilmour tends to be more of a typical Englishman.

You can even see it in the tonality of their voices, the way they deliver. Waters is quite snappy and tight in throat and whinier, and David has this lovely, lamenting, chocolatey smooth, soft, whispery, delicate tone. And that's absolutely perfect for what they wanted to deliver in Pink Floyd. They're almost like light and dark, day and night. It's required in a band, especially when you have lengthy passages of instrumental music as well. That contrast between them is important to engage the listener.

SIDE 1
1. Pigs on the Wing 1   1:24
   (Waters)
2. Dogs   17:01
   (Waters, Gilmour)

SIDE 2
1. Pigs (Three Different Ones) 11:20
   (Waters)
2. Sheep   10:22
   (Waters)
3. Pigs on the Wing 2   1:24
   (Waters)

Recorded at Britannia Row, Islington, London

PERSONNEL: Roger Waters—lead and harmony vocals, bass guitar, acoustic guitar, rhythm guitar, tape effects, vocoder; David Gilmour—lead vocals, lead guitar, acoustic guitar, rhythm guitar, bass guitar, talk box; Rick Wright—Hammond organ, electric piano, Minimoog, ARP string synthesizer, piano, Clavinet, harmony vocals; Nick Mason—drums, percussion, tape effects

Produced by Pink Floyd

Released September 23, 1977 (UK); October 2, 1977 (US)

CHAPTER 10

ANIMALS

WITH NICK BEGGS, HEATHER FINDLAY, AND STEVE ROTHERY

Sullen sister album to *Wish You Were Here, Animals* emerged at a very different time for Floyd, not because of anything external like punk or the events of 1977, but rather due to Roger's loudly ticking internal clock. Sure, the rote narrative says that punk rock was all the rage, and prog bands were on their heels from a barrage of ridicule. But the barrage was minimal and prog bands were not on their heels—the big four or six doing just fine, thanks, in the late '70s. If there was any pressure on the band, it was due more so to the pressure to impress again after two massive albums, that pressure denting heads and creating the foundation for *The Wall,* but also causing charged psychic breakage in the spaces between a small band of non–rock stars coping with the machine grinding fantastically and now also monotonously.

Roger takes charge, and now one person—Roger for three more records, and then David—will lead until Floyd's demise post–*The Endless River*. But Roger doesn't only lead, he drives and all the while quietly seethes. And on *Animals* he sinks his teeth into those who lead, society's rapacious and upper crusts, even as the rapacious and blood-lusted all wind up fat and dying of cancer in the end anyhow, along with the sheep who arrive there without the spoils, aside from a bit of heart-darkening revenge.

Loosely based on (but ultimately quite graphically connected to) George Orwell's *Animal Farm*, *Animals* also provokes ruminations on *1984*. But it's also about 1977, and a hot and rotting Britain, which in a sense does make its relationship to punk salient. Waters and Joe Strummer were spitting at the same things, and in fact they carped with the same caw (tellingly, David takes only one lead vocal). It's just that concerning Floyd, one couldn't conceive of a musical mélange still part of the rock idiom that was farther from punk. It was almost as if punk demonstrated for Roger for the first time how expendable his band was—it's surprising, in a sense, that Waters did not go punk, although he would find his own way to increase the amount and intensity of instilled terror with sound (like explosions!) through the rest of Floyd and into his solo career.

But if there was astringent punk politics in the manifesto Roger slashed across *Animals*, his impatience was also demonstrated in the absurdist and even Python-esque disposition and dispensation of the record. The Monty Python troupe was at its peak in the late '70s. Roger flies a pig above Battersea Power Station (his idea, not Hipgnosis's) while the track list reads "Pigs on the Wing 1," "Dogs," "Pigs (Three Different Ones)," "Sheep," and "Pigs on the Wing 2"—not exactly reading like a treasure chest of smash singles.

Animals would achieve four times platinum, but would take nigh on twenty years to get there. At those numbers (equal to the sales of every punk album in a pile), the record is the laggard among the four world-beaters from '73 to '79. Still, for a record with a couple one-minute-long love songs (to whom? to what?) bracketing thirty-nine minutes of bleakness and bile, that's testimony to an appetite for Roger's worldview, no matter if the experience leaves one ragged and worse for wear by journey's end.

Inner label from a UK pressing of *Animals*.

POPOFF: What type of record do we get out of Pink Floyd with *Animals* versus *Wish You Were Here*?
BEGGS: Roger's searing world overview is developing on *Animals*, and very much as a precursor to *The Wall*, you can see him withdrawing from society at large in his lyrics, or engaging

OPPOSITE AND ABOVE: Onstage portraits of Roger Waters and Nick Mason at the Ahoy, Rotterdam, February 1977.

with it in a very vociferous tone. It's hard to put words into people's mouths when you're reading their lyrics, but I guess the essence of good songwriting is the dialog is left suitably open for people to draw their own conclusions.

But as a fourteen-year-old impressionable Pink Floyd fan, I would come home after school and religiously listen to that album front to back, read all the lyrics and look at and analyze the sleeve, the gatefold with the Storm Thorgerson photograph, this dystopian imagery that was very powerful. Throughout the record, you have Roger Waters making a very pointed comment on society as it was at that particular time in the '70s, politically and socially, and with commerce and industry. It's an angry record and that anger is couched in a lot of allegory.

POPOFF: What do you think the relationship is between the *Animals* album and Pink Floyd as a collective during this new mania at the time—punk rock?
FINDLAY: This is where Pink Floyd really realized they needed a shakeup. We need to move with the times or probably be attacked by this new wave or punk rock that is coming about. Punk was born of a shift that was happening, young musicians rising coupled with the politics of the time, the rise of crony capitalism and people saying, "No more, we're not gonna do this anymore."

Previous to them going into the studio to record *Animals*, the Sex Pistols had already had a little bit of a pop at Pink Floyd as being these boring dinosaurs. Johnny Rotten wore a defaced Pink Floyd T-shirt, and I think they realized they had to do something to move with the times. And obviously being part of a politically changing and probably quite fragile situation, and being of a certain

ABOVE: Capital Radio DJ Nicky Horne (right) talks to Brian James of the Damned (left) and Nick Mason, who produced the punk band's second LP, *Music for Pleasure*.

LEFT: A French edition of *Animals* featuring alternate pink artwork, alongside a radio promo copy.

stature and having a certain voice, maybe they thought it was time to show some responsibility as well. That's where the theme for *Animals* turned into quite a political one, really.

BEGGS: There's something very punk about Roger Waters anyway, and there always was. He had the ability to be angry with a ninja consciousness. If punk was the blunt tool of youth culture, the blunt anger of youth culture, Roger Waters's lyrics were razor-sharp and concise—and precise. I think his anger was more punk than punk at that time.

ROTHERY: All my friends at that time embraced the whole punk–new wave thing, and I was the only kind of holdout. I was still listening to my Genesis and Pink Floyd albums. Some of the new wave stuff I didn't mind, like Stranglers and the kind of more musical bands at the time. Generally, I was more attuned to prog, which happened all the way through to when

I moved down to join Marillion in '79, at the whole tail end of that new wave thing. Because all of that had blown away a lot of the music of that time and it was starting again, like a rebirth of prog.

But Floyd managed to stay relevant through that because of the bleakness of Roger's words. You could slag them off as being one of the prog dinosaurs, but there's so much anger and bitterness involved in Roger's works and themes that even the angry young men of punk could still relate to it.

I was so young, my experience was really just the music press at the time—*Sounds* and *Melody Maker* in the UK—and Floyd still seemed to be the critics' favorite. This is kind of just before the punk– new wave movements swept aside most of those things. Perhaps *Animals* held its own because it's quite a dark, bitter album—powerful but also very bleak.

Gilmour behind the pedal steel at Westfalenhallen, Dortmund, West Germany, January 24, 1977.

POPOFF: Give a little summary of who the dogs are, who the pigs are, who the sheep are in this story.
BEGGS: In "Pigs (Three Different Ones)," there's a direct reference to conservative activist Mary Whitehouse. "Sheep," you have allusions to the kind of proletariat, average human woman waiting at the bus stop. "Pigs" more so represents the corporate bosses. And "Dogs," to me, it seems to take you through the life cycle of an average man trying to make his way in the world, in business, in his place of work— doing deals, underhandedly, sticking a knife in, getting to be trusted by the people that you lie to. And always striving.

Maybe that's the echo back to *The Dark Side of the Moon*, the whole idea of time, and the eternal struggle of man, to make a living, to earn a crust, and never really getting anywhere and dying in want. And using the analogy of the dog is a very apposite tool.

POPOFF: And "Sheep"?
BEGGS: Wow, "Sheep" is a tricky one, because it's hard to talk about that song without my vegetarian credentials showing [*laughs*]. I like the idea of the enraged, psychotic creatures rising up and taking revenge on mankind. They're the tormentors. And, in many respects, it inspired a track I wrote on the recent Mute Gods album called "Animal army." In "Sheep," he said that so well that I wanted to take it further. I wanted to write about the biosphere, so I wrote this song called "Animal Army," which is an extrapolation of that idea.

It's beautiful where he takes the Lord's Prayer and he intersperses it with images of sheep being led into the stainless-steel valley where they're slaughtered. Again, very allegorical and cynical. I don't think Roger Waters is a vegetarian. In fact, I think he's even pro-foxhunting. But I still like the analogy of wreaking revenge on their tormentors, and that for me is what that song's about.

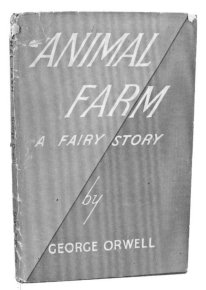

An original 1945 edition of George Orwell's *Animal Farm*—a key influence on *Animals*.

POPOFF: What is the worldview or philosophy expressed by the lyrics of *Animals*?

FINDLAY: I think, initially, it set out to be a movement against capitalism. I know that it's often criticized for being brought back to actually supporting the economic base that that is built upon, just by the fact that it's actually about that in the first place. So, you're taking apart and judging these three separate types or groups of people that the whole country, or any country, could be divided up into.

Obviously, it's loosely based on George Orwell's *Animal Farm*; they needed a theme for an album. It's always dangerous how much you read into somebody's art, but I think it was definitely against what was happening in the government at the time, but then also saying, well, we're British, keep a stiff upper lip, and show up and put up.

Because he wasn't prepared to be all-out like the punk movement where they were rioting and protesting and rising up and trying to create some sort of social revolution. They were really saying, well, we're sitting over here and there's not a lot we can do about it, which is possibly kind of a realist, essential view. But Floyd's fans, the mild side of the rock audience, they were probably fitting in quite nicely with the sheep, happily trying not to rock the boat and listen to this wonderful album and politely nod [*laughs*].

POPOFF: Are you saying that there's a little bit of an apologist stance to the idea of being a sheep? That they should just get on with it and keep a stiff upper lip?

FINDLAY: I think Roger is a bit sympathetic. "Pigs on the Wing" offers hope in saying no matter what these divides are, with a bit of human compassion we can come back around to being here for each other.

I don't think the punks were happy with what was going on, nor do I think the general rock/pop music fans were happy with what was going on. A torrential rainy summer had spoiled crops and water was then rationed when the sun did come. It was a really bad year for politics and weather and the economy in Britain.

But "Pigs on the Wing" also has touches of "Wish You Were Here," the way the chords work. I think it's Roger doing what he does very easily, using three chords to make a folk song. And having this hidden message. It's nice that you're brought in on a very intimate level. To begin with as a listener, you're really drawn in and spoken to in quite a personal way. That sets up a good place for the listener to begin. That theme comes back at the very end of the album as well; you have the bookend, which is typical of a few Floyd albums.

But it's quite gloomy. Roger Waters is saying, "If I didn't care for you," so it's quite a closed but still intimate thing. And at the end it comes back to the same musical theme but he's saying, "I really do care about you," and we can do this if we have some sort of unity between us as humans. It brings everybody

ABOVE: Session guitarist Snowy White (far left), Nick Mason, and Dave Gilmour onstage at the Empire Pool, Wembley, London, March 1977.

RIGHT: A ticket for the band's fourth of five shows at Wembley, signed for a fan by Gilmour and Mason.

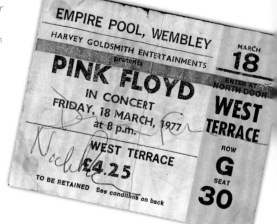

EMPIRE POOL, WEMBLEY
HARVEY GOLDSMITH ENTERTAINMENTS
presents
PINK FLOYD
IN CONCERT
FRIDAY, 18 MARCH, 1977
at 8 p.m.
WEST TERRACE
£4.25
TO BE RETAINED See conditions on back
MARCH
18
ENTER AT NORTH DOOR
WEST TERRACE
ROW
G
SEAT
30

together as humans despite all this segregation and dividing and pigeonholing that happens throughout the middle of the album. It's nice that you have these soft and nurturing bookends to quite an angsty album.

POPOFF: The first full song is "Dogs," with the urgently strummed acoustic guitar. How would you break that one down musically?

BEGGS: It's the longest piece on the record, and therefore it has a very strong sense of journey to it. It's taking you with it. And the chords are building; the way it fades in and climbs, it's moving upward. And there are various crescendos until the end syncopation where everything is very much in staccato and in unison, but it's driving.

I always feel like it's a man's life, using the metaphor of this dog, this down-at-heel animal. Taking every opportunity that life throws at it and taking the knocks as well. Very emotive, prescient piece of writing. Totally exquisite.

It's actually my favorite Pink Floyd album, but in later years I've come to understand that Vince Clarke of Depeche Mode and Yazoo and Erasure had also cited this as one of his favorite albums, if not his favorite Pink Floyd album—very interesting, from a master of electronics. Even he would see the validity of this album for not only its original production but its folk affectation. A lot of it sounds like a folk record.

ROTHERY: "Dogs" is the highlight track to me from a guitar standpoint, including most of my favorite passages of David playing on the record. But it's bittersweet, and quite a difficult album to listen to because it was the album that signaled the beginning of the end of the unity of the band. Roger was sort of angling for more control, which is a shame. When you get onto *The Wall*, there's some great music, but it just doesn't feel like a band in the same way it did on *Dark Side* and *Wish You Were Here*.

If there's a negative to *Animals*, it lacks that sense of unity where you can tell with tracks when different band members have had the freedom to make a contribution as opposed to being told, "You play this here." With *Animals*, it just feels like Roger was kind of suffocating the rest of them artistically.

POPOFF: As a guitarist yourself, and in a band that I imagine you wouldn't mind being placed closer to Floyd under the wide prog umbrella, what do you like about David's playing?

ROTHERY: Oh, his bending and vibrato and choice of notes. He very much works within a simple, on the whole, pentatonic blue scale. But it's his expression that sets it apart. It's a melodic sensibility, along with the emotional resonance, that he sets up in the music. He's one of my main influences. There's a reason he's promoted as the best guitar player of all time in some people's eyes. And even though he's not really a technical player as such, during that period of time, say from *Meddle* through to *The Wall*, his playing is just exceptional.

POPOFF: How about a brief description of how David gets his classic sound from a technological standpoint?

ROTHERY: He usually uses Hiwatt heads, and I think he ran it pretty clean in those days. And with various overdrive pedals. I know Pete Cornish built him quite a few pedals. I think he used a Big Muff on some things, an Echoplex in the old days for the delays. He had the same basic tonal choices that all musicians had at that time.

But the sound doesn't just come from the equipment. It really comes from how you approach the guitar, how you attack each note. So, many tiny details add up to the difference between one player and another. You give two players the same guitar and the same equipment and they will sound completely different. What I

A set of three *Animals* badges, as sold during Pink Floyd's In the Flesh tour, 1977.

Take home pigs, dogs and sheep.

Pink Floyd's "Animals," on Columbia Records and Tapes.

learned from Dave is the value of his almost minimalist approach to playing. He would play just the right part with the right sound. And the sound itself is vital when you're trying to paint those sorts of pictures.

POPOFF: Before we leave "Dogs," Heather, what do you make of this one?
FINDLAY: It's great to have this contrast between David at the beginning and Roger at the end, where you have this big brother dog or uncle dog or father dog speaking to the younger one, and the younger one is trying to weigh in or make his mind up. And that almost speaks of, well, there are dogs, but then there's also a generational gap within a certain societal category or group as well, where the young one might be thinking, "Maybe I don't want to be a dog. Maybe I actually want to be a sheep. Who knows, I might end up being a pig." So, there's an uncertainty among the youth as they're being advised by the elders of their group.

But then toward the end of the song, you realize that the advice that's been given by the elder is being lamented over. There's this whole sense of social unrest, society on the verge of collapse. Even those who think they know what they're doing, and what they're about and where they're going, they're all on a knife's edge.

So, there's this nice interplay between Gilmour and Waters that offers two extremely contrasting personalities and voices—although vocally they are not that far apart here—within one song, that allows that picture to be painted in a less broad way. You can fit a lot more depth into the one song with use of the two voices.

POPOFF: And what do you think of the *Animals* cover art?
ROTHERY: It's a fantastic cover, utilizing Storm's vision and ability to create something that is such a potent image, along with the sly reference to flying pigs and all those connotations. It's an iconic image and probably my favorite Floyd cover, even though I wouldn't say the album is my favorite Floyd album. These days you'd do it all with Photoshop, but in those days you built a huge inflatable pig and you photographed it.
FINDLAY: Floating a huge inflatable pig above Battersea Power Station must've been quite an unprecedented move at the time [*laughs*]. Stylistically and conceptually, it's very British. That's a scene that when you come into London from the south of England, you know that the train pulls in past Battersea, and it's very familiar for anybody from that area of London or the south of England. The significance of the pig itself, well, there's "Pigs on the Wing," and as you've mentioned, the probability of pigs flying, but I also think about the social climbing of the pigs.
BEGGS: I always loved Hipgnosis and I wanted to work with Storm Thorgerson from a very early age. I was an art student and I bought all the Hipgnosis books—*Walk Away René* and the Paper Tiger publications that he was involved with. I was fascinated by him and his colleagues' approach to album art. That was a time when it was a vanguard art form.

When I had a band in the '80s called Ellis, Beggs & Howard, we were discussing who would do the album cover. I told Simon Ellis that I knew Storm Thorgerson. He said, "That's who we should get to do the cover." Storm came in and just blew us away with these great ideas.

He was regaling us with the experiences of shooting the cover for *Animals*, about how he'd come up with this idea for putting the pig between Battersea Power Station's chimneys, although the original idea was Roger's. He'd had lots of ideas for that album cover. But the big story is the way it blew loose and ended up in a farmer's field in Kent. It's an iconic story in itself.

The album cover appears in so many different scenarios. For instance, the incredible film *Children of Men* has some very interesting musical references throughout. And two of those musical references are *Court of the Crimson King*, which is played virtually in its entirety, and a direct visual reference to the *Animals* album cover, a massive reference. And unless you knew what it was, you wouldn't understand. You would just think, oh, there's a giant pig there. But they happen to be in Battersea Power Station. So, it's become an iconic metaphor used by people who are in the know, perhaps to relate some kind of like-minded consciousness between people. Almost like a musical Mason symbol [*laughs*].

POPOFF: Any other details or trivia Storm told you about the shoot?
BEGGS: Just that nobody thought it was a good idea, initially. It was like, what the fuck are you thinking? Really? [*laughs*] They hadn't even really got a particularly good shot. The dirty little secret is that the sky was really foreboding and dramatic on the first day, the pig flew away on the second day, and the shot was gotten on the third day, so they wound up stripping the pig from the third day into the sky from the first day when they couldn't get the pig up in the air.

The actual pig on the album cover is so small. If you look at it on a CD, you think, what is this? It's like a little pink dot. But on a vinyl twelve-inch record you can see that it's a pig. But what is it? Is it a sticker? It's actually a real floating pig [*laughs*], an inflatable blimp they shot between the chimneys of Battersea Power Station. Crazy imagery—amazing.

POPOFF: "Pigs (Three Different Ones)" is fairly angular and funky—it's even got cowbell. But the lyrics are quite biting.
FINDLAY: It's classic Roger Waters, when he gets on a soapbox and he wants to have a bit of a pop in general. I love that he doesn't care, basically, what you think. I never want to be on the receiving end of that guy when he gets going and he says what he wants to. It's kind of *Final Cut* as well as *The Wall* in tone, where

A pig "flies" over Battersea Power Station, London, in September 2011 to commemorate the thirty-fifth anniversary of *Animals*.

he really lets it rip. He can really spit and choke on his words. You can hear in the tone of his voice exactly what's going on.

It's quite spooky about how that song is being used now, where Whitehouse now doesn't refer to Mary Whitehouse, it refers to the White House [*laughs*]. Quite convenient for him. But it must have been inspiring and rousing for fans who were feeling hard done to be supported by one of their musical heroes stating how unhappy he was about the political situation in the country.

Perhaps it gave people a sense of purpose or power, or re-empowered these people to go, "We have to show that famous stiff upper lip and shut up and put up. We have to get on with life. But at the same time we can come together. We've broken into all our groups and divides, but we see the bigger picture and know that it will pass and there will be a new situation for us to deal with in a year or two." It perhaps helped people feel unified in that they weren't the only ones suffering in this particularly bad political year.

POPOFF: Nick, where does Pink Floyd get their funk, so evident in this song?
BEGGS: It's Dave Gilmour, isn't it? And Richard Wright's Fender Rhodes electric piano sound works very well with what Gilmour's doing there. It's white-boy funk with a touch of jazz, but they always did it in a peculiar way, like nobody else. Richard Wright was a jazz student and he understood groove very well. And David always demonstrates a very strong blues sense of things. So, there's the push and pull between those two instruments.

And Roger's just holding it down like he does on everything. Very simple, very uneffected bass parts, which, understated, work very well with Nick Mason's simplistic timekeeping. Extraordinary that they made such a big impression on the music world, when you think about it. And I'm sure a lot of it was borne out of the decade of psychedelic jamming they did. Just jamming all the time at UFO or some other strange happening in London. I'm sure that gave them a great grounding for finding the groove. And it was always the same slow to midtempo, lolloping along, nothing particularly interesting, yet incredibly dynamic and totally engaging. If you were trying to work out the perfect scenario, you couldn't really think these guys were gonna crack it. But it just worked brilliantly.

Ultimately, Floyd were many things to many people. Therein lies the secret of their success. They can be taken to heart by the prog fraternity, but I'm sure they would never see themselves in that genre. Because they were the biggest of that genre, if that's the case; they certainly superseded it. Like so many bands, they don't want to be shackled to a particular type. In the same way that Genesis would never have been happy being a prog band, so they just moved into pop. That was the thing about Floyd—the songwriting was so good that it doesn't really matter what people think of them or what genre they're stuck in. And why would they pigeonhole themselves? I don't think they ever did.

Dave Gilmour and his guitar-playing foil, Snowy White, during Pink Floyd's summer 1977 tour of the US.

FINDLAY: It's amazing, once you go in a bit deeper into Floyd with a view to taking the music apart. For instance, Nick Mason is rarely cited as a drummer people reference for any particular technicality or technique, but there probably aren't many drummers that can drum at that pace and keep the groove. It's the groove that you find between him and Waters that allows Gilmour to have this sort of phraseology, this bluesy, funky riffing that you hear in something like "Pigs (Three Different Ones)." He has to drum so slowly sometimes that he almost stops. And that must be quite tricky in terms of keeping a steady pace. He's often cited as being an uninteresting drummer, even a boring drummer, which I've always found quite sad.

But when you start to notice this relationship between kick drum and snare, it's the feel and groove that's behind that that allows Gilmour to build his funk and blues in there, as well as for Rick Wright to build in his jazz riffs. You need an extremely steady drummer to be able to have jazz and funk phrasing falling behind and in front of the beat when those kinds of choices are made.

POPOFF: Is it a challenge to play as slow as Floyd does? I know Marillion is no stranger to these sorts of tempos.

ROTHERY: It depends how stoned you are [*laughs*]. That seems to be the general consensus [*laughs*]. But no, that's the area of music that they specialized in and excelled at, those more atmospheric, psychedelic soundscapes. Floyd are a great example of putting together the right musicians, where it's all about how they play together. It's not about who's got the best chops. There's loads of better drummers, bass players, keyboardists, and guitarists, but it's what they did together that matters. There's something very special and timeless about what they produced.

But with *Animals*, I can hear the fragmentation. Roger's a bit of a highly creative megalomaniac, really. I think he always wants to have control and he wants it to be all about him. Then again, he's a guy with a lot of vision and a lot of talent. But the truly special moments that happen with Floyd are when it's an ensemble, when you have the right musicians interpreting those ideas in the right way. Someone like David wants to play the guitar; he wants to have creative input. I imagine that at times there could be a lot of conflict, because I think Roger wanted his own way all the time.

POPOFF: Wrap things up for us, Heather. First, why after all these years is *Animals* still a favorite for you, and why do you think many people feel that way today about the record?

FINDLAY: To me, *Animals* really smacks of the '70s. I can put it on and it just seems to encapsulate some of the angst of that time, yet some of the hope. Somehow it creates a really good painting and tapestry of that era. That was the year I was born, so I see this in retrospect and place it with other music of the time. For example, it doesn't have a disco element at all, but there's something about the funk and the guitars and the placement of the synths that suggest that disco was going on at that time, if that makes sense.

Although I'm not sure I agree it's a top favorite of too many Floyd fans, I've seen in the last year videos of "Pigs" being shared a lot. Particularly Roger Waters's performances from last year. It's quite spooky to see that the political themes are still at large, that it still fits with the political themes of today and in some ways more than ever. I still see young kids wandering around with their *Animals* Pink Floyd T-shirts. It's certainly standing the test of time, but in terms of across the board as a Floyd fan, I'm not sure how *Animals* ranks. I would say it probably doesn't rank as one of the top Floyd albums.

But the politics is quite prescient. In "Sheep," for example—which is a great driving tune, by the way—Roger's warning of the danger of just going along with things for the sake of it. People aren't taking responsibility for who they follow and who they choose as a leader. He's telling us, don't just settle for hearsay, and do research and look at things. It's such a theme of importance at the moment with all the political stuff that is going on.

People don't get out and bother to vote and they don't really care to read the political manifestos offered to them. They just lazily go with what they've always gone with or don't vote at all. As a result, you get the group of sheep that just go along with whatever's served them, be it religion or politics or whatever. Without really thinking about, what do I want? Is this really what I want? Am I doing it because my family does it? Or because we've always believed in this or voted for such and such? Whether or not it had an effect, Roger was trying to empower society at that particular time to stand up for themselves and to be responsible for the future of their country.

CHAPTER **11**

THE WALL

WITH NICK BEGGS, RALPH CHAPMAN, STEVE HACKETT, AND JORDAN RUDESS

SIDE 1

1. In the Flesh? (Waters)	3:16
2. The Thin Ice (Waters)	2:27
3. Another Brick in the Wall (Part 1) (Waters)	3:21
4. The Happiest Days of Our Lives (Waters)	1:46
5. Another Brick in the Wall (Part 2) (Waters)	3:59
6. Mother (Waters)	5:32

SIDE 2

1. Goodbye Blue Sky (Waters)	2:45
2. Empty Spaces (Waters)	2:10
3. Young Lust (Waters, Gilmour)	3:25
4. One of My Turns (Waters)	3:41
5. Don't Leave Me Now (Waters)	4:08
6. Another Brick in the Wall (Part 3) (Waters)	1:48
7. Goodbye Cruel World (Waters)	0:48

SIDE 3

1. Hey You (Waters)	4:40
2. Is There Anybody Out There? (Waters)	2:44
3. Nobody Home (Waters)	3:26
4. Vera (Waters)	1:35
5. Bring the Boys Back Home (Waters)	1:21
6. Comfortably Numb (Waters, Gilmour)	6:23

SIDE 4

1. The Show Must Go On (Waters)	1:36
2. In the Flesh (Waters)	4:15
3. Run Like Hell (Gilmour, Waters)	4:20
4. Waiting for the Worms (Waters)	4:04
5. Stop (Waters)	0:30
6. The Trial (Waters, Ezrin)	5:13
7. Outside the Wall (Waters)	1:41

Recorded at Britannia Row, Islington, London; CBS Studios, Manhattan, New York; Producer's Workshop, Hollywood, California; Studio Miraval, Le Val, France; Super Bear, Berre les Alpes, France

PERSONNEL: Roger Waters—vocals, bass guitar, synthesizer, acoustic guitar; David Gilmour—vocals, guitars, bass guitar, synthesizer, Clavinet, percussion; Richard Wright—piano, organ, synthesizer, Clavinet, bass pedals; Nick Mason—drums, percussion

GUEST PERFORMANCES: Bob Ezrin—piano, Hammond organ, synthesizers, reed organ, backing vocals; James Guthrie—percussion, synthesizers, sound effects; Jeff Porcaro—drums; Joe Porcaro—snare drums; Lee Ritenour—rhythm guitar, acoustic guitar; Joe (Ron) di Blasi—classical guitar; Fred Mandel—Hammond organ; Bobbye Hall—congas, bongos; Frank Marrocco—concertina; Larry Williams—clarinet; Trevor Veitch—mandolin; New York Orchestra—orchestra; Phil Taylor—sound effects; New York Opera—choral vocals; Vicki Brown—backing vocals; Joe Chemay—backing vocals; Stan Farber—backing vocals; Jim Haas—backing vocals; Islington Green School Choir— backing vocals; Bruce Johnston—backing vocals; Jon Joyce—backing vocals; Toni Tennille—backing vocals; Clare Torry—backing vocals; Harry Waters—spoken vocals; Trudy Young—spoken vocals

Produced by (in alphabetical order) Bob Ezrin, David Gilmour, Roger Waters; coproduced by James Guthrie

Released November 30, 1979

f *The Dark Side of the Moon* represents Pink Floyd happily and efficiently making bleak music, and *Wish You Were Here* and *Animals* represent uneasy questions, first in the incubator that was the band, second in the petri dish that was a rotting Britain, *The Wall* represents the idea that the answers to all of Roger's questions turned out to be the worst imaginable.

But the action-packed concept for *The Wall* is more *Wish You Were Here* than *Animals*, and the magnifying glass is focused not so much on the whole band as on the character Pink, whose mind is shattered by the demands of fame. Roger has said that the final straw was when he found himself spitting at a noisy fan during a concert inside Montréal's imposing and impersonal Olympic Stadium in July 1977, fatefully the last show of the band's In the Flesh Tour supporting the laconic and cynical *Animals* album.

The perversity of his protest shook Roger to the core, and the result was this fascinating and satisfyingly tidy concept concerning a rock star building a wall around his fragile psyche, one rather large white brick at a time. The hope and the creative tension come from the deeper philosophical discussion as to how one disassembles the wall and rejoins humanity.

Making the record as tax exiles atop a mountain on the beautiful French Riviera, but living their days down by the sea, Pink Floyd was playing out the middle chapters of the power struggle between Roger and the rest of the band. It is fortunate for rock history that Roger pressed his will upon David, Richard, and Nick like a mental terrorist, emerging as the sole tormented writer of every song but four on this double album.

Holding the fraught sessions together was a practical people person, producer Bob Ezrin, who had to not only corral the cats but work on Roger's story like a Printer's Row editor *and* commandeer the most sonically complicated record that either he or the Floyd had ever kneaded into sourdough—which is saying a lot. Offering moral support as much as anything, along with the ability to create a chaos that he alone could own, Ezrin also injected the idea of key guest performances. Some were simple and surgical; others, such as the use of Michael Kamen for orchestration and a school choir famously belting out, "We don't need no education," lent appropriate bombast to the task at hand.

At the end of the day, the artists were cut up beyond repair, but the art was out: *The Wall*—along with *In Through the Out Door*, *The Long Run*, and fresh sounds from the Knack and the Cars—saving a moribund 1979 from the disastrous record sales year it was shaping up to be. Of all those, *The Wall* would rule rock talk for the next eighteen months, up and down high school halls and in the pages of a music press that seemed addled by this sense-overloading provocation, not able to decide

ABOVE: Waters sings "Outside the Wall" with an all-acoustic backing that includes Mason (left) on guitar, Gilmour (second right) on mandolin, and Wright (right) on accordion.

LEFT: Label from the Columbia pressing of *The Wall*.

if it was the greatest album ever made or mere juvenilia with its virtual torrents of bells and whistles even by Pink Floyd standards, let alone those of bands that would never consider dialog from groupies, headmasters, and judges parts of their normal stock and trade.

Even outside its entertaining cinematic touches, *The Wall* felt like an overtly commercial Pink Floyd album due simply to the fact that despite its double-album sprawl, the songs were short, many of them quite conventional and self-contained, and even then quite rocky and, weirdly, often in the realm of disco. Not like they were trying to "work" anything—nevertheless, it worked famously. *The Wall* coughed up a good six to ten hit singles and/or perennial classic rock radio tracks on its way to diamond certification—and the shiniest of diamonds to boot, not the cheat of a double getting counted as two records, but more than twelve million bought and paid for copies of *The Wall* at its nearly double retail price.

All told, it's quite an achievement—as well as testimony to the smarts and open-mindedness of Floyd fans—that a record as depressing, stylistically divergent, jarringly dynamic, and, well, twice as long as a regular fun-time spin could command so much attention and sell so well. Then again, the happy results at the cash register might just come down to the quick pace and consistent quality of Roger's tall tale. As the cliché goes, a good song proves itself by whether it holds up when rendered with just a voice and an acoustic guitar. As corollary, one would have to say that *The Wall* counts as solid storytelling by virtue of the entertainment value found in the lyric sheet alone.

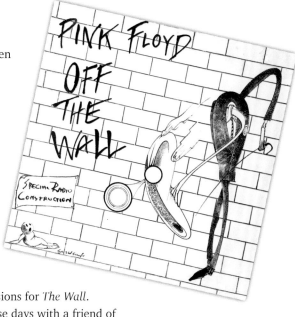

POPOFF: Let's start with this: What did you think of *The Wall* when you heard it for the first time?

RUDESS: My personal story of *The Wall* is a pretty interesting one, because I was actually at one of the sessions for *The Wall*. Just a total, crazy coincidence. I was hanging out in those days with a friend of mine, who went by the name of Blue Ocean. He was a drummer in New York City and he was invited to put together a bunch of snare drum players to play on what turned out to be "Bring the Boys Back Home."

I was at his house when he was arranging that and he said, "Come on down. I'm organizing a bunch of drummers to play on something, like snare drum. Do you play the snare drum?" "Oh yeah, I can play the snare drum, sure." I had played some snare drum in third grade. So, we went down to the studio, one of the big studios right in Manhattan, and we walk in; beautiful, beautiful room—big live room.

I go in and they've got all the snare drums set up and all these people there. Still didn't know who it was for or what it was. I start playing the snare drum, along with all these guys. The guy who was leading the group, after a few measures of playing, he looked at me and yanked his thumb like, take a hike [*laughs*]. "No, that ain't happening." [*laughs*] I got canned from my *Wall* appearance. Looking back, it was more humorous than anything else. Because I was tanking out. We were all really, really stoned. We go down to do some snare drum thing, which I thought was amusing in itself.

But when I got told not to play, I was able to wait in the control room. And in the control room, they kept on playing, "Bring the boys back home!" I'm hearing this opera stuff, right? And the snare drum. I'm thinking, "What is this record? Who is this?" It wasn't until later when we left and it was all done that I found out that was for an upcoming Pink Floyd album. Pretty weird album, I thought. Didn't sound like Pink Floyd to me [*laughs*].

POPOFF: None of the Pink Floyd guys were there, obviously, because you would have recognized them, I assume. But was Bob Ezrin there?

ABOVE: "Special Radio Construction" promo LP containing eight songs *"Off" The Wall*.

BELOW: Voice actor Gary Yudman emcees onstage at the Nassau Coliseum.

RUDESS: Bob Ezrin was there. He was the one who fired me. "You. Stop." [*laughs*] One of my claims to fame.

POPOFF: Nick: How about you? What do you remember about that time, late 1979?
BEGGS: There's a very strange story with me in relation to *The Wall*. I had totally bought into *Animals* in such a massive way, more than any of their other records. And at that time my mother had contracted cancer; she was dying. When I was reading about *The Wall*'s impending release into the market, and then it came out, I picked up pretty quickly that this was the story of a man who was folding. He was coming apart at the seams. Because I understood what Roger was saying in *Animals*. You could see, in *Animals*, that this guy was on the edge. I understand that later on, a lot of *The Wall* concept was crystallized for Roger during the *Animals* tour, when he actually started to become very angry with the audience. I could see that this was the story of a man's life falling apart.

Because of what I was going through, the impending death of my mother, I couldn't bring myself to listen to the record because I knew it was a visceral open sore and that I would find it hard to listen to it. When I eventually did listen to it years after, I concurred that I was justified in not listening to it because I was very fragile.

From a more mature, emotionally stable headspace, I listen to that record and it's just incredible. The psychology involved in it, the bravery to tell that story, to take your balls and your cock and put them out there for the world to stick a knife in, is absolutely incredible. Because that's what Waters did. He bore his

LEFT: The "Teacher" peers over the wall at Nassau Coliseum, February 27, 1980.

RIGHT: Gilmour flanked by drummers Willie Wilson and Nick Mason at the Nassau Coliseum, Long Island, New York, February 27, 1980.

soul to the world in such an extraordinary way. When you get to "Comfortably Numb," there's not a dry eye in the house, is there? You listen to that song and the lyrics go so deep that it takes the punctuation of Dave Gilmour's guitar solo right at the end of those lines to really make you understand the sincerity of it. It's probably one of the greatest rock songs ever written.

CHAPMAN: My brother brought that album home when it came out. I was thirteen and I found the writing on the sleeve—that sharp cursive writing that is barely legible—I just found it an unnerving visual document. Listening to it, it was not something I comprehended at all.

POPOFF: Okay, I don't want to make you recount the specifics of the story, but could you articulate a bit about the theme of this record, about building the wall with those blocks and then tearing it down?

BEGGS: The wall is a metaphor for his alienation and self-exile, his self-induced exile from society. Psychologically speaking, he's using the wall as a metaphor to represent what we do, what he did in this instance, but what many people do, which is withdraw rather than confront the issues as they see them in their lives. It's a type of psychosis, I suppose.

Earls Court, London, August 1980.

Each brick in the wall is an event, building a sequence of events that amalgamate in him retracting or retreating a little bit more. Until "Goodbye Cruel World," and the very last brick goes in and the light goes out. From there on, it's "Is There Anybody Out There?" The wall is complete, and you have the perspective of a man in self-imposed exile from the world. That's what it's about.

But, the ray of hope is, of course, he realizes through his own self-analysis that he has to tear down the wall, even though his alter ego is the thing that does it. He doesn't want to do it himself because he's too frightened. He sees it as being exposed before his peers. Isn't that a powerful thing? For us all to be exposed before our peers. How terrible! I've got this recurring nightmare that one day people will realize that I'm really shit. That I'm not this great musician they all think I am. And I'm really not. I'm just an average guy who can do a few things quite well and tries to make a living from it.

And in his loftiness, he's ascended this monolithic path to this massive state of fame and fortune and high regard. He's being stripped of everything and exposed before all his peers. That's the worst thing he could see. And yet it's his saving grace, because he realizes that in his vulnerability, he's found out who he really is, and can begin again. So, that's the hope of it. The last piece of music, "Outside the Wall"—he's so fragile and delicate and human and quiet, yet it's . . . it's so beautiful.

RUDESS: It's not unlike Roger Waters to think of big conceptual things that you can look at a lot of different ways. I was lucky enough to see *The Wall* show at the time and then also when Roger came back and did it as a solo artist. But just this big idea of creating a wall, and then doing it live as well . . . Who does that? [*laughs*] It's so over the top.

But he's talking about blocks, whether it be a political block or a social block or something as far as relationships go. On the surface or below the surface he was talking about all that stuff, while also taking a lot of risks with his words. I don't know how accepted all his lyrics would be if he put them out again today. He's definitely skating on some thin ice. And he's gotten even more political these days. But *The Wall* will go down in history as a really important album, because of both the music and the concept.

POPOFF: To address just one specific brick in the wall, the public school system seems to have scarred so many older British rock musicians I've interviewed over the years. Why is this one of the bricks for Roger?
BEGGS: The English public school system is very often populated by boys who felt that their mothers and fathers didn't love them enough. You know, sent them off, were done with them. Leaving your child in an institution where the primary love of the parent is no longer available 24/7, I would say that would be a pretty good brick in the wall for anyone. I know a lot of people who've been to public school and they carry scars from it. But the parents think they're doing the right thing. Well, don't all parents think they're doing the right thing? And we fuck up every stage of the way. I'm not making a judgment. I'm just saying that we all fuck it up.

Tickets for the first and fourth shows in the band's first run of *Wall* shows at Earls Court, as well as a pair of badges from the second run.

HACKETT: "Another Brick in the Wall" is really talking about when you first get messed up. This seems to be a recurring theme in Floyd: these sadists, in the name of education, messing with delicate young minds, with very little protection for young kids. I know that Genesis went through this. I know that at school they were not allowed to go to the local record store, and of course that's compulsory, isn't it? So, they have violence inflicted on them by a system that, on one hand, they're resisting, but on the other hand, they're supposed to be the sons of the privileged, having this kind of education.

I know we've talked about this, but there were so many people messed up by the British system. Or the Scottish system, which was supposed to produce high achievers. From what I've been told, the Scottish system wasn't really the greatest system, because although it produced geniuses and what have you, I was told you either learned or you got battered. Which doesn't work in every instance. Sanatoriums are full of people who didn't quite make it, and many on the outside are still trying to anesthetize themselves from the effects of having been invalidated early on. British education has got quite a lot to answer for.

PINK FLOYD PRESENT THE WALL IN CONCERT

LOS ANGELES SPORTS ARENA FEB. 7, 8, 9, 10, 11, 12, 13. NASSAU COLISEUM NEW YORK FEB 24, 25, 26, 27, 28.

Gerald Scarfe

I remember, for instance, I happened to be in the boys' loo at the time when there was a raid by the prefects, and they were trying to round up all those who were smoking. I wasn't at the time, but it didn't make any difference with the headmaster. I remember being hauled up in front of him, and I saw on his desk, he had a book—I was reading it upside down—called *The Fundamentals of Brainwashing*. Now our headmaster had been a New Zealander, but he'd been a Japanese prisoner of war. I remember thinking, isn't this guy supposed to be an educator? Not a brainwasher.

But he liked to get drunk and beat boys. And the thing is, I don't think that was so unusual at the time. He said to me, "Oh, smoking again, Hackett? Why not opium?" I thought, I can't take this guy seriously anymore. So, I said, "It's too expensive, sir," which I think disarmed him. Imagine what would happen today. I probably should've said, "Well, it would be very interesting, sir, if the press got ahold of this, if you're suggesting that I should take opium. How do you think they're going to feel about that?" But you don't really think about that as a kid. You think, oh well, they've got the right to do anything to us that they want. And you've got a choice. Either go along with it or get expelled.

I remember a teacher perforating some kid's ear drum. Because the teacher cracked a joke in class and the boy laughed at it and then he hit him. Really nasty stuff. The boy was a musician too. He could read music and play the piano and accordion very well, and the headmaster perforated his eardrum and the kid ran out of the classroom. All I heard afterward was that the teacher was required to apologize to him.

Japanese and US pressings of the single release of "Another Brick in the Wall (Part II)."

POPOFF: Sticking with this song, what do you make of the three different versions of "Another Brick in the Wall?" What is Roger doing across those?
BEGGS: He's taking us on a journey and revealing themes. It's the whole reprise idea, which you get in progressive rock a lot. You get it in classical music, and that reference is probably more appropriate. He's developing the theme each time as well. He adds another color, or another sequence of notes, which then leads you into the next piece of music in true concept album format. Because it's hard to just write forty songs and make them work together. If you take forty songs and have three of them cross-reference, then you're able to draw different sides of the record together in a very cohesive way. That's not the first time they did that. They did that on *The Dark Side of the Moon*, they did it on *Wish You Were Here*, and they did it on *Animals*. Again, a well-trodden path for that band.

POPOFF: I hear disco on this one, plus somewhat on "Young Lust" and "Run Like Hell." Where do you think that comes from?
CHAPMAN: I hear it only on "Another Brick in the Wall (Part 2)," and my understanding is that was Ezrin. Now that you mention it, "Young Lust," maybe,

but I never thought of it that way. Because I keyed into the lyrics and Gilmour's performance, the idea of "I'm just a new boy, stranger in this town."

And "Run Like Hell," now that one is more Krautrock to me. I'm speculating, but it seems to me, when you brought up Krautrock when we talked about *Obscured by Clouds* and the unfettered feel of Nick Mason's drumming, that was the last moment when he had those kind of rhythms, where the tempo swayed because he was swinging.

By the time you get to *The Wall* and Bob Ezrin, I imagine they stuck poor Nick on a click track. And the upside of that is you can get this marshal rhythm. That's how I read "Run Like Hell"—marshal jackboot rhythm, this idea of the military oppressor. I didn't read disco.

"Another Brick in the Wall," the disco, to me, is opportunism, commercial opportunism, almost like a piss take on disco. But also acknowledging, well, this would be a great single. I would imagine that there was a desire to create something that could sell the record.

BEGGS: I know exactly why that is: because they happened to have been listening to Nile Rodgers, who was recording near them. And they'd heard him playing some disco stuff. Chic and all that disco stuff was really happening. And David just came in and he started playing that riff. And Roger really liked it. It's even a Stratocaster, which is also Nile Rodgers's type of instrument—Fender Strat. A clean, rhythmic syncopated groove. Very white boy, but it really worked. White-boy disco [*laughs*].

POPOFF: What do you know about the problems with Rick Wright at this point, or the breakdown in band relations in general?

BEGGS: Him and Nick Mason were the ones who were ostracized the most. But from what I understand, Rick and Roger had the most tempestuous relationship. Roger was so strong a personality, and Rick was such an effusive, more diminutive chap. I don't think he was very verbose. And I'm sure Roger would have had the upper hand in trying to get his ideas across. This is opinion, and I'm happy to be proven wrong on these points, but that's the way I read it.

And Dave was of more use to Roger, because he was the virtuosic soloist. Also, he was the one who had a voice and vocal style that worked so well between what Roger was trying to spit at the world and the softer, more soothing sounds of the lyrics that were to be sung by David Gilmour. For instance, when he's singing in the context of the mother's lyrics. It's a light and dark thing, as if David represents light and Roger represents the darkest and the bleakest of blacks. Which again is an incredible thing; you get a wonderful juxtaposition.

CHAPMAN: I agree. I love the duet combination of Roger and Dave. That was a band that was blessed with three excellent vocalists, one extraordinary vocalist in

Dave and one extremely unique singer in Roger. Whenever they utilized that, as in the duet in "Mother," it's extraordinary. With Dave taking on the role of the mother. And, of course, "Mother" also works because they brought in Jeff Porcaro, who gives this incredibly silky, smooth performance with those buzz rolls that he does. The genius behind that is that either Bob or Roger or Dave, or a combination, recognized that Nick wasn't capable of giving them the sound they needed and they found the exact right guy who could do that. And that took vision and a complete engagement in their process. I have an enormous amount of respect for that.

HACKETT: I recall that later, after things had fallen completely apart, Roger Waters controversially said that he thought Floyd were a spent force creatively. I believe it was David who said that the only thing that was a spent force was Roger. I know that Roger assumed command and then fired Rick Wright.

I wouldn't presume to know for sure, but I know how individuals in bands try to unseat other members, and then once they've done that the band is finished [*laughs*]. We've got a similar situation with Genesis. The people who own the name are Tony and Mike, but they choose to do nothing with it. Meanwhile, I often play Genesis tunes, as does Phil occasionally. I think Mike does too. But autonomy becomes terribly important in a band, and bands like Floyd and Genesis are competitive within the ranks.

For bands to become very successful, usually there's a very gifted control freak who's very intelligent and puts his arguments across with a rare degree of force. But it often means that those bands cease to exist after a certain point, or find there are insufficient grounds to work together, which has gotten to be the case for Jethro Tull—it seems to be there's no version of Tull anymore, and yet Ian Anderson totally agrees with me about this.

Drummer Jeff Porcaro, who plays on *The Wall*'s "Mother," with his band Toto in 1981.

Those who feel they know best, they want the control, and writing music is perhaps not best done with a shared pen. It doesn't really work, and if it does, it doesn't work for very long.

You can look at the Stones, and you know for a fact that although other guys were writing songs within, or important riffs, they weren't getting the credits. It's still Jagger/Richards, those two guys who have apparently written everything. And the Beatles effect, where it's Lennon and McCartney that seem to write most of it, but then they have this other genius in the ranks, rather embarrassingly, named George Harrison. By the time they're doing *The White Album*, he's coming up with the strongest songs, to my mind, and has developed something that ranks alongside the others. But he will forever be thought of as the new boy and our kid.

If only characters in bands were as philanthropically developed with their music as they are with their money. Some people in bands remain in the fetal stage sociologically and they haven't learned to share. And when others evolve to the same level of creative capability, these same people are still unwilling to share and so you get a great falling out.

The idea, when we all die, is to be able to meet each other in heaven and say, "Yeah, actually, you were really good at that. But I wasn't generous enough to admit that you were writing songs that were just as good as mine." That's how I suspect it will all go when we survive this mortal coil and meet up, as I suspect we all will, in some form of afterlife. It's better to bury the hatchet now, but people who create world-class bands are very driven and not necessarily ready, even in their dotage, to lay aside differences and embrace the idea of equality.

POPOFF: Well put. So, in a sense, *The Wall* is an example of this idea that writing is best done by oneself.

RUDESS: Sure, I suppose. It was the start of Roger Waters really having what feels like that much more of a controlling factor in the band. To me, at this point in time, he didn't get so far that it was over the top. It was still like a fresh thing; it was this fresh creative energy going into this massive project. And even though there was a lot of tension in the band, how Rick Wright was not as involved, and then he got a job as a hired gun and that's very sad, I still feel they were able to keep it together as a group and keep that energy focused—and tell this story as a band. Where I feel like on *The Final Cut*, Roger Waters started to get a little bit too self-absorbed and wasn't listening to Pink Floyd anymore. But *The Wall* was a real trip and totally worked and was very powerful.

The cover art and inner sleeve for the Japanese single release of "Comfortably Numb" b/w "Hey You."

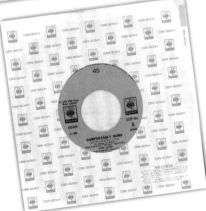

POPOFF: To touch upon some more of the specific songs on the album, what are a few highlights?

RUDESS: One of the songs that I cover on solo piano a lot is "Hey You," and I just think that whole tonality is really nice. There's a ton of ninth chords, minor ninth chords, that are really special. It's just one that deeply resonates with me. And like so many people, I have to agree to the greatness of "Comfortably Numb." I've played it a million times on piano, I've played it with a bunch of bands. It's a classic. The guitar lead at the end is just one of the best guitar leads to ever have happened. It's something you always go back to whenever you're thinking about creating an expressive lead. You think, well, "Comfortably Numb" is the role model [*laughs*].

HACKETT: I really appreciate "Comfortably Numb" as well. There's a sense of the idea of disassociation, the idea of acceptance, resignation, but not being particularly happy about it. There are many levels on which you could take Floyd. Although Genesis was more sophisticated harmonically and rhythmically than Floyd, I don't think we addressed social issues in quite the way that Floyd did. I think that was there throughout all of Floyd's works, whereas Genesis perhaps was taking a more populist stance.

BEGGS: "Comfortably Numb" is one of the greatest songs ever written—a heartbreakingly heartfelt, beautifully open wound, an open-hearted song. You go and see *The Wall* live and grown men and women are openly weeping to that song.

POPOFF: As Dream Theater's keyboardist, what are some of the bright spots from that side of the stage?

RUDESS: *The Wall's* an album filled with beautiful colors, and a lot of those colors seem to be orchestral colors, and there's also a lot of sound effects. And a lot of those sound effects aren't necessarily coming from the keyboards. They come from whatever way they were creating them or using libraries. Those kind of stick out in my mind as being sonic elements.

I think, from the keyboard point of view, it's quite basic. You have a lot of piano, a lot of organ. Again, it's more like a functional approach. I can't point to a really great color, although the orchestrations are really very tasteful. I love "Hey You"; there's some really nice piano stuff, and of course "Comfortably Numb" is so beautiful. The mixture of the orchestra in that makes it real special. When Dream Theater did "Comfortably Numb," I was the one who had to figure out how to do the orchestration because we didn't have an orchestra. That was a nice experience, to be able to be the orchestrator of that.

CHAPMAN: The thing about *The Wall* is that there are songs that are great because they're great transition moments in the story. They may not be the best songs but they serve a purpose so beautifully. But as a standalone song, I always go back to "Nobody Home." That, to me, although it's a basic piano-driven piece, is the giant on that record. "Mother" is big as well, and I appreciate the dramatic chorus vocals on "The Show Must Go On."

"Young Lust" is interesting, because aside from the scorching guitar work, Gilmour convincingly shows us he can be a rock singer. Like Wright's voice, it's this secret weapon that they called on occasionally, and probably not enough for some people. But when you did hear it, you thought, wow, what an interesting—and convincing—side of Gilmour.

But when I listen to his guitar work, not just on *The Wall*, he's like Brian May—myriad influences. Everyone from Hank Marvin to George Harrison to Paul Kossoff to Eric Clapton to Peter Green. I prefer him to all those guys.

POPOFF: More Eric Clapton than anybody, do you think?

CHAPMAN: No, because Gilmour believed in the magic of machinery, delays and loops, which Clapton never really indulged. When Clapton finally did start exploring the role of guitar synthesizer in the mid-'80s at the behest of Phil Collins, he was shat on for it. Meanwhile Gilmour, going back to something like *Obscured by Clouds*, he always had the steel guitar in his back pocket, the pedal steel. He was an acoustic player, but as we saw on *The Wall*, he was quite an adept nylon player. He could play just as well as Clapton, but he's got far more to offer. Which again is why I love Brian May and Steve Hackett. Those guys seemed to transcend their basic British blues roots and have taken on so many other things.

BEGGS: Gilmour is playing the fretless bass on *The Wall* as well. You can hear it. It's much more fluid and melodic and expressive than what Roger would've done. David is somebody who has a real strong sense of harmony and melody, but it's very simple and effective. I love that about him. It's one of the most beautiful things about his playing. He always picked a very simple handful of notes and put them in such an exquisite order.

POPOFF: As Jordan alluded to, there are a lot of effects on the record that don't necessarily come from the keyboards or synthesizers.

BEGGS: I love the way that Roger used spoken dialog throughout the record. I like the way he opened: "I've got a little black book with my poems in it." And that is shouted. He has it shouted at the beginning of the track before he starts to sing the lyrics. It's a beautiful segue, very clever.

But again, this refers to a tried and tested formula that Floyd implemented throughout their career, using spoken word and recorded dialog from various sources—individuals, roadies, people on the street, friends—and just dropping those in. Plus the constant drone of the TV in a few places, where you're being drawn into the world of this myopic, introspective lunatic, where you have the TV speaking as a wallpaper while the music unfolds around it. It always draws you back into the room, which is a strange kind of asylum where he's holed up. And various people are introduced there. There's a groupie that comes in who wants to take a bath with him. And still the TV is playing. And he's talking about the amount of shit on television. And he can't get through to his wife in the UK. When he calls, no one's home. And still the TV's playing. And it's very brooding.

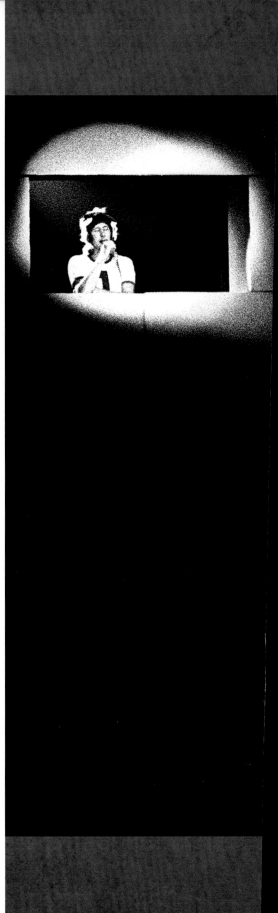

POPOFF: Decades after the fact, why do people still speak about *The Wall* so reverently?

CHAPMAN: Personally, there's nothing about *The Wall* I don't like. Sonically, it's a splendor. The arrangements are extraordinary. Over a sprawling double album, the narrative holds together. There are so many instances of the full range of human emotion. I'm not a songwriter, but as a writer, if you can capture all the different elements of what it is to be human, it's an extraordinary feat. I found he does that.

Roger goes from fat and psychopathic wives and to "Young Lust" on the next side, but then into where he presents Pink as very sympathetic, by using sound, by having him calling home to the wife and a guy answers the phone. There's just an enormous amount of universal humanity that runs through it, with much of it addressing sense of betrayal. But aside from all that, the hooks are there.

But we have to remember that it's Roger's record. Wright is most notably marginalized, but obviously Roger is writing everything. In that sense, if they say *The Final Cut* is not a Pink Floyd record, then I would say *The Wall* is not a Pink Floyd record. Sure, it's got Waters, but there's also Ezrin, who is a huge presence on that record, who allegedly took the long ramblings and the eccentricities of Waters's writing and his demos and helped shape them into a coherent narrative. It wasn't a guy in Pink Floyd who did that. You have a song like "The Trial," this outrageous piece of work that is pointedly a cowrite with Bob Ezrin. You have Jeff Porcaro on "Mother." You have rhythm guitar players, you have Beach Boys and Toni Tennille singing on it.

BEGGS: It wasn't just Bob Ezrin. There were a lot of other people involved, including Michael Kamen. Because the bulk of the band, they were in different camps at that point. They had fractured into an us-and-them scenario. This was Roger with a do-or-die mentality for getting the story told. And he was gonna do it his way and everybody else was gonna do it or be damned. The story is, after that album, he was trying to get rid of them, but really, *they* got rid of *him*.

CHAPMAN: Yes, an interesting way to put it, but for the time being, in the aftermath of spitting at that fan, as much Roger conceived of Pink Floyd as a band playing behind a wall, he also conceived of Pink Floyd in terms of a much broader definition, of having the control to do exactly what he wanted. In essence, even though Gilmour fans and Gilmour himself would disagree, *The Wall* is where they start being sidemen to Waters's vision. Even *Animals* is about Waters being gradually more ambitious. *Wish You Were Here* is the last Pink Floyd record, if you really want to split hairs. It's the one where everyone contributes; certainly Richard Wright is a huge part of *Wish You Were Here*.

Anyway, I think *The Wall* is a perfect piece of work. It's a record that you have to have some interest in the human condition to appreciate. It's not a record where you say, I want to be entertained. I don't want to think about negative things. It's not one of those records.

The Wall at Earls Court, London, August 7, 1980.

POPOFF: There's definitely a bleakness to it. Even though there's the glimpse of a process, it doesn't feel like much of the wall is really, for all intents and purposes, compromised by the close of the story.

CHAPMAN: No, there are suicide notes on that record, but there's also dabbling into totalitarianism and neo-Nazism; that's what was leveled at it. There are certainly lyrics on that record that you would never get away with today. "And that one's a coon! Who let all of this riffraff into the room?" Because as an artist now, you're not allowed to tell stories like you were back then. For better or worse. Of course, some would say that you shouldn't be allowed to use words like that.

BEGGS: It's in 3/4, so it's waltz time and has this kind of old-worldly, jingoistic, nationalistic, pseudo–marching band feel. But it's drunk and it's lazy and feels like men lifting steins of beer, singing this rallying song. It's almost a racist chant. Because he goes through a litany of people that he hates. That one's a coon, that one's a queer. It's his fascist alter ego identifying with the Nazi imagery. He's very clearly linking fascistic imagery with the fascist that he thinks he's becoming through this endless bout of touring, isolation, rejection by his wife, drugs, sleep deprivation, and hatred of the audience that seem to want him to play the old stuff all the time. You don't get more punk than that—and remember, this was the tail end of punk. So, even the soldiers of the revolution were tired and washed-up. But not Roger. Roger kept on spitting bile at the world in the most eloquent way.

CHAPMAN: I'm always amazed that it achieved so much commercially, because it's an unrelenting record. You have something like "Don't Leave Me Now," which in my mind is far more difficult to listen to than anything on *The Final Cut*. There's no compromise made on "Don't Leave Me Now," as far as how he sings that, what the lyrics are—it's as bleak as it gets and it's probably, right at that moment, as bleak as Pink Floyd would ever get.

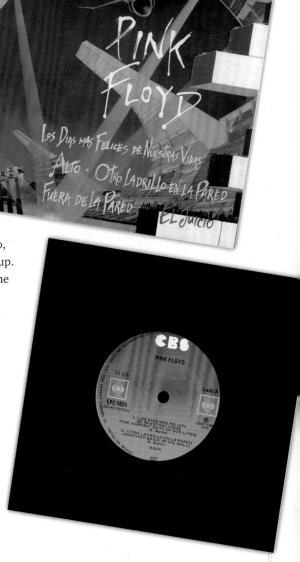

A five-track picture-sleeve EP of songs from *The Wall*, released in Mexico in 1980, with track titles translated into Spanish.

CHAPTER 12

THE FINAL CUT

WITH RALPH CHAPMAN, ROBERT CORICH, AND NICK BEGGS

SIDE 1

1.	The Post War Dream	3:02
	(Waters)	
2.	Your Possible Pasts	4:22
	(Waters)	
3.	One of the Few	1:23
	(Waters)	
4.	The Hero's Return	2:56
	(Waters)	
5.	The Gunner's Dream	5:07
	(Waters)	
6.	Paranoid Eyes	3:40
	(Waters)	

SIDE 2

1.	Get Your Filthy Hands Off My Desert	1:19
	(Waters)	
2.	The Fletcher Memorial Home	4:11
	(Waters)	
3.	Southampton Dock	2:13
	(Waters)	
4.	The Final Cut	4:46
	(Waters)	
5.	Not Now John	5:01
	(Waters)	
6.	Two Suns in the Sunset	5:14
	(Waters)	

pink
floyd
the
final
cut

Recorded at Mayfair Studios, Primrose Hill, London; Olympic Studios, Barnes, London; Abbey Road Studios, St. John's Wood, London; Eel Pie Studios, Twickenham, London; Audio International, London; RAK Studios, St. John's Wood, London; Hookend Manor Studios, Reading, UK; The Billiard Room, Sheen, London

PERSONNEL: Roger Waters—lead vocals, bass guitar, acoustic and electric guitars, synthesizers, tape effects; David Gilmour—guitars, vocals; Nick Mason—drums, tape effects

GUEST PERFORMANCES: Michael Kamen—piano, harmonium; Andy Bown—organ; Ray Cooper—drums, percussion; Andy Newmark—drums; Raphael Ravenscroft—tenor saxophone; Doreen Chanter—backing vocals; Irene Chanter—backing vocals; National Philharmonic Orchestra—various instrumentation

Produced by Roger Waters, James Guthrie, and Michael Kamen

Released March 21, 1983

If one song is a microcosm for what befell Pink Floyd circa *The Final Cut*, it's "When the Tigers Broke Free." Pink Floyd had built *The Wall*, and the album had broken the band. The film that followed would destroy what was left, and an adjunct album to be called *Spare Bricks* was doomed from the start. But the seed of *The Final Cut* is in this one song written at the time of *The Wall* but prophetically rejected because it was too personal to Roger's biography, namely how his father, Eric Fletcher Waters, died in the war.

A work like that was bound to stick in Roger's craw, and by affect and effect both good and cancerous, the song essentially expanded to become an entire album destined

to be increasingly too personal for David. For a fading Nick Mason and Rick . . . well, who cares?

Then Margaret Thatcher went to war over a distant pile of rocks called the Falkland Islands in a Keystone Kops affair that Jorge Luis Borges famously called "two bald men fighting over a comb." This war rankled Roger and he drew parallels to losing his father in the Battle of Anzio, where he and his fellow sacrifices found themselves helplessly defending Italy, only to be overrun by German Tiger tanks. But there are echoes of *Animals* in Roger's stated, wider goals for the album, namely a denunciation of Thatcher's brutal Tory rule and how it had further rotted out a once great empire already in decline through the late '70s.

The resulting précis-turned-thesis was forged and hammered into shape by Roger's creative drive, which was twice as powerful here as it was during *The Wall* (which had doubled Roger's sense of purpose on *Animals*, which in turn doubled up how much Roger we got on *Wish You Were Here*). A territorial clash was inevitable, and the only other writer in the band, already faded, essentially gave up the ghost.

What emerged to very little fanfare is a record pretty much derided by fans and critics alike during its quiet early life, although now many a deep Floyd fan put *The Final Cut* among their (warily respected) top few.

ABOVE: Waters, Gilmour, Mason, and Wright leave the stage together at the Los Angeles Memorial Sports Arena, February 1980. By the time of the band's next tour, in 1987, only Gilmour and Mason would be permanent members of Pink Floyd.

BELOW: Label from an original Italian pressing of *The Final Cut*.

ABOVE: Bob Geldof in a still from the film adaptation of *The Wall*.

INSET: Promotional program produced in 1982 for Alan Parker's film version of *The Wall*.

Whether justified or not, the main complaint—to net it out bluntly—was this: the album was too slow, too quiet, too non-rock, too orchestrated. Without Bob Ezrin around to bring the best out of Dave and Roger and act as a constant reminder to write some rock 'n' roll with choruses and resolutions, Roger essentially built the album with Michael Kamen, the end mélange turning out to be something that sits neatly as the first of Roger's solo albums, with the untidy technicality that it was issued under the Floyd banner.

Lacking enough guitar, bass, and drums, *The Final Cut*'s concept, heavy on World War II, tended to enforce grumblings that the album contained too much gosh-darn old-timey, soundtrack-y music, which in turn was enforced by the storyline—known to the press-reading Floyd follower—that the album in fact was a left turn from what was to be an actual soundtrack album. It also didn't help that the album had a subtitle, and a foggy one at that—*A Requiem for the Post-War Dream*—and, quite simply, that there's a sense of anticlimax when a band follows a double record with a single (more acutely so if that double is heralded as one of the great records of all time—Fleetwood Mac didn't have this problem with *Tusk*, nor did The Clash with the triple *Sandinista!*).

Back to "When the Tigers Broke Free." The song also represents one of the many myths about Floyd and *The Final Cut*. All it takes is a quote or two from, say, David Gilmour, to write the narrative that *The Final Cut* is a bunch of *Wall* leftovers, when in fact, "When the Tigers Broke Free" was the one main fleshed-out composition (although not even recorded at the time). The song itself doesn't even show up on *The Final Cut*; that is, until Roger does some dangerous, or at least messy, rewriting of history and starts wedging it in subsequent reissues.

True, *The Final Cut* builds upon several story points from *The Wall*, but it is anything but an also-ran. Indeed, the record must be applauded for sounding very little like *The Wall* and for giving birth to Roger Waters's magnificent solo works, particularly the likes of *Amused to Death* and *Is This the Life We Really Want?* These are two notable classics among four very strong records that celebrate the smorgasbord of devices that make *The Final Cut* a thought-provoking symphony of sound, a regal feast as it were, food for thought, ear candy as dessert, followed by a boozy aperitif.

"When the Tigers Broke Free," a non-album single released by Pink Floyd in the period between *The Wall* and *The Final Cut*.

POPOFF: Could you lay out the series of events leading up to the building and release of *The Final Cut*? How and why do we get this record?

CHAPMAN: They were doing a movie with the idea that they would then do a quasi-soundtrack album that would collect the rearrangements of *The Wall* tracks that they did, the re-recordings they did for the film, and they would find a home for "When the Tigers Broke Free." But Waters was constantly locking horns with Alan Parker, the director of the movie, and it dissolved into this extremely contentious, acrimonious relationship that completely spoiled it for Roger. It was a ruinous experience for him.

And it was splintering the band. By that point Wright had been fired, and they'd put him on salary to do the tour. I don't think Roger was even thinking about anything other than, "I have my own ideas and I want to move this band forward." Because Pink Floyd was still his vehicle. It reminds me of one of his heroes, Lennon, where in the waning moments of the Beatles, Lennon was putting out songs like "The Ballad of John and Yoko," which had nothing to do with the Beatles. But at that point, that's the only vehicle he had.

And it seemed unthinkable from a business point of view, and probably from an emotional point of view, to split Floyd to see this vision through. Instead, Roger said to Dave, "I don't want any material from you now that Rick is gone. I don't want any of your material. This is my project. This is the next Pink Floyd project, and if you don't like it, fuck you; I'll dissolve the band, or I'll take my marbles and go home" kind of thing. And Gilmour, as history bears out, still craving that structure, capitulated. And he agreed to his name being removed from the producer credits and not being a producer, but still demanding, of course, producer points on the record, which is very shrewd.

CORICH: Yes, Rick was cut out, due to all those problems with *The Wall*. They'd definitely had a falling out and he was not about to be included. I think Gilmour wanted him to play, but then again, at times, David didn't put his foot down hard enough. But it's interesting—you listen to Dave Gilmour's solo album, *About Face*, which was out exactly a year later, a split second in Pink Floyd time; no shortage of great material. Imagine, if Gilmour was going to supply material, there's what it might have sounded like.

So this was Roger's album through and through. And it was most likely, I suspect, also one to satisfy the delivery of something to the record company. And it has been said he was the only one who was really writing anything at the time. Can they complain? Mason wasn't writing much, Dave Gilmour essentially demurred, and Rick Wright had been ejected from the band. There you go. Roger was absolutely in control. Gilmour's been on record saying that he's basically a session musician on this one—in his own band.

And he wasn't that pleased about it, was he? But you've got to say, his guitar playing on it is sublime, although it wasn't as in-your-face as on previous works. Still, it's quite a rounded album, a gentle album in many ways, but it's got some violent parts to it too.

POPOFF: How does Britain's entry into the Falklands War affect Roger?

CHAPMAN: While all this is happening, I think it was in April 1982, the Argentineans invade the Falkland Islands. And Thatcher, whose popularity is in the toilet, and the country is dying and everyone hates her, comes up, either consciously or subconsciously, with this plan to defend the Falklands.

And we see it now, which is one of the reasons I love *The Final Cut* even more today. History keeps repeating itself. We see it in Syria, with Trump sending cruise missiles into Syria. If the people realize what a schmuck you are, often the only thing you can do is bring nationalism into the picture. How do you bring nationalism into the picture? You start a war. Because anyone who doesn't support your country when you're in a war is treasonous.

I think that's what Maggie did. She thought, here's my opportunity to take the country's mind off rampant unemployment and blah blah blah, so she sends this armada down and fights for these meaningless islands—not symbolically meaningless, but strategically meaningless, economically meaningless—it's a war that's simply about pride.

Roger sees this, and sees the destruction of the *Sheffield*, the British ship, and he sees the destruction of the *General Belgrano*, which was the Argentinean ship, and he says—again, this is my conjecture and my belief—this is all bullshit. My father died completely in vain. This is "The Post War Dream"—what happened to the postwar dream? What happened to recognizing that war takes young people's lives and unless you're fighting for freedom or something noble, then it's criminal. It's fundamentally evil.

So, he goes through that, coupled with *The Wall* film experience, coupled with his own sense that he was on a roll as a writer and had something to say and felt an obligation to say it. I think it was the playwright Edward Albee who said if art is merely decorative it's a waste of time. I think Waters, especially because he was a follower of Lennon and Dylan, thought, "I have a pulpit, I'm going to use it. Not to preach, but to say what needs to be said. To provide a dissenting voice, especially in wartime." That's when you need to hear someone saying: you know what? This is not an honorable fight. It's about nothing more than power.

CORICH: But it also feeds a young man's basic or maybe morbid fascination for all things military. My friends and I, we all followed the Falklands War; certainly where I grew up—New Zealand. We followed it every hour, every day pretty much, while it ran. To hear an album that absolutely references what happened and the effects of that, I found quite fascinating.

And I found it fascinating coming from a little country—a colony, a well-to-do place all in all, like Canada, where you didn't want for anything—that I could hear anger in Roger's lyrics about this conflict that I thought I understood. But I realized I didn't understand the sense of anger and outrage that could be taking place at home in England.

And that comes out palpably. He writes about the leaders of the day, Galtieri and Reagan and Thatcher. Roger's a clever writer, very politically motivated, and he's not afraid to say what he thinks, which I've always admired. I don't always agree with what he writes about or even like it all, but no one can say he's a man who will not write about his convictions.

POPOFF: Dispel for me the myths about *The Final Cut*.

CHAPMAN: The myth for me of *The Final Cut* is it's a knockoff; it's all the shit bits of *The Wall* that weren't used, that Roger sort of cobbled together. Another myth is that it's somehow not a Pink Floyd record. Another myth is that it's this depressing polemic, that it's Roger still moaning about his father. In my mind, that was something that I certainly ascribed to. I hated *The Final Cut* for years and years and years—until I got some living in me.

I was seventeen when that record came out, and in my early to mid-twenties a friend of mine from college, a guy named Uwe, said to me, "No, you actually have to listen to *The Final Cut*." Because there are certain records—and you know this—where groupthink comes into play, where you're pressured to think, "Yeah, that's the shit one." *Love Beach* from ELP is always the one that comes to mind. "Fuck *Love Beach*—that sucks." I've met so many people who have never actually heard that record.

Final Cut did get a five-star review from *Rolling Stone*, so it wasn't like it was completely vilified. But it was released among this uncertainty with the band and the sense of infighting that was starting to spill out into the public. Then Gilmour heaps more on the idea that *Final Cut* was just songs the band had already rejected. The album was never allowed to be just listened to.

Luckily, when I got some living under my belt, it was a record I returned to. My country didn't go to war with Argentina, so that wasn't my access point. I wasn't a political animal. I was someone who was growing up and having relationship issues and dealing with rage issues; life was not going the way it was supposed to go.

That was my entry point to *Final Cut*. When there's a line like, "Button your lip. Don't let the shield slip" or "Take a fresh grip on your bulletproof mask"—that's just universal. It may be about a war vet who is trying to hide his pain, but the magic of so much of that record is that it's universal in its message of anguish. It's on those levels that I reached *The Final Cut*, which so few people choose to do.

Again, if you're told that *Wish You Were Here* is about Syd Barrett, you go, "Fuck, that's great. It's about Syd Barrett, man. He got high, lost his mind, and they miss him." Okay, that's simply one level. On another level it's about yearning and loneliness and finding companionship and finding peace. "The Final Cut," "Paranoid Eyes," "The Gunner's Dream" . . . there are all these different songs that hit on the human heart, songs that really have nothing to do with what Waters is saying other than this is the human condition.

That's why I get frustrated when people dismiss it. Because they're not actually listening to the poetry of it. I could conjure so many lines. There are so many examples of Waters exploring personal vulnerability, although it may be couched in this larger narrative. But it's an emotional record. If you have any feeling, it doesn't matter that it's about Eric Fletcher Waters. It doesn't matter that it's about this ridiculous race to build the best car or the best ship. It's not about any of those things. That's just imagery. It's about betrayal and loneliness and life and death and vulnerability. On those levels it's an absolutely perfect record.

CORICH: Well put; and yes, I agree, those are the myths—that it should've been a Roger Waters solo album or that it's just lots of leftovers and outtakes from *The Wall*. And whether you accept his choice of subject matter, Roger had a lot of issues. He was trying to deal with family and the loss of his dad, as well as not knowing his dad.

I might be the only person on the planet who likes listening to *The Final Cut* more than I like listening to *The Wall*. *The Wall* is a brilliant piece of music, but now I find it a bit turgid to listen to, which is maybe due to the running length. *The Final Cut* is a weird one because I figure you have to listen to it start to finish, and when you do that, it dispels the myth that it's uninspired or not exquisitely constructed.

It's a musical album, but it's got a story to it that might be even tighter than that of *The Wall* and flows better than *The Wall*, again, because it was condensed into forty-four minutes. Whereas *The Wall* was always an effort to listen to. Great tracks, some of which you'll play over and over again, and there is nothing like that on *The Final Cut*. But *The Final Cut* flows like an album to the point where it feels like one epic song.

As much of an uncommon fan as I am of the record, there's not a track that I can pick off and say, "Oh, I'm going to play it over and over again." To me it's not that kind of album. It commands undivided attention. The other day, I traveled across London on the tube, and I went for a walk through St. Katharine Docks where in 2017 they had terrorist killings, and it turned out in that instance to be a very therapeutic album for me, very reflective, especially in light of the politics on it being, unfortunately, evergreen. But I also firmly believe it might have more resonance for those of us who grew up with it and experienced it in real time.

POPOFF: Let's look at some of the individual songs on here, starting with the most obvious, "Not Now John," the big single.

CORICH: When I first heard that one, I thought, that's great, someone used the "fuck" word in a song properly. Something you say as a young man all the time, someone's put it properly on record, and you've got a monstrous beat going with it as well. It's a powerful song, yet it's also got Doreen and Irene Chanter doing soulful female backing vocals, which is an occasional Floyd tradition. It feels like a song Roger wrote for himself, and not really his band, which just happened to be around; it feels like an anthemic crescendo moment on one of his solo albums. It's violent lyrically but it's also fun. Sure, it's political and serious, sort of an *Animals* lyric, but hearing it with your mates or on the radio, it was also, "Yeah, let's get on with this. Fuck this, let's get down to the pub and have a drink."

CHAPMAN: The "Fuck all that, we've got to get on with these" kind of thing, this unfeeling, almost sociopathic, we've got to bring the Russian bear to his knees, we've got to outproduce, we've got to profit, profit . . . it's revealing the truth of what war is about, which is often about profiteering, and what capitalism is often about, which is about profit at all costs. And Roger has pointed out that the character in "Have a Cigar" is the same character in "Not Now John." Thematically, it's "Have a Cigar" part two, couched in a larger and much more disastrous outcome. It's not simply about exploiting a rock band, it's about exploiting humanity at any cost. It's about profiteering.

As far as the actual performance, I find it fascinating that the one time he uses Gilmour as a vocalist is for a so-called rock part. Now, Gilmour may still be the only one in that band who could convincingly sing a rock 'n' roll song—that's up to debate. Even "Have a Cigar," they got in Roy Harper. Waters expressed regret about that, since he tried "Have a Cigar" and couldn't pull it off. Maybe if you asked him now, he'd say, "Maybe I could've sung 'Not Now John,' but at the time, I didn't feel I could pull it off."

Because I can't see a stylistic reason why Gilmour was chosen to sing that. I don't understand that, and I can't believe it's because they needed a single. If you were going to use Gilmour as a singer, you would have used him on "The Final Cut" or on some of these songs that, in theory, could've used that softer voice. But instead, he uses him for something that he wasn't exactly the greatest at. There's an irony to it. Who knows? Waters being the type of guy he is, maybe it was intentionally ironic. But I don't necessarily believe that Gilmour sang it better than Waters would have.

CORICH: I prefer David's voice through and through. Maybe with Mason and Gilmour not really doing very much on the album, Roger had to step up and take most the vocals because

UK pressing of "Not Now John," the sole single drawn from *The Final Cut.*

pink floyd not now john

he had no choice. They didn't want to sing his songs, so Roger had to sing them. I prefer David's voice, and I agree: On "Not Now John" we get his aggressive higher gear and not his usual soothing, dreamy style. Roger's got that nagging English voice; he obviously puts his passion in there and doesn't hold back.

POPOFF: What are some other highlights on the record from a lyrical standpoint?

CHAPMAN: There's a line in "Paranoid Eyes," a song I continually come back to, which again reveals this record to me not as a political polemic, but an album of humanity. Roger writes, "The pie in the sky turned out to be miles too high." In the context of "Paranoid Eyes," it's about this guy who comes back from the war and he's succumbed to alcohol-soft middle age. He's forced to hide his pain and the secrets of what he saw in wartime. He's not allowed to be a war hero. He has to keep it all shut up inside.

But what's so appealing about that line is that I would say 90 or 100 percent of the people that I know, if I asked, "Did the brass ring turn out to be much harder to grasp than you thought?" they would all say yes. Maybe that's because I don't hang out with rock stars and multimillionaires. But for the most part, one can't escape the universal message of a line like that.

Yes, *The Final Cut* is political, and yes, it's about the rage against war and the powers that be—Reagan and Brezhnev and Thatcher. Yes, on the surface it's a political record. But just below it's a record about very human, very universal characteristics of disillusionment, suffering, failure, pain, secrecy, trying to attain some degree of peace of mind—all those things that make this record age with you, become more and more relevant as you move forward in life.

That's why I return to "Free Four" and how he painted this so beautifully when he said, "The memories of a man in his old age/Are the deeds of a man in his prime." Roger instinctively created a timeless image. God willing, when I'm eighty and I'm listening to "Free Four," I'll say, "You're right, Roger. My memories are everything I did when I was young and vital, and could've, should've, and maybe did do something meaningful."

A much more dramatic lyric is "The Gunner's Dream," ostensibly about a guy blown out of his airplane and falling to his death and looking down and saying goodbye to his relatives, and also, incredibly, imagining his service. It's a beautiful image. When you imagine "After the service when you're walking slowly to the car" coming from a guy who's falling to his death, it's consciousness-shifting. It's astounding, that much artistry in a handful of lines.

Then he shifts to this idea of contemporary England and what life should be about. It's a place to eat, a place to sleep, not worrying about some cop or secret policeman kicking your door down. There are the Falkland Islands on this record, but Waters pulls in contemporary events as well, referencing the twin bombings in London in July 1982 by the IRA.

And the last verse of "The Gunner's Dream" seems to be about his sense of responsibility to get this message out. It's the idea that if you go back to war for the wrong reasons, they all died in vain. Not just that those who fight war for the wrong reasons die in vain, but maybe that all soldiers, including Eric Fletcher Waters, died in vain if wars continue. Roger wants to feel his father didn't die in vain, but he's conflicted about it.

POPOFF: "Two Suns in the Sunset" is contemporary as well, or even prescient and worried about the warfare of the future, namely that it could be nuclear.

CORICH: Yes, and it sets a pattern. Moving forward into his solo records, Roger's often alluded to nuclear war, final war, devastation, on albums like *Amused to Death*. I'm pretty sure Roger knew the Nevil Shute book On the Beach from 1957, quite well-known at the time, about nuclear holocaust or nuclear devastation, albeit from afar, watching it happen in the northern hemisphere from the vantage point of Australia.

Drummer Andy Newmark, who appears on *The Final Cut's* "Two Suns in the Sunset," pictured at a Rex Smith session at Mediasound, New York City, 1979.

But Roger writes about the big issues of the day, making his albums topical, and in some instances quite dated with some of the references. But in the early 1980s, no one really knew what was happening. You had the Russians with Brezhnev with his finger on the trigger. And you didn't really know how Reagan was going to react, or overreact. We all could conceive of a nuclear war breaking out at any moment.

The Final Cut is an antiwar album through and through, from the past into a possible apocalyptic future. The album's last track, "Two Suns in the Sunset," opens with the First World War coming up to the Second World War. And it's complex enough to look at the role of money in war and then just big money and the abuse of it in the economy. Roger was so far ahead of his time, because this is what the world is about right now. It's about all those references in "The Post War Dream."

We've been through a couple of Gulf Wars that no one should've been involved in, certainly not the second one. And we've got big figures that, in my opinion, should have been up for war crimes, like Tony Blair. And you've got the situation with big corporate money, countries run by corporations and not by governments that are actually looking after their people. This album is about that, but it's also about, subliminally, the consequences. Which is why I appreciate *The Final Cut* so much today and find new things in it.

Bottom line, *The Final Cut*, for me, hasn't dated much at all. Whereas, say, *Meddle* is dated; I love it to death, but the music is of the period. But someone could've recorded *The Final Cut* two years ago, a year ago, slightly different lyrics and tone; it's not completely off what someone would put out today.

CHAPMAN: To Robert's point about Tony Blair, on "The Fletcher Memorial Home," Roger calls out Brezhnev and these world leaders, the Latin American meatpacking glitterati. What is the word I'm looking for? These cretins. And there's that great line where he says, "Did they expect us to treat them with any respect?" But it's this idea that these are all crazy lunatics, these people, who should be pitied, not revered. Of course, in wartime, you revere your leader because you're forced to. And Waters is saying, no, these are lunatics. They should be locked away so they can't send young men to die.

POPOFF: I'd like to get a few words on just how great this record sounds. Is it possible that it's the very best-sounding Pink Floyd album ever, or the one that certainly handles all these sonically challenging effects with the most grace and sympathy?

CHAPMAN: It was recorded using a new system called Holophonics. And it's funny, Waters's third solo album, *Amused to Death*, was recorded in QSound. There was always a part of Roger interested in achieving these broad, rich sonic pictures. Holophonics was a recording process that allowed the stereo to sound three-dimensional without using Quad sound.

There's whispering and the sounds of being at a bar and tons of different pieces of recording. I'm sure Waters was thinking, "I want to put you in the bar. I want you to hear the glasses over here and I want you to hear the billiard balls clanking over there." Because Quad had fallen out, certainly by the early '80s. There was this quest still to find ways of achieving that but still on a stereo tape.

Roger eventually commissioned a 5.1 mix of *Amused to Death*, and I could only dream of a 5.1 mix of *Final Cut*. Of course, it will never happen, because of the record's reputation. But I agree, sonically *The Final Cut* is not stale, it's stunning. One figures with Mayfair and Eel Pie and RAK and all these different studios, that Roger was constantly searching for the right places to find the sounds in his head. I imagine a certain studio had a great drum room, and a certain studio had a great room for strings, and so on.

If you ever want to test headphones, it's one of the records I reach to. But why? I guess it's because of Michael Kamen, plus James Guthrie was there. The album had to sound mighty. It was an album that certainly had a righteous rage about it, but it had a royal righteous rage, if that makes sense. It had to be huge. It had to match the power of the voice in his head. Roger was never a guy who interpreted power as screaming guitars and feedback. He interpreted it as enveloping sound.

MICHAEL KAMEN

ATCO RECORDS

A promotional portrait of Michael Kamen, who stood in for Richard Wright on *The Final Cut*.

Waters's third solo LP, *Amused to Death*, from September 1992.

POPOFF: Still, the reality is, it's far from universally loved now, and it didn't exactly take the world by storm when it came out back in 1983.

CORICH: No; the critics, all the English newspapers, New Zealand, Australia, America, anything you read about, it didn't rate highly. I think there were a few reasons for that. Yes, it was a departure from the Floyd of the '70s, but then, bands had to grow. And that's the secret of a band like Pink Floyd—they were innovative, and the next time out they innovated again.

But as I stressed earlier, to me, this was an album that needed to be listened to as a body of work. A lot of journalists have the attention span of a gnat. If they don't get it in the first two or three minutes, it's a shit album. And A&R people would be even more ruthless or quick to react.

You've got to look at times as well. MTV was a couple years in, at the height of its power. The early stages of this current disaster we have now was just starting, namely the one-hit wonder or at least the single, or the single with that perfect video. And now it's all about the one song. Pretty soon we might not have albums anymore, and something like *The Final Cut*, a work of art that depends on being framed as an entire album, looks like an anathema.

POPOFF: Ralph, despite how it was received at the time, you are calling for a reassessment.

CHAPMAN: If I stuck with the opinions I formed when I was nineteen, twenty, twenty-one, I would find that pathetic now as a fifty-one-year-old. Yet there's something about albums—and I'm sure other types of art—where, even though people's lives have gone through changes, they cling to opinions about things like records like a blanket from their childhood.

The Final Cut is one of those records where you can't. It's not like Pink Floyd wasn't always about raising very unpleasant ideas about paranoia and insanity. Read the lyrics to "Time"; those are some of the most depressing lyrics you'll ever read. And unlike "Time," the thing about *The Final Cut* is that there's so much tenderness and vulnerability in the lyrics throughout this record that it's not depressing—it's life. And you can say life is depressing, but Roger is out there saying, "I know how you feel." He's being life-affirming.

Sure, *The Final Cut* is a universal record about criminals and bullies, and betrayal and loss and frustration, and a refusal to understand and learn from history. It's about the perils of greed and capitalism, but most importantly, it's about what a struggle it is to be a human being. And it devastates me that Roger

A promotional portrait of Dave Gilmour, taken in New York City in 1984.

has aligned himself with the pro-hunting Countryside Alliance, because it seems completely at odds. But people are contradictions. But that's Roger's betrayal to me [*laughs*], is that he got in bed with those people.

But the last thing I want to say is that on *The Final Cut*, not only did Roger Waters have his shining moment as a lyricist, as good as anybody in the entertainment industry, but that he was also an extraordinary vocalist. With what a lot of people think is a limited voice, he brought out so many colors and ranges of emotion. His message was clear. He was like Olivier, a performer able to convey a monologue that made you weep. I must've heard and listened to that record five hundred, a thousand times, easily, and it always stops me in my tracks. And each time, I can't help but think this guy understands me.

THE FINAL CUT **187**

CHAPTER 13

A MOMENTARY LAPSE OF REASON

WITH ROIE AVIN AND ED LOPEZ-REYES

SIDE 1

1.	Signs of Life (Gilmour, Ezrin)	4:25
2.	Learning to Fly (Gilmour, Moore, Ezrin, Carin)	4:53
3.	The Dogs of War (Gilmour, Moore)	6:11
4.	One Slip (Gilmour, Manzanera)	5:04
5.	On the Turning Away (Gilmour, Moore)	5:38

SIDE 2

1.	Yet Another Movie (Gilmour, Leonard)	5:56
1a.	Round and Around (Gilmour)	1:31
2.	A New Machine Part 1 (Gilmour)	1:46
3.	Terminal Frost (Gilmour)	6:17
4.	A New Machine Part 2 (Gilmour)	0:39
5.	Sorrow (Gilmour)	8:49

Recorded at Astoria Studios, Hampton, London; A&M Studios, Hollywood, California; Audio International, London; Britannia Row, Islington, London; Can Am Recorders, Tarzana, California; Cherokee Recording Studios, Hollywood, California; Mayfair Studios, Primrose Hill, London; Village Recorder, West Los Angeles, California

PERSONNEL: David Gilmour—guitars, vocals, keyboards, and sequencers; Nick Mason—electric and acoustic drums, sound effects; Richard Wright—piano, vocals, Kurzweil, Hammond organ

GUEST PERFORMANCES: Bob Ezrin—keyboards, percussion, and sequencers; Tony Levin—bass guitar, Stick; Jim Keltner—drums; Steve Forman—percussion; Jon Carin—keyboards; Tom Scott—alto and soprano saxophones; Scott Page—tenor saxophone; Carmine Appice—drums; Pat Leonard—synthesizers; Bill Payne—Hammond organ; Michael Landau—guitar; John Halliwell—saxophone; Darlene Koldenhaven—backing vocals; Carmen Twillie—backing vocals; Phyllis St. James—backing vocals; Donnie Gerrard—backing vocals

Produced by Bob Ezrin and David Gilmour

Released September 7, 1987

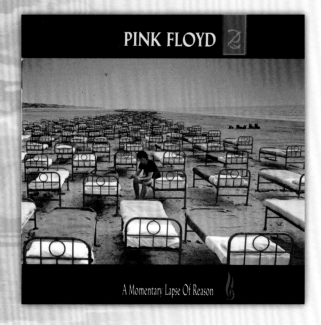

A Momentary Lapse Of Reason

I f you prefer an extinct Pink Floyd, then sure, complain about *A Momentary Lapse of Reason*. But the fact is, with the album falling out of a process that began as work toward a third David Gilmour solo album, a valuable brand was given renewed life. And once living, it went live—Pink Floyd, until its demise two conventional yacht rock studio albums and a new age record later, would pretty much exist and thrive in the memories of millions as a concert experience. Sure, the albums sold in crony capitalistic quantity, but now that they are gone, the Gilmour-led version of Pink Floyd will be remembered for bringing so much joy to fans perfectly happy to have had not one but two compromised Floyds flowin', David's and Roger's, the latter of which kept a second sub-brand gleaming in his showy celebrations of *The Wall*.

With Roger officially gone from the band in December 1985, it was less than a year later that work commenced on *A Momentary Lapse of Reason*. David's second solo album, *About Face*, issued in March 1984, was a valiant, emotionally stirring affair, but "Blue Light" and "Love on the Air" failed to propel the record past gold in the states—still a decent certification, except for maybe Pink Floyd.

With plans for a third solo album wobbling, the more exciting prospect of reviving the Pink Floyd name found David collaborating again with Nick and bringing in Rick, even if for legal reasons he couldn't be classed as an official member. Also returning was Bob Ezrin of *The Wall* and *About Face*—a key partner in forming David's soundscapes into songs. Ezrin was point-blank honest about it: he could have worked with Roger on what became *Radio K.A.O.S.*, but found working with Gilmour easier; to boot, the prospect of their labors being labeled Pink Floyd appealed greatly.

Still, sessions on David's houseboat were conducted with no decision as to whether the results would be solo or Floyd. The writing was a struggle, and the music wasn't sounding particularly Floyd-ish (according to the label's Stephen Ralbovsky). In the end, collaborating with an outside writer, Anthony Moore, proved to be the spark. Even though Gilmour ultimately carried the load, it was the sumptuous MTV-friendly "Learning to Fly," built up from a Jon Carin demo, that became the new record's calling card.

TOP: Mason, Gilmour, and Wright at Britannia Row Studios, London, November 1986.

INSET: Canadian CBS Records issue of *A Momentary Lapse of Reason*.

"One Slip" and "On the Turning Away" followed as singles, while the oppressive and blustery "The Dogs of War," riding fan support, became essentially the record's second-most everlasting track. All told, the band—in order of incursion, David, Nick, Bob, Rick, Anthony Moore, and Jon Carin—efficiently constructed a record for the demanding mid-'80s, through dint of hard work and crafty brand-positioning by way of playing to type. Missing something as nebulous as a strong creative concept proved surmountable, with the successful completion of the task abetted by the fact that three of four members were aboard, one being the guitarist and the friendlier of the band's two singers. David framed the album as a return to a better balance between lyrics and music, and a large swath of the customer class agreed.

Once the totals were tallied, however, the UK wasn't buying it, with the record stalling at gold. But Canada sent *Momentary Lapse* triple platinum and American fans bestowed upon the Floyd impressive quadruple platinum status, vaulting the record to #3 on the *Billboard* charts, where it couldn't get past the *Whitesnake* juggernaut or Michael Jackson's *Bad*. Pink Floyd was firmly part of the pop culture fabric once again as lawsuits with Roger over the name were resolved. More importantly, the album was supported by a tour and, within fourteen months, the *Delicate Sound of Thunder* live album, on which more than half of *A Momentary Lapse of Reason*'s wares were displayed for a second time.

POPOFF: What are the circumstances leading up to this record? There's the long gap since *The Final Cut*.

LOPEZ-REYES: Gilmour and Waters are wrapping up their solo tours in 1985, which forces them to give renewed focus to the Pink Floyd brand and where that was going. The animosities were there, but they hadn't quite reached the point of saying, okay, what's gonna happen to Pink Floyd? Gilmour seems to be a lot more focused on his work toward a third solo album, but at the same time there's the realization that they had to resolve the Pink Floyd thing and then figure out how to move forward without Roger Waters as part of that brand. My understanding is that Gilmour continued working on material for a third solo album, and as the record label was pushing them to do a Pink Floyd album, they're getting into a legal battle. It was never clear that this was going to be Pink Floyd material. I think what cemented it as Pink Floyd material for Gilmour were the unfolding legal circumstances combined with an increasing amount of Pink Floyd veterans coming on board, like Bob Ezrin and Andy Jackson.

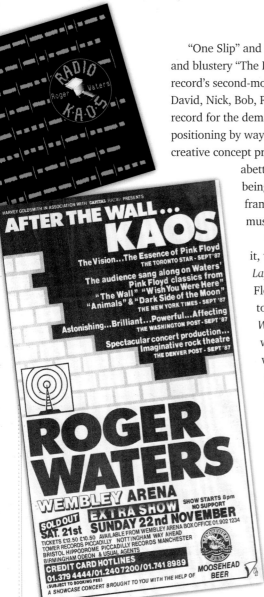

ABOVE: Roger Waters's concept album *Radio K.A.O.S.* was released in the summer of 1987, a few months before *Momentary Lapse*.

OPPOSITE: Gilmour in Detroit circa 1984, around the time of the release of his solo LP *About Face*.

AVIN: The coalescing of a strong team definitely helped. Anthony Moore helped cowrite a couple of songs lyrically: "On the Turning Away," "The Dogs of War," and "Learning to Fly." They needed some help making the album; that's apparent. When it used to be just the four of them, they could do it, but this was largely a Gilmour solo album turned into a Pink Floyd album. And to get it to that point, they needed a lot of help. Nothing necessarily wrong with that, but that's also maybe the disconnect between the new fans and the old fans who might not feel it's a Pink Floyd album. To me it definitely is a Pink Floyd album, but they needed some help, at least for this first time when they were trying to do it without Waters.

POPOFF: What's happening with Rick Wright at this point? Why couldn't he be fully involved?
LOPEZ-REYES: This is one of the more curious aspects of how that album developed. There was a legal agreement that included a clause that said that he could not rejoin the band as a full member. That was written in there when Wright was removed as a band member during *The Wall* even though he was brought back as a contract member to play live.

There are several accounts explaining that Gilmour and Mason were investing so much in this album that they weren't ready to share the profits. They weren't sure how it was going to turn out. It seemed like they counted on it being successful to some degree, but they weren't ready to divide that with a third person who would've been coming in quite late. It was Rick Wright's wife at the time who approached David Gilmour about Wright participating in that project when she heard that this was going on. It took them a while to reintegrate him into the band. In fact, Wright was not photographed inside the album sleeve originally, although he was added in newer editions of the album.

POPOFF: Where does *A Momentary Lapse of Reason* rank in the catalog for you?
LOPEZ-REYES: This my favorite Floyd album, believe it or not. This album is a manifestation of David Gilmour's vision for the band, ultimately, despite how it evolved, in the same sense that *The Final Cut* is an expression of the band filtered through Roger Waters's dominant voice. *The Final Cut*, in a way, represents the peak of that Roger Waters era. People might argue that, in reality, it's a Roger Waters solo album, and logistically you can see that argument. But they made an effort to preserve certain qualities that represented Roger Waters's voice and yet put it through that Pink Floyd filter.

I'd place *Momentary Lapse* as the other bookend to this really chaotic period with all this uncertainty—it's a legitimate Pink Floyd album that compares to *The Final Cut* in that sense. This time

Rick Wright performs with his short-lived band Zee in New York City, 1984.

Gilmour's voice is filtered through that Pink Floyd sound. This point in the timeline is marked by an ebb and flow where one band member is more assertive than the other, and with *Momentary Lapse*, the historical circumstances gave Gilmour that place.

POPOFF: **What is Bob Ezrin's contribution to the record? One might argue that—again historical circumstances—he's second in command here.**

LOPEZ-REYES: There's the question about whether he had deliberately chosen to work with this version of the band as opposed to Roger Waters, and there are conflicting accounts of what exactly happened during this period. But it seems to me like Ezrin was always comfortable working with people who had very strong opinions and voices, artists from different genres and different backgrounds and musical strengths, including Lou Reed, Alice Cooper, Kiss.

But what Ezrin also brought to this, to the Gilmour camp and *A Momentary Lapse of Reason*, was a sense of emancipation. I honestly think it was purely accidental that for some reason he ended up dealing with the Gilmour side of this split. A lot of it had to do, apparently, with family pressures that he had. Gilmour was being more pliable and was offering to work with him with a lot more flexibility. And that was certainly something that lured him into that project.

The Astoria houseboat where much of *A Momentary Lapse of Reason* was recorded is shown docked on the River Thames at Hampton Court.

I also think he saw an opportunity to give new voice and breathe new life into the band. People forget that by *The Final Cut*, the band was losing steam, not just artistically but commercially, and this was a chance to revitalize that. And Ezrin seems to really succeed in doing that with bands. With Kiss, for example, the band had three stiffs with their studio albums. The live album did well, but Bob really helped them make a great record with *Destroyer*. It seems that he can take bands to the next level. I think that's the place he saw himself fitting with Pink Floyd with this new era.

POPOFF: Before we look at the music, tell me a little bit about this album cover, with the beds on the beaches.
LOPEZ-REYES: It was a really complicated and expensive album cover. They took seven, eight hundred beds, depending on what source you read, out into an area called Saunton Sands in Devon, southern England. Basically, they took them to the beach, and when they first attempted to take the picture, it started to rain. So, they had to take all the beds, put them back in storage, and it took them two weeks to go back out, reassemble the entire thing, and that's when they managed to get the cover that they finally got.

The shot includes elements of the album. The beds themselves are reflective of the lyrics in "Yet Another Movie" with "the vision of an empty bed." And you've got the hang glider, which is a representation of "Learning to Fly," and the five dogs of course, referencing "The Dogs of War." I'm not sure if Thorgerson thought that those were the anchor tracks on that album, but those are the ones represented in that picture for whatever reason. I actually own a lithograph signed by Storm. I think they made three hundred of them. I picked it up at his flat and got to talk to him about this. It's my favorite album cover, which might be odd, but I'm partial to the Gilmour era, even though I love all of Pink Floyd's work.

POPOFF: Sticking with the wrapper, how about the title? Why did they call it this?
LOPEZ-REYES: They were struggling to find a title, and they were concerned about how Roger Waters might be able to use and abuse the album title to criticize them. Eventually they kind of realized that there was no way to settle on a title that he wouldn't criticize or find a way to mock. They basically picked a lyric out of the song "One Slip."
AVIN: Yes, it's part of the chorus: "A momentary lapse of reason/ That binds a life for life." My feeling is that maybe it's kind of giving

Roger Waters a little nudge, poking him with a stick or something, suggesting maybe leaving Pink Floyd was a momentary lapse of reason [*laughs*]. Not the best idea in the world. But I always felt like that's what they were trying to do with that title. But this is also one where there were known working titles, like *Of Promises Broken*, *Delusions of Maturity*, and *Signs of Life*, which also all can be related to the breakdown in relations.

POPOFF: Into the record, it's funny, there's a long intro called "Signs of Life," over four minutes, where not much happens. But then that collapses into the majesty of "Learning to Fly." And given how great that song is, the dramatic build somehow now seems justified. What can you tell me about "Learning to Fly"?

UK pressings of the three singles drawn from *Momentary Lapse*: "Learning to Fly," "One Slip," and "On the Turning Away."

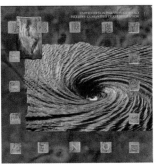

AVIN: The story is David Gilmour was interested in taking flying lessons, and Nick Mason joined him. They eventually bought a plane together, although I'm not sure if that was before or after the album. The lyrics are quite literally about piloting a plane and the view and the sensation, but it also gives a nice setup for learning how to make a new album without Roger Waters. That's definitely something that you can read into it. That was a good first single; it has sort of a hit element to it. In the live version, that opening drum thing with the percussion elements was played up to pretty dramatic effect. The song's got a great groove, and so it makes sense to hear it open unadorned.

LOPEZ-REYES: The interesting thing to me about "Learning to Fly" is that it's Jon Carin's first full thrust into the Pink Floyd camp in the sense that he developed the original demo. This is where he begins to integrate into the band very fully. The fans could never have accepted it, but he is someone who could have easily been added later as a member. He has integrated so well with Roger Waters now and is using his skills in his band. So, that's one of the paramount things about "Learning to Fly."

I also agree that there's not only the element of Gilmour and Mason conveying what they were doing as a hobby, but also expressing what they were doing with the band, moving forward. It's that sense of emancipation; they're taking off and taking the band in a new direction. Lyrically, it's a beautiful piece.

I'll also agree that the song lends itself to such magic live. I only got to see them do it on the *Division Bell* tour, and it's a shame that it hasn't been done on David Gilmour's solo tours, but there's something truly powerful about the song being on that opening segment of the album.

As a kid, this was the song that really hooked me into Pink Floyd. Two, three in the morning, I would lie awake listening to my radio through headphones, waiting for heavy metal and hard rock bands to come on, on this mixed-format radio station. I had ignored Floyd for the most part; didn't really know about them. And this was the song, with all the special effects and that guitar sound, that really captivated me and pulled me into this passion I have for the band.

POPOFF: Just to clarify, are you saying that Jon Carin really wrote the song?
LOPEZ-REYES: He had already constructed this demo, but then he developed it with David Gilmour. When I had a chance to ask Carin about it once or twice, every time that we've talked about it he essentially confirms that this is something he had already constructed when he came into the band. But I know the lyrics were largely written by Anthony Moore and Gilmour, and of course there's Mason's contributions. But musically this is where Carin most definitely injected the texture of his playing into the band. That carried out in the rest of the band's history.

People forget that there are two versions of the video for "Learning to Fly," which I think proves that the band saw that song as a critical statement. Not just in terms of the hobby that Mason and Gilmour had, but also in terms of what it represented symbolically about the band, namely kicking off with new leadership and Gilmour feeling that sense of emancipation.

When I asked Thorgerson about the first version of the video—which aired for no more than a week, and is impossible to find; it was on YouTube for a while but then they took it down—he didn't think much of the difference. But I know there was a great deal of investment in both versions of the video. I did an interview with Lawrence Payne, the young Native American fellow who was in the video, and he said that it was just crazy, the amount of money spent and the extras that were picked up. It seems that a larger investment was made on the original version of the video. But the second version is the one that most people are familiar with.

POPOFF: Take us on a tour of a few highlight tracks besides "Learning to Fly."
AVIN: The last song, "Sorrow," is a favorite for me—and also for them because they played it live, as do bands like The Australian Pink Floyd Show and Brit Floyd, the sort of approved touring tribute bands. Phenomenal song, with the heavy guitar tone at the opening and then the massive solo at the end, as well as the bass line that kind of drives the song. Amazing.

An overhead view of the *Momentary Lapse* stage setup, taken on the first US leg of the tour in the fall of 1987.

Side two of the album is where they go back to the old kind of Pink Floyd weirdness with these two interludes, "A New Machine" in two parts, which bookend "Terminal Frost." And that song I particularly like as well. While it's driven by what sounds like a drum machine, it very much feels like a Pink Floyd song to me, and it has an awesome breakdown in the middle, with the female background vocals/choir thing going on. I always thought that was an underrated track.

LOPEZ-REYES: I'll agree on "Sorrow"; that's an incredible guitar piece. I think any guitar player, even guitar players who are more passionate about the Waters era, will recognize "Sorrow" as an incredible piece. The way it was recorded and the way it's executed . . . the only pity is that it uses a drum machine. Nick says that David wrote it entirely by himself on his houseboat over a weekend. The beginning was recorded in the L.A. Memorial Sports Arena, which has since been demolished. They captured something really powerful. As the last song on the album, thumping away with that heavy guitar, it's a strong statement that says this is a new era for Pink Floyd. There's something special about it being at the end of the album. I'm looking to the future but I'm also feeling nostalgic.

POPOFF: Any comment on "On the Turning Away"? Nice ballad that could've been a solo album song for David. There's something very *About Face* about it.

AVIN: Great ballad, but to me the best part of that song is the last two or three minutes where it's just Gilmour soloing, where he just goes off. It's a great live number, for sure, and I believe they used to close the first set of their shows with that, which always felt kind of right. They may have played one more song. When I inspect this record song by song, there are some good songs on it, but as a whole it's missing that heavy weight of concept, as well as the darkness of the classic-period material.

LOPEZ-REYES: "On the Turning Away" is one of those songs that had commercial appeal; it's one of the few songs that people that are not fully into Pink Floyd would recognize as, oh yeah, that's Pink Floyd and still really love that song. They point to that song when they think about this album as much as they do "Learning to Fly." It's also a song that gave Gilmour a chance to express his political voice, which is more compassionate, less partisan and less vitriolic, in a sense, than Waters's. That's no criticism of Waters's expression, but without him, the politics are more compassionate and subtle.

Another one I enjoy is "Yet Another Movie"—incredible track, underrated, a track where Pink Floyd makes very good use of space. Jim Keltner is the drummer, studio musician, and his use of space is brilliant, minimalist, fascinating. That song conveys a darkness in terms of Gilmour's thinking, both lyrically and musically. I'd call that the peak of Gilmour's achievement in terms of song construction. It's indicative of what Pink Floyd could have done moving forward, had it not tried to go in a safer direction, in my opinion, with *The Division Bell*.

POPOFF: Anthony Moore gets a credit on "On the Turning Away." What is his story?

LOPEZ-REYES: They were having a really hard time without Roger in the sense of songwriting. And they brought in all these new people to help them write songs. It seems to me that eventually Anthony Moore is where they land, or at least Gilmour lands, as the one outside contributor that he feels most comfortable with. They're the same age, similar background—he was with Slapp Happy and Henry Cow—similar upbringing, and maybe it's just being in the right place at the right time. The songs that he contributed are songs that became paramount to that album. There was just good synergy with him in particular.

POPOFF: We should probably talk about "The Dogs of War," because that's pretty aggressive and hard to ignore. Describe that one musically and lyrically.

LOPEZ-REYES: What's interesting about "The Dogs of War," on the subject of digital and analog, this is a place where you see a lot of the digital coming through, especially the sound effects of the dogs. It's also interesting that this is the piece that introduces Scott Page into the Pink Floyd camp. Another story with the analog versus digital is that despite all the digital technology, they were still dealing with analog recording equipment and needed to be economical with it.

One thing Scott Page has shared with me is his sense of uneasiness with what they were recording over when adding his saxophone part. Apparently, Tom Scott and David Sanborn, as well as John Helliwell of Supertramp, had all recorded potential saxophone parts for that song. Pink

Meet the press: the three Floyds attend a photo call in Versailles, France, June 9, 1988.

Floyd was looking for a different vibe, though, and recruited Page, who worked on the track with the realization they were recording over the parts these guys had laid down before him. Page, as someone who admires all these saxophone players and feels they are geniuses, thought it was crazy that stuff was being erased!

But, yes, "The Dogs of War" is quite reminiscent of the older records, and I think a lot of older fans recognized that. If anything, that's the one song here that manifests some of the Waters spirit in this new era of Pink Floyd. It has that sense of aggression and tone.

AVIN: I agree, "The Dogs of War," another great song. Funny, it has that sax solo, which was a weird thing that Pink Floyd, as a heavy, moody progressive rock band, was always able to get away with and do well. But I agree, that song plays into the classic sound; it lives in that world of "Money" and "Have a Cigar" and some of those bluesy tracks they did.

But I'd have to say, this is one of those songs where it becomes clear that on this record the drums are horribly overproduced. I don't want to make it sound like I don't like the album—I like it a lot—but it requires a frame of reference, as a fan. It's a major band with such iconic work; like your grandmother knows *The Dark Side of the Moon*. That lays a heavy burden on whatever a new album might've been at that time. There's that massive reverb, wall of sound thing going on that was prevalent then. Genesis was doing that with those pop records, and Yes got into that with *Big Generator*. Every band suffered from that a little bit at the time.

POPOFF: Ed, what else did Jon Carin tell you about working with Floyd?
LOPEZ-REYES: I guess the most interesting thing was he gave me a very full description of this

"Peace Be with You" track that hasn't been released. He said that it had monks chanting in it or a choir, something to that effect. I've read it had to do with David Gilmour's feelings toward Roger Waters. But apparently it was a very delicate and beautiful piece and something that probably would've integrated well into the album. He gave me the sense that it was crossing the line from demo stage to something that could've been finished in the studio.

POPOFF: Did he say anything about what the houseboat studio, Astoria, was like?
LOPEZ-REYES: No, but I've read a lot about Astoria; I'm fascinated by the studio. I know that the dining room was basically the actual studio where the band played, and the living room, I believe, was turned into the control room. So, it's a tight space. It's a historical vessel; it's registered with National Historic Ships UK. A fascinating studio, but it's not used much anymore.

POPOFF: What do you think the current knowledgeable fan assessment of this record is? How has *A Momentary Lapse of Reason* aged?
LOPEZ-REYES: My sense is people who really get into Pink Floyd for the Waters era, many of them have had a visceral negative reaction to *A Momentary Lapse of Reason*. They still don't consider it a Pink Floyd album. My sense is that this is a lot more political and a bit more falling in line with pop culture around the history of the albums than an objective assessment.

Program from the 1988 tour, and a ticket from Berlin's Reichstagsgelande (the latter signed by Richard Wright).

I personally got introduced to the band through *A Momentary Lapse of Reason*, and having come in through that vessel, it's an important hinge, a pivot point where you listen to it and go, "Where did this band come from?" And you can't help but be fascinated with the back catalog as much as *Momentary Lapse*. But it also projects and gives you a sense of where the band could go. People who love guitar playing and people who truly appreciate David Gilmour's voice in the band will love the album.

But it really is David's album, much more so than *The Division Bell* would be, where Rick and Nick are back. Those guys both felt undermined by their experiences with Roger Waters. And based on those, they'd become timid about their playing. Rick Wright had more of a limited role just based on the legal issue that he was facing with the band in terms of reintegrating, but Nick Mason did feel that sense of discomfort, and he may have also been somewhat intimidated by the use of drum machines. At this point people didn't necessarily diminish drum machines the way we do now, and I feel that he might have felt threatened by them. There was a lot of insecurity there in the beginning.

Pink Floyd onstage at Feijenoord Stadion in Rotterdam, June 13, 1988, in a reconfigured lineup that included Tim Pratt (fourth left) and Guy Pratt (second right).

That said, Scott Page told me that when people like Jeff Porcaro sat in on soundchecks every now and then, they couldn't get that Pink Floyd sound. So, Nick Mason was always critical in that sense. I do know that *A Momentary Lapse of Reason*—and I asked Nick Mason this recently—I know that they'd re-recorded the album with him on drums all the way through. And I hope that sees the light of day. He answered this question from me during an AOL broadcast, so it's on record.

POPOFF: When would they have done that?

LOPEZ-REYES: I'm not sure, but it was certainly before *The Endless River*. This goes back at least ten, fifteen years. I didn't ask him when, but I know that they did re-record the parts to give it that fuller Pink Floyd sound. That's something that could come out with a reissue of the album, perhaps along with "Peace Be with You."

AVIN: Looking back on *A Momentary Lapse of Reason* now, some people might argue that the band was missing its key writer, the person who sets the tone for

each album, the person who was the soul of each album—Roger Waters. And if you were a fan who grew up in the early '70s, *A Momentary Lapse of Reason* might be hard to get into. It didn't have a conceptual basis, and as Gilmour admitted, the record was hard to write. He missed Waters for that conceptual angle.

David Gilmour's solo records were sort of the opposite of Pink Floyd. They were very straightforward, had this rock, bluesy thing going on, and largely focused on his guitar work. And they were never overly popular; they didn't sell that well. So, while *A Momentary Lapse of Reason* does sound more like Pink Floyd than his solo albums, it's missing the Roger Waters aspect. Again, if you were not brought up on *Wish You Were Here*, *Animals*, and *The Dark Side of the Moon*, there's a lot to like on it. But if you came up in the '70s, it may be a little harder to get into. Even for me, being in the young bracket, going back into the album now, I'm not sure it holds up as well.

And Roger himself, when he heard the record, there's a quote where he called it "facile" and "a quite clever forgery." He said the songs were poor in general and Gilmour's lyrics were third-rate. Upon reflection, Richard Wright apparently agreed, saying that Roger's criticisms were fair and that it's not a band album at all.

LEFT: Program from the 1989 run of shows, with which the *Momentary Lapse* tour extended into a third year.

BELOW: Artwork for the live LP *Delicate Sound of Thunder*, along with the label from an Italian pressing of same.

CHAPTER 14

THE DIVISION BELL

WITH ROIE AVIN, ED LOPEZ-REYES,
AND JEFF WAGNER

1. Cluster One   5:56
   (Music: Wright, Gilmour)
2. What Do You Want from Me   4:21
   (Music: Gilmour, Wright; lyrics:
   Gilmour, Samson)
3. Poles Apart   7:03
   (Music: Gilmour; lyrics: Gilmour,
   Samson, Laird-Clowes)
4. Marooned   5:29
   (Music: Wright, Gilmour)
5. A Great Day for Freedom   4:17
   (Music: Gilmour; lyrics: Gilmour, Samson)
6. Wearing the Inside Out   6:49
   (Music: Wright; lyrics: Moore)
7. Take It Back   6:12
   (Music: Gilmour, Ezrin; lyrics:
   Gilmour, Samson, Laird-Clowes)
8. Coming Back to Life   6:19
   (Music: Gilmour; lyrics: Gilmour)
9. Keep Talking   6:10
   (Music: Gilmour, Wright; lyrics:
   Gilmour, Samson)
10. Lost for Words   5:13
   (Music: Gilmour; lyrics: Gilmour, Samson)
11. High Hopes   8:34
   (Music: Gilmour; lyrics: Gilmour,
   Samson)

Recorded at Astoria Studios, Hampton,
London; Britannia Row, Islington, London;
Abbey Road, London; Metropolis Studios,
Chiswick, London; Creek Recording Studios,
London

PERSONNEL: David Gilmour—guitar,
vocals, bass, keyboarding, programming;
Richard Wright—keyboards, vocals; Nick
Mason—drums, percussion

GUEST PERFORMANCES: Jon
Carin—programming, additional keyboards;
Guy Pratt—bass; Gary Wallis—played and
programmed percussion; Tim Renwick—
guitars; Dick Parry—tenor saxophone; Bob
Ezrin—keyboards, percussion; Sam Brown—
backing vocals; Durga McBroom—backing
vocals, Carol Kenyon—backing vocals; Jackie
Sheridan—backing vocals; Rebecca Leigh-
White—backing vocals; orchestra—various
instrumentation

Produced by Bob Ezrin and David Gilmour

Released March 28, 1994

I f the band that crafted *The Dark Side of the Moon* were
a blue-collar band that could still see mass fame only
in others, so too is there a sense that the builders of *A
Momentary Lapse of Reason* were at ground level. Six-and-
a-half years on, David Gilmour had rejuvenated the band
with himself as a bigger part of its tenor, but also with the
idea that a collective approach required no apologies.

Indeed, David's reengineering of the band was—fingers
crossed—accepted by the fanbase, or some overlap of
the old fanbase with swaths of new fans. The studio
album sold, tickets sold, the band's first live album,
Delicate Sound of Thunder, sold. The smooth sounds of
the '80s were over, grunge was the rage, and along with

it, an analog aesthetic. Serendipitously, mid-'90s radio, fans, and journos found themselves grappling with the concept of classic rock, and here was one of the big half-dozen, still touring and still relevant, about to deliver a studio album that would sell multiplatinum, and then keep touring, at the top quartile of that half-dozen.

So, an emboldened Pink Floyd committee featuring on the marquee more Nick and more Rick—with Bob Ezrin, David's wife, Polly, Jon Carin, Guy Pratt, Dick Parry, Michal Kamen, and a bevy of background vocalists, along with engineer Andrew Jackson—assembled a steady album as rooted as the metal sculptures on the cover.

Admirably lacking bells and whistles, *The Division Bell* is rendered somewhat even and oppressive, level-headed, earnest. It's made by committee but it very much reflects the voice, guitar, and personality of David Gilmour, making it consistent and of a pair with *A Momentary Lapse*. But the record also reflects a confidence that the band is valid, and that its leader knows who is a valid part of the team. After all, three of the four are here anyway, and none of them are pikers. The team knows, as well, that even if Floyd are renowned for gloss, a plush and no-expense-spared '70s sheen will do just fine.

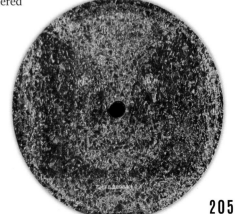

205

Closeups of Wright and Mason at the Rose Bowl in Pasadena, California, April 1994.

Despite some complaints from the tastemakers on the advisory board who debated the insularity and sterility inevitably resulting from being so impossibly upper-crust, *The Division Bell* was a record with a goodly clutch of songs even skeptics regarded as quite good. "What Do You Want from Me" explored themes of alienation with suitably dark, heavy, bluesy music that linked to louder Floyd of the '70s. "Keep Talking" added to this theme with a panoramic and similarly heavy arrangement—languid, scooped out, but again, unapologetic of its stadium rock authority. Finally, "High Hopes," musically poignant if a bit rote, found David presciently putting his papers in order while staring at a loaded gun. Summed up by this bitter close, *The Division Bell* resonated as deep, heavy, and lasting, but also as a little cold, respectable, and hard to love.

POPOFF: What are the main adjustments with *The Division Bell* coming off *Momentary Lapse*? What is the personality or vibe of this second record for David without Roger?

LOPEZ-REYES: In my opinion, the main difference is that the band regroups for a more coherent Pink Floyd effort—Jon Carin and Guy Pratt truly integrate into Pink Floyd. And, perhaps ironically, the sound is more loyal to the more popular Pink Floyd sound. These are brands, and legally I'm sure these new guys could never have become Pink Floyd members. And fans would've said Guy Pratt could never be an official Pink Floyd member. I understand that completely. But from a technical standpoint, this record marked their full integration into the band and, fortunately, as we would get no more except for *The Endless River*, that carried over into the David Gilmour solo era.

AVIN: When I first heard "Keep Talking" on the radio, and they said it was from a new Pink Floyd album that was coming out, I was really, really happy. I was impressed with that song because it immediately sounded like classic Floyd. It

wasn't attempting to be an obvious hit single with a catchy chorus. That's sort of how the rest of that album played out. It's a better version of what they were trying to do with *Momentary Lapse of Reason*, and it holds up better, years later, as an album, even though it might not have had the big hits. It's not as overproduced and it's a little warmer and it's a bit more diverse.

I just really like it, but I'm going to say that it's divided among some of the fans I know. *Momentary Lapse* had the hits, "Learning to Fly" and "Dogs of War," but the older classic-era fans definitely like *The Division Bell* more. Reviews showed that; they expressed that it sounded more like a cohesive band. It's known that they wrote it more together. It wasn't a Gilmour solo effort. It was, in fact, the three—Wright, Mason, and Gilmour—writing it together, which added to the effect of it being an authentic Pink Floyd album.

POPOFF: How is David doing without Roger? Is it working?
WAGNER: When it came time for Gilmour to really step up and be a leader in the band with *A Momentary Lapse*, that's probably my least favorite Floyd album—but I love *The Division Bell*. I think David was strengthened by the guys around him at the time of early Floyd, but you hear a real lack of Waters on

TOP: Gilmour and Mason at Joe Robbie Stadium in Miami, Florida, on the opening night of the *Division Bell* tour, March 30, 1994.

INSET: From left: guitarist Tim Renwick and backing singers Durga McBroom, Sam Brown, and Claudia Fontaine onstage at Joe Robbie Stadium.

Momentary Lapse. It's obvious that he's not there. No disrespect to Gilmour—massively important in this Pink Floyd puzzle—but not enough can be said about Roger Waters's leadership.

Momentary Lapse is just them going, okay, what now, right? The main creative driver has left. But I think there was some feeling of freedom there, because *Final Cut* was essentially a Roger Waters solo album, with the other guys coming in and out of it. On paper, it should've been this greatly freeing and wonderful new direction. And in some cases, it is. But to me, it's a little bit like those mid-'80s Rush albums, where it sounds so of its time. I hesitate to use the word "dated," because of course it's going to sound dated. Things from '69 should sound like '69 and things from '87 should sound like '87—that's not a bad thing. But it's a little uncomfortable-sounding in that they're kind of trapped in '87, with some of the sounds and the production.

But with *The Division Bell*, seven years later, the band seem very comfortable as Gilmour, Wright, and Mason. *The Division Bell* kind of admits, hey, we're all older now. We're not the band we used to be, but we're still Pink Floyd and these are the things we want to address lyrically and this is the music we want to make. And it just has a unified feeling to it. It's a more confident step away from the Waters era than *Momentary Lapse* was. Maybe *Momentary Lapse* was always going to be doomed to fail. Doomed to fail—it sold how many bazillion copies? It did really well, and that's wonderful for Gilmour and the rest, but I think, creatively, the second one is the better album. The one thing I don't like about *The Division Bell*, it tends to kind of all bleed together. It's lacking momentum; there's that mid-paced tempo, and it's pretty oppressive. Still, there's a mantra or hypnosis there that I kind of enjoy.

POPOFF: What is that odd title, *The Division Bell*, supposed to denote?
LOPEZ-REYES: It's the call they make in parliament, when they have to count the votes for each side, if I remember correctly. But it's also symbolic of that division between people when there's lack of communication.

POPOFF: And the album cover?
AVIN: Storm Thorgerson has these big metal statues of faces looking at each other. They look like they're talking, and when you look at them, they make sort of a third face. Those things were put in the Rock and Roll Hall of Fame. It's become one of those iconic Pink Floyd covers that everybody knows.
LOPEZ-REYES: To me, it's a depiction of common ground. Ultimately, there's a human commonality we all share, which is where we're supposed to connect as human beings. There's something more profound and something more divine, in a sense, about that space that we don't necessarily connect in when we're so

focused on our own views and the things that are important to us as individuals and not thinking about the overall picture of people and what's important.

I've also heard that it represents the band's relationship with Syd Barrett. There's always that ghost of Syd Barrett somewhere in a lot of Pink Floyd's work. The cover was made in several formats. There were some heads made of cement, some were made of metal, and there's a version of the cover that, instead of having the lights between the two figureheads, it has some red flags. And they're beautiful covers. I've bought Storm prints before, and if I had a chance to buy *The Division Bell*, the version I would get would be the one with the flags. I don't know the symbolism between the flags and lights, but it reminds me of *Animals*, in the sense that it looks like animation but it's actually a true picture.

AVIN: Syd Barrett hangs over the band in all the albums. *Wish You Were Here* and *Dark Side* both have songs about him, and he influenced a lot of where Roger Waters came from lyrically.

POPOFF: Let's dig in. What are a couple of your favorite tracks and why?

LOPEZ-REYES: "Poles Apart" has a haunting sound. The guitar work is reminiscent of classic David Gilmour during the Waters era. And "Marooned" is incredible—you can see I'm a huge David Gilmour fan [*laughs*]. Those are the two tracks that stand out to me most. And "Keep Talking" is also great. The guitar's very aggressive and fresh. Lyrically, they start getting more into concept. It's not a concept album, but there you get some abstraction. And the tempo, although still languid, it's got a heavy groove, which made it a great live selection.

AVIN: "Keep Talking" has the Stephen Hawking sample from an old British Telecommunications commercial. And it has that delay guitar effect that is famous from "Run Like Hell," which became a signature Gilmour effect, which adds a nice touch. With a delay, you play one note, and you can set it to how quickly you want that note echoed. You play it once and repeat that note again every 0.2 seconds, and it'll just play that note on repeat. If you ride two or three guitar strings repeatedly against each other with that effect, it creates this wall of a hundred guitar strings playing. I'm sure he has the most massive rig with all sorts of things on it, but any guitarist can simulate that effect with a delay pedal and a guitar.

Another highlight for me is "Wearing the Inside Out," written by Anthony Moore and Rick Wright, who also sings it with Dave. That was a nice touch, a reminder that he did sing, for example "Time," back on *The Dark Side of the Moon*. It's nostalgic, having him be more involved in the writing. With that album, I like all the songs that were mellower and slower. I thought those had more of that Pink Floyd–esque nature about them. "Poles Apart" is one, with the acoustic guitar and a nice chorus. "A Great Day for Freedom" is another one, an amazing song about the Berlin Wall coming down.

LOPEZ-REYES: "A Great Day for Freedom" is one of those tracks I didn't find as accessible. Whether it's the tempo—something about it didn't draw me in as much. But like "On the Turning Away," it was an opportunity for Gilmour to express political views in his own tone, in his own voice, which was missing during the Waters era. He's coming through at a more personal level, imparting his political views clearly and simply. In that sense it has some commonality with the political statements you see throughout *A Momentary Lapse of Reason*.

POPOFF: A personal favorite is "What Do You Want from Me," with those impassioned backing vocals and the adversarial tension in the lyric, harkening back to *The Wall*. What do you make of that one?
LOPEZ-REYES: A lot of guitar players agree that's a really strong Gilmour track, a powerful guitar piece. That's the one that got the most critical recognition, and it was even nominated for a Grammy. That song spoke to people who weren't necessarily as invested in the band as a lot of us are. It was a track that casual fans could relate to. And yet it's not a pop song. It's aggressive and Gilmour is strong and almost raspy of voice. In some ways it revisits the common ground he had with Waters as far as the demands they faced from the audience. It's interesting that Gilmour played that song during the 2016 tour. I didn't think that would be the one to resurface, but there it was, the second night at the Hollywood Bowl in Los Angeles. I was blown away.

POPOFF: And this is one of fully five tracks to which Polly Samson contributes lyrics. David and Polly would marry during the tour for this album. What does she contribute?
LOPEZ-REYES: Obviously, she has a very personal relationship as soon-to-be wife of Gilmour. And that connection gave him that sense of comfort to be able to write with her. And as the person who was leading Floyd, he thought that was a good fit at the time. The songwriting on the album is phenomenal, so I have

Dave Gilmour and future wife Polly Samson attend a National Youth Theatre event at Grosvenor House, London, 1992. Polly contributed lyrics to five of the tracks on *The Division Bell*.

no criticism. People can criticize her for meddling with such a huge historical entity in rock music—the whole Yoko Ono story—but I think Gilmour knew how to give her the opportunity to participate in their work and it was a good synergy. She's a great writer in her own right, an actual writer of novels and short stories, and so that the space was well-deserved in that sense. It was a good call on his part to integrate her into what he was doing with *The Division Bell*, and that's underscored by her contributing even more in his solo career.

AVIN: That turned out to be tremendous. There was some concern about her being involved, from what I've read. But she did write the lyrics to "High Hopes," which is one of the great songs the band ever made, really.

POPOFF: Yes, "High Hopes" is another high point on the record. What's the power of that song?

AVIN: It works on two levels. It closes the album effectively, and it also closes, it turns out, the Pink Floyd chapter, right? The lyrics, the music, the grandiose production . . . it signified a closing up of shop for the band. Everything about the song works; it's the best song they did between the two albums. Lyrically, it's looking back on David's childhood and recreating the imagery of the old world, and then reflecting on what it was like to be in the band and how things maybe fell apart and became what they are now, but it's kept abstract and metaphorical.

LOPEZ-REYES: "High Hopes" is a song that a lot of people, my wife included, love on that album. I personally am not as keen on it, perhaps because I feel there's some monotony to it. But I can see why people are passionate about it. I think people like the songwriting and the imagery that went with it. We've graduated fully into the importance of visuals. Pink Floyd always had great visuals, but when you see the song live, the video footage that goes with it, people found that very appealing and striking. I really do think the appeal in part is tied to all those visuals. But I don't find it as accessible, and in part, that's because of the tempo, and there are a couple like that for me on some classic Pink Floyd albums. But, hey, it seems like it's universally approved and liked as a track.

WAGNER: Oh my God, "High Hopes" is one of the greatest Floyd songs ever, period. So profound. I'm not somebody who leans as heavily on lyrics as some other people, but "High Hopes" for me lyrically is just, wow, that's just the human condition and that's growing old right there and it's so beautiful. "High Hopes" is wonderful. It's interesting that the song turned out to be a false ending, and that "Louder than Words" on *The Endless River* ended up serving the function that this song seemed to be destined for; but in my mind, this is far and away the superior track.

POPOFF: And into the deep tracks, where is there some magic on this record?

AVIN: Well "Coming Back to Life" is a favorite, and a little bit different. Midway through it has this weird cowbell drumbeat thing that seems out of place but it works. Plus, that's got one of the best guitar solos on the album, in terms of melody.

LOPEZ-REYES: That song has great longevity because it's essentially a pop song. It's one of those songs that has universal appeal. I don't mean to sound sexist, but I find that a lot of women really appreciate that song. That's not a bad thing; those are the kind of tracks that made the band more accessible to women

Picture-disc editions of the two UK singles drawn from *The Division Bell:* "Take It Back" and "High Hopes."

and that's one thing that was accomplished with *The Division Bell*. Maybe reaccomplished, because *Dark Side* had that broad appeal. It appealed to sensitivities that the band hadn't appealed to for a long time. It lived on in Gilmour's solo career as well.

"Wearing the Inside Out" is probably the one gigantic track that people tend to overlook. One of the best performances of that song was in that David Gilmour acoustic show from 2001, when Rick Wright guested. When you hear that performance of it, you can't help but go back to *The Division Bell* and go, how did I skip this track when I was playing the album? Or how did I not find it memorable? And it echoes so much of Rick Wright's solo work, *Broken China* and *Wet Dream*, that it really gives you a sense of the impact Wright had on the band overall, and then particularly on that album. And it's sad because we know he was working on a solo album when he passed away. I don't know if that material ever had vocals or anything on it. But "Wearing the Inside Out" is a great gateway into his solo work, and to the genius that was Rick Wright in his own right.

I feel that the band was very cognizant that they had to overcome the apprehension the fans had expressed about *A Momentary Lapse of Reason* being a true Pink Floyd album. From that sense, not only was Rick Wright being more assertive now, but Mason and Gilmour and the production team were probably giving him more space, because they understood that Rick Wright played a critical role in shaping the sound of Pink Floyd. As they got older, both Mason and Gilmour recognized that Rick was such a paramount element in that Pink Floyd sound. The combination of Wright being assertive and the band needing more of a "Pink Floyd–sounding" album contributed to his presence on the album being more pronounced.

POPOFF: And what of Nick? What is his importance in the tale?
AVIN: I don't think his name is ever mentioned on the top drummers lists or anything, but he's a solid drummer. Pink Floyd wasn't about individual instrumentation—showing off what each of the guys could do on his instrument. They were about the songs, the lyrics, the overall mood and vibe, and sort of building a wall of sound with each guy contributing. Nick Mason filled that gap fine. But is he ever mentioned in the top drummer lists? I don't think anyone would ever make that case.

POPOFF: The album is pushed into the marketplace in spring 1994. What
kind of rock world greets these guys in the mid-'90s, and how well do they
perform in that marketplace?

AVIN: For one, it's the mature phase of the grunge era. Hair metal is gone, Pearl
Jam's big at this point and Nirvana's big at this point, even though a week after
the album comes out, Kurt Cobain kills himself. Pink Floyd comes out and still
sells millions of albums—because they're immune to trends. They just do what
they do and people like it. It sold less than *A Momentary Lapse of Reason*, but
again, it didn't have the massive MTV hit, because MTV at that time was all about
rap and grunge. But they were immune to the power of MTV, I suppose. As for
their classic rock competitors, Genesis had a huge album in late '91 with *We Can't
Dance*. Van Halen put out *Balance* in 1995. Eagles put out *Hell Freezes Over* in late
'94. There were still classic rock bands that could sell albums.

   If you were a progressive rock band, you didn't really rely on singles. How
many hit singles did Yes have? You could go back and count on one hand the

hit singles that band had over that long career. So, that genre is blessed with really loyal fans who are just happy that the bands are still around.

POPOFF: And when the band went out on tour, was the new record well represented? Did it seem like they were proud of it?
AVIN: They played a good half of it. Then, I believe, they added the entire *Dark Side of the Moon* on the *Division Bell* tour, which they played during the second half, along with some of the hits. And they released the live album *Pulse* right after that, May '95, which was from that tour. And *Pulse* had "What Do You Want from Me," "Coming Back to Life," "High Hopes," "Keep Talking," and "A Great Day for Freedom." So, *The Division Bell* was well represented. From *A Momentary Lapse of Reason*, they only had "Learning to Fly" and "Sorrow." The second disc is classic Rock and Roll Hall of Fame [*laughs*]. It's the entire *Dark Side of the Moon*, and then "Wish You Were Here," "Comfortably Numb," and "Run Like Hell."

POPOFF: Looking back, as these records are written into history, considered, and reconsidered, how is *The Division Bell* framed and how should it be framed?
AVIN: I've made this analogy with Genesis as well. Some of these iconic '60s and '70s bands are unlike anything we'll ever see again. Because they were made of members who all added amazing contributions to the music, that when you removed one member, you later could see what was missing. Genesis is a perfect example. If you listen to Steve Hackett's solo albums, you can see what his contributions were when he was in the band. When you hear Phil Collins's solo albums, you can hear what's missing on his solo albums, where there's a lack of Genesis. That goes for each member. When Steve Hackett left, the acoustic guitar dropped out. They lost the acoustic guitar—like, they never did it again!

The *Division Bell* tour ended with a two-week run of shows at Earls Court, London.

Pink Floyd is the same thing. When the four of them were at their peak, everything was working, because each guy filled that certain gap that you can hear is back when any of them are gone. Roger Waters was the conceptual, lyrical guy, and when he was gone, that part left. That's the same with the music. If you go listen to Roger Waters's albums, it's missing melody, it's missing guitar solos, it's missing the things that Gilmour and those guys brought in.

LOPEZ-REYES: Between the two albums, even now, years later, I find that people tend to like *The Division Bell* more. They find it more relatable, they find it more loyal to the traditional sound, the Waters-era Pink Floyd sound. The production is more confident, the technology is better, there's more depth and completion to the sound, the instrumentation is more natural, more analog, no drum machines as far as I know, or at least fewer of them. The majority of fans I speak to find it more palatable. But the fans who really get into the nitty gritty of details and song construction, and especially those who love David Gilmour's guitar playing and his thinking, tend to very quietly say that *A Momentary Lapse of Reason* is the better album. There are fewer of those, but I do encounter them.

WAGNER: What is important with *The Division Bell* is that it's pretty obvious from the very beginning that others are involved, rather than just the core three. You could of course see that on stage where they had this greatly filled-out lineup. But I think they weren't afraid to become more of a collective at that point. They're embracing it. Whatever worked, right? Whatever brought *The Division Bell* to life. Mason was kind of like checking out at that point. So, you're left with Gilmour leading the charge, and Wright in there, but maybe not always 100 percent there. If you listen to *The Division Bell*, it's a bit like some of the later Gilmour solo records. But, hey, they did it as Pink Floyd, and it has every right to be Pink Floyd as much as *The Final Cut* has a right to be Pink Floyd. I'm sure some would say that none of those are Pink Floyd albums, but it is what it is [*laughs*].

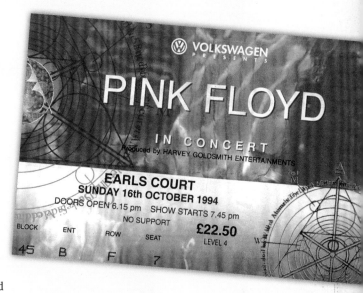

ABOVE AND OPPOSITE: Ticket and program from one of Pink Floyd's fourteen Earls Court performances.

CHAPTER 15

THE ENDLESS RIVER

WITH ROIE AVIN, ROBERT CORICH, AND ED LOPEZ-REYES

1.	Things Left Unsaid (Gilmour, Wright)	4:26
2.	It's What We Do (Gilmour, Wright)	6:17
3.	Ebb and Flow (Gilmour, Wright)	1:55
4.	Sum (Gilmour, Mason, Wright)	4:48
5.	Skins (Gilmour, Mason, Wright)	2:37
6.	Unsung (Wright)	1:07
7.	Anisina (Gilmour)	3:16
8.	The Lost Art of Conversation (Wright)	1:42
9.	On Noodle Street (Gilmour, Wright)	1:42
10.	Night Light (Gilmour, Wright)	1:42
11.	Allons-y (1) (Gilmour)	1:57
12.	Autumn '68 (Wright)	1:35
13.	Allons-y (2) (Gilmour)	1:32
14.	Talkin' Hawkin' (Gilmour, Wright)	3:29
15.	Calling (Moore, Gilmour)	3:37
16.	Eyes to Pearls (Gilmour)	1:51
17.	Surfacing (Gilmour)	2:46
18.	Louder than Words (Gilmour, Samson)	6:36

Recorded at Royal Albert Hall, London; Olympia Studios, London; Britannia Row Studios, London; Astoria, London; Medina Studios, Hove, UK

PERSONNEL: David Gilmour—acoustic and electric guitars, bass guitar, piano, keyboards, synthesizer, EBow, effects, vocals, backing vocals; Richard Wright—organ, synthesizer, keyboards, pipe organ, strings; Nick Mason—drums, Rototoms, percussion, gong

GUEST PERFORMANCES: Bob Ezrin—keyboards, bass guitar; Damon Iddins—keyboards; Andy Jackson—bass guitar, effects; Gilad Atzmon—tenor saxophone, clarinet; Guy Pratt—bass guitar; Jon Carin—synthesizer, loops; Anthony Moore—keyboards; Durga McBroom—backing vocals; Louise Marshal—backing vocals; Sarah Brown—backing vocals; Chantal Leverton—viola; Helen Nash—cello; Honor Watson—violin; Victoria Lyon—violin; Stephen Hawking—voice sample

Produced by David Gilmour, Phil Manzanera, Youth, Andy Jackson, Bob Ezrin

Released November 7, 2014

I ntended as a tribute to Rick Wright, deceased from cancer on September 15, 2008, at the age of sixty-five, *The Endless River*, through its near completely instrumental span, also serves as a final act of defiance toward those who would stress Roger and his wordsmithing as more important than the plush soundscapes David was wont to prefer, vocals or none.

The raw material of the project derived from extra material recorded during the *Division Bell* sessions, as Rick explained it, on "four DATs of five or six hours of music." These first served as the building blocks for a piece that engineer Andy Jackson had edited down to about an hour, amusingly and provisionally titled "The Big Spliff."

218

But credit to David and Nick—and Phil Manzanera, Guy Pratt, Youth, John
Carin, engineer Damon Iddins, and, delightfully, Gilad Atzmon, with his clarinet
and tenor sax—the final flow of *The Endless River* finds a complete retooling
beyond "The Big Spliff" into a developing display of short instrumental tracks,
culminating in beyond-elegant and distinguished closer "Louder than Words."

The album retains faithfully the focus on Rick, whose posthumous presence
renders the atmospheres airy, bright, and New Age-y. Around him, quite often the
full band joins in, represented in likeminded gleam of fidelity on what has got to
be the most tactile and viscerally clear and clean production job in a catalog that
lives to impress on fine stereos.

Floyd's famously slow pacing is also retained, and the album has a curious
relationship with melody. Although chord changes are typically erudite and
emotionally sophisticated, one's brain is hard-pressed to ascribe structure to the
relaxed but relentless journey toward . . . what?

One has to say, toward an album that annoyed almost everybody, the obvious
reason being the curious refusal to have David say something overtop. Inclined

to be a man of few words anyway, the effect is faithful to the overriding brief: namely to let the now passed Rick Wright live and continue to speak through his ebbing and flowing washes of synth and all manner of stealth soloing, often in conversation with Gilmour's comfortably numb guitar. Indeed, David made no apologies for the approach, adding, in effect, that it's for the old-school Floyd-head framed by headphones, who finds the full-length trip inviting and just doesn't see eye to eye with the immediacy of a downloading generation flitting from artist to artist one track at a time.

Ultimately, this is all lipstick on a floating pig, for any and all rationalizing fell mostly on deaf ears, the vast majority of Floyd followers (the author vehemently included) finding this a messy and qualified end, an adjunct to the catalog that has to be impatiently explained, rather than the fifteenth and final—and bravely rule-breaking—Pink Floyd album that it was intended to be.

POPOFF: Explain why suddenly we get this mostly instrumental Pink Floyd album showing up a decade after *The Division Bell*.

LOPEZ-REYES: When I was backstage at the Gilmour show at the Hollywood Bowl, I was talking to Scott Page and Jon Carin about the album and why they did it. The band had essentially picked up pieces from *The Division Bell* they had seriously considered releasing. There was enough done to rework the pieces. I think—just my theory—that they had maybe considered putting some of that material on David Gilmour's solo album that eventually came out as *Rattle That Lock*. It was being done concurrently, as far as I know. I interviewed one of the backup singers, Sarah Brown, who also sings with Simple Minds, and she told me that when she went in, there was no hint about it being Pink Floyd or David Gilmour. They just worked on background vocals for what eventually became *The Endless River*. So, a lot of the material is left over from *The Division Bell*, but it was reworked enough that it deserves consideration on its own merit as a good album. I personally think there could've been no better way to close the Pink Floyd history than with that album. The fact that there are lead vocals on only one track gives *The Endless River* a sense that it's a ghost of an album. That's not a negative connotation—I think the record represents the ghost of Pink Floyd.

POPOFF: Interesting. But why do you think Polly, for example, or Anthony Moore, weren't asked to write more words for this material?

LOPEZ-REYES: At that point Gilmour's really focused on putting out a strong lyrical album with *Rattle That Lock*. Perhaps they felt the one track they ended up choosing to close *The Endless River* was a powerful track in its own right in terms of the lyrics and the vocal. It's the perfect closing, just the right space to work with Polly, as far as that album went. The focus was on Richard Wright and the pieces he left behind from *The Division Bell*, the legacy he could no longer help continue constructing.

OPPOSITE: Wright in his pomp at the Los Angeles Sports Arena, April 1975. A key cog in the band from the start, Wright passed away on September 15, 2008, aged sixty-five.

AVIN: There was a lot of material left over from *The Division Bell*. They wrote a good number of songs, something like sixty-five, and they had a number ranking system that they created from zero to ten that would determine which songs they proceeded to work on further and record. Richard Wright died in September of 2008, so this was conceived as a tribute, using the unfinished demos and then finishing them.

POPOFF: Concerning Richard, there's "Autumn '68," which is a title in reference to "Summer '68" from *Atom Heart Mother*.
LOPEZ-REYES: They used an organ piece recorded at the Royal Albert Hall of Richard Wright rehearsing or just fiddling around with a piece he had created, I guess, during one of those shows back in that era. It was an exquisite addition, in my view.
CORICH: The album is a very noble tribute to Rick Wright, who was the unsung hero of Pink Floyd. Allegedly there's still a lot more sitting around in the can to do another two or three of these. Now, being a producer, and working with engineering of music, I absolutely am stunned by some of the cleverness and the simplicity of Phil Manzanera, who had a big part in putting this together. What a job he did, using basically things that were left on the cutting-room floor.

Manzanera's adept at working with older technology in the sound field as well as newer technology. Did David pick the right person? I'd say so. Of course, Andy Jackson and David are a big part of the assembly as well, but the results to me definitely sound and feel like Floyd. It may not be as ambitious as *The Division Bell* or *Animals* or whatever else they've done, but it captures the essence of Floyd for me. Funny enough, a lot of this was done on David's houseboat; that just shows you what technology can do.

Nick Mason—the driving force behind *The Endless River*—in New York City, November 3, 2014.

But the album is almost defined by Rick's keyboards, which are all over it. This is what it's about. It's a huge testimony to someone who David was clearly very close to and who was missed. Without going overboard about it, they did a good thing. Maybe if the fans really understood that, some wouldn't be so critical.
AVIN: But I can understand the fan response. It's obvious that everyone would have preferred an album of songs. It's clearly not one of their best but it's nice to listen to once in a while [*laughs*]. And "Louder than Words," the one song with lyrics—great song. It's one of those that when a band puts out something like that and hadn't put out something in a long time, and when you know there's never going to be another because a member died or they broke up . . . it's like putting on an old pair of shoes.

POPOFF: How about a little critique of "Louder than Words" as a song?

LOPEZ-REYES: What's really compelling about "Louder than Words" . . . the production order of tracks is such an important thing, and it's being lost in the era of iTunes and downloading, the era of the one song or the three songs instead of full-scale albums. When you hear the album all the way through, there's something truly uplifting about that song. It gives such a strong sense of closure that it would almost be criminal to release another Pink Floyd album, even if they could. Polly and David delivered what they had to deliver to give the band closure on such a permanent basis.

The lyrics are beautiful, the music is incredible; it's uplifting and sad at the same time. You're basically saying farewell, but they also talk about the tension between people, especially the band members. It's a powerful statement, and at the very, very end you can barely hear Rick Wright saying something like, "Go

The one-off reunion of Pink Floyd and Roger Waters (plus sax player Dick Parry, second left) for Live 8, Hyde Park, London, July 2, 2005.

Gilmour, Waters, Mason, and Wright take their final bow together. Live 8, Hyde Park, London, July 2, 2005.

ahead and complain." There were forces that created tension, but what beautiful words and beautiful music came from that tension for those many years. "Louder than Words" really captured that.

POPOFF: How about two or three other highlights on the record?
LOPEZ-REYES: Besides "Louder than Words," there's a trio of tracks, "Allons-y (1)," "Autumn '68," and "Allons-y (2)," that are the peak of the album for me—those three tracks bleed together. David Gilmour's guitar playing sounds so lively and crisp and clear. There's something so Gilmour and so Pink Floyd about the way the guitar piece is written for both of those bookends, that it just ties something together really well. And the fact that they bookend the piece with Richard Wright, and that organ at the Royal Albert Hall, that, to me, is the essence of the album right there, the anchor piece. Even though it's an upbeat and up-tempo part of the album, it's still somehow haunting, which evokes for me the Pink Floyd of the past.

"Skins" is also interesting. Nick Mason was always underrated as a drummer. He may not be a technical drummer in terms of fills and things, but this is one track where he gets to shine and go a little crazy. The other one I like is "Talkin' Hawkin'" with the spoken excerpts from Stephen Hawking, which obviously evokes his sample on *The Division Bell*. That's such a powerful piece because "Keep Talking" is such a powerful part of *The Division Bell*. If you really pay attention, the album contains reminders of all these strong points about the band throughout its history.

CORICH: You've got the best of all your little songs, things like "Unsung," "On Noodle Street," "Night Light," "Allons-y" one and two; these are all interlinked pieces of music and for me it works. Now, I don't smoke dope now, but I can absolutely imagine that if you sat down with some recreational marijuana, *The Endless River* would sound absolutely stunning as a composed, complete album. When I first heard this I liked what I was hearing, but I kept thinking, when the hell is he going to sing? And, of course, he doesn't—until "Louder than Words." You listen to this album properly and you give it time, and when finally arrive at "Louder than Words," I think you understand what the concept of the record is about. You understand that through that one song, and through the title of the song itself and how the lyrics are about not needing to speak to communicate, that there was a purpose to what came before. It's a nice way for the band to go out, especially for a band that had already said that they never were going to tour again.

POPOFF: What is the significance of this cover art, and how does it speak to you?

LOPEZ-REYES: I interviewed the young Egyptian man who did the album cover, Ahmed Emad Eldin, and it turns out that the piece had already been made. When it was made, there was no relationship to Pink Floyd. Aubrey Powell, who of course was part of Hipgnosis with Storm Thorgerson, was involved and he found that an appealing image. If you look at the artist's work, this is by far his brightest piece of work; everything else is very dark. It was almost like it was meant for Pink Floyd somehow [*laughs*]. His work has a lot of Middle Eastern or North African influence.

The title is a quote from "High Hopes" on *The Division Bell*, which, as fate would have it, is a sort of sister song to "Louder than Words." One interpretation is that the music carries on. That no matter what contention exists, and who passes away and will eventually pass away—we're all human beings going down that path—the music will carry on. That's the symbolism I get from the title.

POPOFF: And I'd say that the multiple images from the video for "Louder than Words" reinforce that kind of reading.

LOPEZ-REYES: The video, I wasn't as keen on [*laughs*]. I'm not sure having the cover come to life, with the guy floating in the sky, works that well. But I found the imagery of the families and the boat on what was once the Aral Sea far more appealing. It was certainly reminiscent of what had been done for the "Marooned" video. There's something very captivating about that material. The old footage of the band playing together during *The Division Bell* era was also appealing; that was great, those little bits and pieces that few fans had seen. But I could have done without the floating guy. All told, I almost got the feeling the video was as much a tribute to Storm Thorgerson as the album was to Rick Wright.

POPOFF: There are no hard feelings with you? Having to deal with this as the band's last album?
CORICH: No, not at all, and like I said, I did get sort of halfway, or even a third of the way through, wondering, when are they gonna sing? You had the few words at the beginning, and then you've got Stephen Hawking doing his bit, and then after you hear that, and you hear the album progress and you lose yourself in all that Rick Wright and the also substantial amount of David Gilmour doing exactly what he does best. When you hear that, you realize he didn't need to sing. That's it—I thought he didn't need to sing. Is it *The Division Bell*? No. Is it *The Division Bell Part 2*? No, it's not! Is it the best thing Pink Floyd ever did? I'm not going to say it is. But being a person who has always enjoyed Pink Floyd's music, and having no problem with surrendering to the band's long instrumental passages, it's better to have something like this than nothing. People can rubbish the band all they like; it's up to them. They didn't have to listen to it or buy it.

POPOFF: But still, is there something frustrating and even aggravating, having the catalog end with *The Endless River*? Is it a messy end to the catalog?
AVIN: It doesn't have that effect on me. Because you know what the meaning behind the record

Rehearsal for the *Endless River* launch event at Porchester Hall, London, November 10, 2014, with lights by Peter Wynne Wilson.

is; how it came to be and what it was for. A messier end would be David Gilmour going with three other members that have never had anything to do with Pink Floyd and putting out a new album and calling themselves Pink Floyd.

POPOFF: Do you think this is the end? Do you see any way that they might carry on?

LOPEZ-REYES: I think this is it. From a fan's perspective, I don't think it would be right to do any more. Gilmour has carried on with this quite thriving solo career. He's showing a very different creative mind, both musically and lyrically speaking. He's even evolved a lot as far as his solo work goes, from the 1978 album and *About Face*. He's evolved past the Pink Floyd sound. I'm not saying that's better or worse, I'm just saying he's moved on. From a business standpoint, I don't think Gilmour, being legally in charge of this brand, is interested in doing any more with it.

Roger Waters certainly flies the Pink Floyd flag more fully in his live performances, but his solo work has certainly moved in a different direction, although *Is This the Life We Really Want?*, which is excellent, reminds me of *Animals* to some extent. They've both moved on. Nick Mason is not as keen on putting a lot of time into drumming anymore, certainly not for a new studio record, even if he said he would do a live reunion. But without Rick Wright, and being past the reunion at Live 8 in 2005, I'd say *The Endless River* is the proper way to bow out.

AVIN: I don't think there's any appetite for them to carry on. I'd be shocked. Roger Waters is having more success than he could've dreamed with *The Wall* tours and a follow-up to *Amused to Death*, twenty-five years later, with *Is This the Life We Really Want?*. Across the divide, David Gilmour's playing arenas all over the place, so for them to play Pink Floyd music, at this point they probably just don't need the hassle, right? They're like, why bother? We're all good, you know? [*laughs*]

OPPOSITE: Still raging against the machine: Roger Waters performs *The Wall* in Dusseldorf, Germany, September 6, 2013.

ABOVE: Gilmour's 2015 LP, *Rattle That Lock*, and Waters's first solo effort in twenty-five years, 2017's *Is This the Life We Really Want?*.

PHOTO CREDITS

A = All; B = Bottom; L = Left; M = Middle; R = Right; T = Top

Alamy Stock Photos: front endpaper, Ronald Grant Archive; p2, Roger Tillberg; p15, Interfoto; p33A, Pictorial Press Ltd.; pp34–35, Roger Tillberg; p44, Moviestore Collection Ltd.; pp50–51 and 52, Tony Byers; p68A, Philippe Gras; p90T, Pictorial Press Ltd.; p956, Everett Collection Inc.; p126B, Lebrecht Music and Arts Photo Library; p149, John Stillwell/PA Images; p158BL, Lewton Cole; pp176–177, Collection Christophel; p193, Peter Lane; p213, Interfoto; pp214–215, Lenscap; back endpaper, Collection Christophel; back cover, AF archive. **AP Images:** p14; p84, Lucy Young/Rex Features; p181, Bob Child; p207A, Marta Lavandier; p222, Drew Gurian/Invasion; p228, Henning Kaiser/picture-alliance/dpa. **Author Collection:** p6; p75; p78; p80M; p89M; p90M; p147; p162; p190M; p203B; p208A; p212. **Robert Alford:** p131A; p151A; p191; p198. **Crazy Diamond:** p9B; p10; p11, p17M; p23; p24TandM; p27; p29; p37MandB; p38T; p39A; p40; p47B; p63; p64B; p72A; p77B; p93B; p97B; p105; p107B; p109M; p117; p123B; p127; p132; p134B; p136B; p139; p142MandB; p156M; p157T; p163M; p175B; p189M; p203BM; p205B; p211B. **Getty Images:** pp4–5, Michael Ochs Archives; p9T, Andrew Whittuck/Redferns; p12, Adam Ritchie/Redferns; p13, Andrew Whittuck/Redferns; p17T, Andrew Whittuck/Redferns; p19T, Nick Hale/Hulton Archive; p19M, GAB Archive/Redferns; p20, Michael Putland/Hulton Archive; p25, Baron Wolman; p42, Jorgen Angel/Redferns; p45, Brian Shuel/Redferns; p47T, Ullstein Bild Dtl.; pp58–59, Shinko Music/Hulton Archive; pp66 and 67, Michael Putland/Hulton Archive; pp70–71, Jorgen Angel/Redferns; p73, Hans-Jurgen Dibbert–K&K/Redferns; p80T, Gijsbert Hanekroot/Redferns; pp82 and 83, INA; p85, Bob Thomas/Bob Thomas Sports Photography; p86, Shinko Music/Hulton Archive; p88, Jorgen Angel/Redferns; p93T, Shinko Music/Hulton Archive; p94, Mick Gold/Redferns; p98T, Fin Costello/Redferns; p98M, Science & Society Picture Library; pp99 and 100, Michael Putland/Hulton Archive; pp104–105, Gijsbert Hanekroot/Redferns; p108T, Michael Putland/Hulton Archive; p109B, Gijsbert Hanekroot/Redferns; p110T, Mirrorpix; p111, Michael Ochs Archives; p114, Nigel Osbourne/Redferns; p115, David Redfern/Redferns; p116, Ray Moreton/Hulton Archive; p120, David Warner Ellis/Redferns; p123T, Nik Wheeler/Sygma; pp124–125, Nik Wheeler/Sygma; p126T, Mick Gold/Redferns; p129, Nik Wheeler/Sygma; pp134–135, Michael Putland/Hulton Archive; p137, Michael Putland/Hulton Archive; p142T, Erica Echenberg/Redferns; p145T, David Redfern/Redferns; p153, Corbis Historical; p156T, Waring Abbott/Michael Ochs Archives; p157B, Waring Abbott/Michael Ochs Archives; p158BR, Waring Abbott/Michael Ochs Archives; p159T, Waring Abbott/Michael Ochs Archives; p160, Denis O'Regan; p165, Michael Ochs Archives; pp168–169 and 170, Rob Verhorst/Redferns; p172T, Peter Still/Redferns; p172B, Donaldson Collection/Michael Ochs Archives; p175T, Michael Putland/Hulton Archive; p184, Bobby Bank/WireImage; p185, Michael Ochs Archives; p187, Laura Levine/Images Press; p192, Larry Busacca/WireImage; pp194–195, SOPA Images/LightRocket; p200, Rob Verhorst/Redferns; p202, Rob Verhorst/Redferns; p205T, Chip HIRES/Gamma-Rapho; p206A, Denis O'Regan; p219, Jo Hale/Getty Images Entertainment; p220, Jeffrey Mayer/WireImage; p223, Mick Hutson/Redferns; p219, Brian Rasic/Getty Images Entertainment; pp225–226, Brian Rasic/Getty Images Entertainment. **National Archives:** pp118–119, Erik Calonious/NARA record 8464439. **Brad Norr:** front cover; p1. **REX Features:** p37T, Ray Stevenson; p56, Crollalanza; p89B, Bayerische Rundfunk/Ortf/Kobal; p189T, Richard Young; p210, Richard Young. **Andrew Smyth Collection:** p16A; p79A; p97TandM; p112A; p113A; p136TandM; p145B; p146A; p159M; p161A; p163T; p164A; p166A; p173A; p176B; p178; p182; p196A; p201A; p203T; p211TandM; pp216 and 217. **Laurens Van Houten via Frank White Photo Agency:** p28; p30; p31; p54; pp64–65; p69; p77T; pp140 and 141; p143. **Voyageur Press:** p8; p18; p21A; p22; p36; p38B; p43A; p46; p49; p53; p60; p62; p74; p76; p92; p102; p106; p107T; p108M; p110M; p118B; p122; p138; p144; p155; p174; p186; p188; p190T; p191B; p203TM; p204; p218; 229A. **Frank White Photo Agency/Laurens Van Houten:** p28; p30; p31; p54; pp64–65; p69; p77T; pp140 and 141; p143.

ABOUT THE AUTHOR

At approximately 7,900 (with more than 7,000 appearing in his books), Martin Popoff has unofficially written more record reviews than anybody in the history of music writing across all genres. Additionally, Martin has penned seventy-three books on hard rock, heavy metal, classic rock, and record collecting. He was editor-in-chief of the now-retired *Brave Words & Bloody Knuckles*, Canada's foremost heavy metal publication, and has also contributed to *Revolver, Guitar World, Goldmine, Record Collector*, bravewords.com, lollipop.com, and hardradio.com. In addition, Martin has been a regular contractor to Banger Films, having worked on the award-winning documentary *Rush: Beyond the Lighted Stage*, and also the eleven-episode *Metal Evolution* and ten-episode *Rock Icons*, both for VH1 Classic. Martin currently resides in Toronto and can be reached through martinp@inforamp.net or martinpopoff.com.

ROIE AVIN, editor and writer of *The Prog Report*, is an avid progressive rock fan and has years of experience working in the music industry in marketing and social media, as well as publicity for a leading progressive rock label, while also heading up his own Royal Avenue Media. He is also a US correspondent for the UK's *Prog* magazine, the premier publication for progressive rock music worldwide.

CRAIG BAILEY is host of *Floydian Slip*, a syndicated Pink Floyd radio program. He started the show in 1989 at his college radio station and, after graduating, hosted it for more than a decade in the Burlington, Vermont–Plattsburgh, New York, market. In 2009, operating as sole proprietor, he established the Random Precision Radio Network, which has grown to include several dozen stations in the United States and abroad that air *Floydian Slip* each week. A lifelong Vermonter, Craig produces, markets, and distributes his show from the secret basement broadcast lab of his Shelburne home. Network roster, broadcast schedule, and other details are at floydianslip.com.

Don't even think about trying to pigeonhole **NICK BEGGS**. The British bassist, Stick player, and songwriter has a footprint stamped across a range of genres including prog, pop, Celtic, funk, and soul. Collectively, his own band and project releases have sold more than three million copies. He's the prime architect of Kajagoogoo, a synth-pop band that catapulted to success in 1983 with the global smash "Too Shy." Beggs later embarked on a career that found him working with some of the biggest names in rock and pop, including Belinda Carlisle, John Paul Jones, Howard Jones, Gary Numan, Maddy Prior, Cliff Richard, Midge Ure, and Seal, to name a few. In the progressive rock universe, he's performed with Steve Hackett, Steve Howe, Rick Wakeman, and Steven Wilson. Beggs also had a brief career as an A&R man for Phonogram Records in the early '90s and is a celebrated illustrator best known for *Dangerous Potatoes: 13 Stories about Evil Vegetables*, a series of quirky children's stories.

RALPH CHAPMAN's current project is scripting and producing a series for Canada's national broadcaster, CBC, in which he tells the story of the network's legendary music and video archive. Previously, he served as writer and associate producer on the VH1 series *Rock Icons*. Prior to that, he served the same roles on the critically acclaimed eleven-part series *Metal Evolution*. Chapman was also part of the creative team behind the Juno Award–winning documentary, *Rush: Beyond the Lighted Stage*, which also took the Audience Award at the Tribeca Film Festival in 2010. Chapman continues to work with Iconoclassic Records as a project producer, notably overseeing the reissue campaign of the Guess Who catalog. He continues to develop projects with Banger Films and on his own with his production company, Wesbrage Productions, while contributing to various music-related websites in his spare time.

ROBERT CORICH is a remastering engineer and record producer who started his career as an IBM mainframe operator, engineer, and consultant, writing courses and books on mainframes and operating systems, often lecturing all over the world. His love of music moved him into the audio world, first as a studio hand and then into engineering and production. He specialized as a mastering engineer, reworking catalog and remastering for the likes of Uriah Heep, Status Quo, Chris Squire, Nazareth, Rainbow, Gentle Giant, and Magnum. Corich has also been involved in writing extensive liner notes and appearing as a critic in the *Inside* band documentary series. Corich is also the author or coauthor of over a dozen books on classic rock acts.

DENNIS DUNAWAY is the bassist, songwriter, and conceptual artist for the original Alice Cooper group, who were inducted into the Rock and Roll Hall of Fame in 2011. The band's *Billion Dollar Babies* album reached #1 in America and the UK in 1973. Their song "School's Out" was inducted into the Grammy Hall of Fame in 2016, and in 2017 the Music Business Association presented the band with Outstanding Achievement Awards. In 2015, Dennis released his autobiography, *Snakes! Guillotines! Electric Chairs!: My Adventures in the Alice Cooper Group*. The Alice Cooper group, who have remained good friends since the band's multiplatinum run in the early '70s, reunited in 2017 for the *Paranormal* album, following the record with a tour of the UK. Dennis also records and tours with Blue Coupe, which features the Bouchard brothers of Blue Öyster Cult fame and Tish and Snooky of Manic Panic.

By the age of nineteen, **HEATHER FINDLAY** had studied art at college, spent increasing amounts of time in the studio, and begun playing various acoustic gigs. Following one such gig, she was asked to join UK progressive rock band Mostly Autumn, with which she recorded about a dozen albums and EPs and toured internationally during thirteen years with the band. She has supported Blackmore's Night (as well as created cover art for the band), collaborated with Arjen Lucassen, and toured and guested on stage with both Uriah Heep and Jethro Tull. In January 2010, Heather made the decision to part company with Mostly Autumn and launch a solo career.

STEVE HACKETT is renowned as an immensely talented and innovative rock musician. He was lead guitarist with Genesis as part of their classic lineup with Gabriel, Collins, Banks, and Rutherford, appearing on six of the band's albums, including the acclaimed *Selling England by the Pound* (a favorite of John Lennon). As he embarked on his solo career, he developed his exceptional range, pushing musical boundaries into exciting areas and inventing techniques such as "tapping." His solo career went from strength to strength, and the mid-'80s saw not only solo hit single "Cell 151," but also the Steve Hackett and Steve Howe super-group GTR. Steve worked further with many renowned musicians such as Paul Carrack, Bonnie Tyler, John Wetton, and Brian May, who has credited Steve as an early influence. Steve has approximately twenty-five studio titles to his name as a solo artist. Had Steve not been busy with his gold-certified act GTR, there was a pretty good chance he would have ended up working with Roger Waters, who was embarking on the early stages of his solo career.

LEWIS HALL is bassist and vocalist in UK Pink Floyd tribute act Think Floyd, now celebrating their twenty-third year of existence. As the band has developed musically, they have taken on fresh challenges and performed the complete albums *Dark Side of the Moon* and *Wish You Were Here*, Pink Floyd's 1972 film *Live at Pompeii*, plus iconic tracks including "Dogs," "Echoes," and "Atom Heart Mother." For their 2002–2003 tour, Think Floyd's *Through the Wall* show included most of *The Wall* and featured local schoolchildren helping bring to life tracks like "Another Brick in the Wall (Part 2)," "Goodbye Blue Sky," and "The Trial." Think Floyd also helped set up the internationally renowned Rhodes Rock Festival, an annual event on the Greek island of Rhodes. A typical Think Floyd show includes all the well-known classics as well as lesser-known tracks from albums such as *Ummagumma* and *Obscured by Clouds*. Hall has played in and continues to perform with non-cover acts too, and is adept at jazz, classic rock, funk, blues, and of course, progressive rock.

Multi-instrumentalist **PAUL KEHAYAS** has over two decades of composition, performing, and production experience. His music has been featured in a variety of award-winning feature films, documentaries, and television programs, including *Satan Lives*; *Manson, My Name Is Evil*; *Super Duper Alice Cooper*; *We Are Savvy*; and *Rock Icons*. Paul has covered dozens of Pink Floyd songs over the years and spent more than a month's rent to purchase his cherished mono copy of *Piper at the Gates of Dawn*. He currently plays in Hollow Earth.

Educated in Middle Eastern and Arabic international relations and political science, **ED LOPEZ-REYES** has worked and served on boards of directors in academic, non-profit, political, public service, and public relations endeavors. Widely published in these fields, Ed is owner and chief consultant of Wolf & King Strategies, where he is responsible for work in public, government, and entertainment relations. A guitar player and concert enthusiast, Ed is also a music feature writer and contributing editor specializing in the post–Roger Waters era of Pink Floyd, working mostly with authoritative Pink Floyd site brain-damage.co.uk and the *Floydian Slip* blog.

STEVE ROTHERY is the original guitarist and longest continuously serving member of UK progressive rock act Marillion, who, through four decades, eighteen studio albums, and myriad other releases, have sold fifteen million albums worldwide. Steve has also issued two albums as part of a duo called the Wishing Tree, as well as one solo album, 2014's *The Ghosts of Pripyat*. Rothery is also the founder of the British Guitar Academy.

Voted "Best Keyboardist of All Time" by *Music Radar* magazine, **JORDAN RUDESS** is best known as the keyboardist and multi-instrumentalist for platinum-selling, Grammy-nominated prog rock band Dream Theater, who have sold an estimated twelve million albums worldwide. At nine, he entered the Juilliard School of Music Pre-College Division for classical piano training, but by his late teens he had grown increasingly interested in synthesizers and prog rock. Against the counsel of his parents and tutors, he turned away from classical piano to try his hand as a solo progressive rock keyboardist. Jordan owns the successful app development company Wizdom Music and is the author of two keyboard technique books, including *Total Keyboard Wizardry: A Technique and*

Improvisation Workbook. Musicians all over the world subscribe to Rudess's Online Conservatory, which offers a full range of courses in everything from harmony and rhythm to improvisation, ear training, and technique. In addition to working with Dream Theater, Jordan has recorded with myriad other acts and appeared on dozens of albums.

KYLE SHUTT is guitarist for Texas heavy metal heroes the Sword, who have released a half-dozen well-regarded loud records of retro-metal since the band's inception in 2003. In 2017 Shutt assembled a band to record and tour *Doom Side of the Moon*, a rockin' version of . . . you guessed it. The Sword have supported many of metal's most critically acclaimed bands, including Clutch, Lamb of God, Opeth, and Metallica.

JEFF WAGNER is the author of *Mean Deviation: Four Decades of Progressive Heavy Metal* and *Soul on Fire: The Life and Music of Peter Steele*. He also contributed to Martin Popoff's *Rush: The Illustrated History* and *Rush: Album by Album*. Jeff lives in Greensboro, North Carolina, and became a Pink Floyd fan with his first viewing of *Live at Pompeii*. When not listening, cycling, or watching Washington Nationals baseball, Wagner works for prog rock record label InsideOut Music.

A COMPLETE AUTHOR BIBLIOGRAPHY

Iron Maiden: Album by Album (2018)

The Clash: All the Albums, All the Songs (2018)

Led Zeppelin: All the Albums, All the Songs (2017)

AC/DC: Album by Album (2017)

Lights Out: Surviving the '70s with UFO (2017)

Tornado of Souls: Thrash's Titanic Clash (2017)

Caught in a Mosh: The Golden Era of Thrash (2017)

Metal Collector: Gathered Tales from Headbangers (2017)

Rush: Album by Album (2017)

Beer Drinkers and Hell Raisers: The Rise of

Who Invented Heavy Metal? (2015)

Sail Away: Whitesnake's Fantastic Voyage (2015)

Live Magnetic Air: The Unlikely Saga of the Superlative Max Webster (2014)

Steal Away the Night: An Ozzy Osbourne Day-by-Day (2014)

The Big Book of Hair Metal (2014)

Sweating Bullets: The Deth and Rebirth of Megadeth (2014)

Smokin' Valves: A Headbanger's Guide to 900 NWOBHM Records (2014)

The Art of Metal (coedit with Malcolm Dome; 2013)

Black Sabbath FAQ (2011)

The Collector's Guide to Heavy Metal: Volume 4: The '00s (2011; coauthored with David Perri)

Goldmine Standard Catalog of American Records 1948–1991, 7th Edition (2010)

Goldmine Record Album Price Guide, 6th Edition (2009)

Goldmine 45 RPM Price Guide, 7th Edition (2009)

A Castle Full of Rascals: Deep Purple '83–'09 (2009)

Worlds Away: Voivod and the Art of Michel Langevin (2009)

Ye Olde Metal: 1978 (2009)

Gettin' Tighter: Deep Purple '68–'76 (2008)

All Access: The Art of the Backstage Pass (2008)

Ye Olde Metal: 1977 (2008)

Ye Olde Metal: 1976 (2008)

Judas Priest: Heavy Metal Painkillers (2007)

Ye Olde Metal: 1973 to 1975 (2007)

The Collector's Guide to Heavy Metal: Volume 3: The Nineties (2007)

Ye Olde Metal: 1968 to 1972 (2007)

Run for Cover: The Art of Derek Riggs (2006)

Black Sabbath: Doom Let Loose (2006)

Dio: Light Beyond the Black (2006)

The Collector's Guide to Heavy Metal: Volume 2: The Eighties (2005)

Rainbow: English Castle Magic (2005)

UFO: Shoot Out the Lights (2005)

The New Wave of British Heavy Metal Singles (2005)

Blue Öyster Cult: Secrets Revealed! (2004); update and reissue (2009); updated and reissued as Agents of Fortune: The Blue Öyster Cult Story (2016)

Contents Under Pressure: 30 Years of Rush at Home & Away (2004)

The Top 500 Heavy Metal Albums of All Time (2004)

The Collector's Guide to Heavy Metal: Volume 1: The Seventies (2003)

The Top 500 Heavy Metal Songs of All Time (2003)

Southern Rock Review (2001)

Heavy Metal: 20th Century Rock and Roll (2000)

The Goldmine Price Guide to Heavy Metal Records (2000)

The Collector's Guide to Heavy Metal (1997)

Riff Kills Man! 25 Years of Recorded Hard Rock & Heavy Metal (1993)

See www.martinpopoff.com for complete details and ordering information.

INDEX

About Face (Gilmour), 102, 178, 189, 199, 229
"Absolutely Curtains," 93
"Across the Universe," 90
"Alan's Psychedelic Breakfast," 63, 65–66, 70, 72, 107
Albee, Edward, 179
Alice Cooper, 24, 26–27, 32
Alldis, John, 63
"Allons-y (1)," 224–25
"Allons-y (2)," 224–25
AMM, 11, 19
Amused to Death, 63, 177, 184–85, 229
Anderson, Ian, 165
"Animal Army" (Mute Gods), 143
Animal Farm (Orwell), 139, 144
Animals, 61, 123, 136, 138–53, 155, 158, 163, 171, 175, 182, 203, 209, 222, 229
"Another Brick in the Wall," 161, 163–64
"Any Colour You Like," 103, 107
"Arnold Layne," 9, 11–12
"Astronomy Domine," 10, 16, 21, 47, 49, 53
"Atom Heart Mother," 62–63, 74
Atom Heart Mother, 9, 44, 55, 62–75, 79, 83, 94–95, 98, 103, 105, 222
Atzmon, Gilad, 219
"Autumn '68," 222, 224
Avin, Roie, 190–203, 206–17, 221–29

Bad (Jackson), 190
Bailey, Craig, 24–35, 48–61
Balance (Van Halen), 213
"Ballad of John and Yoko, The" (Beatles), 178
Beach Boys, 8, 61, 171
Beatles, 15, 17, 31, 53, 61, 65, 85, 87, 90–91, 165, 178
Beck, Jeff, 117, 119
Beggs, Nick, 139–53, 157–73, 178–87
Big Generator (Yes), 200
"Big Spliff, The," 218–19
"Bike," 10, 15, 19
Black Sabbath, 41, 47
Blackberries, 132
Blue Cheer, 37
"Blue Light," 189
Blue Öyster Cult, 41
Bolan, Marc, 96
Borges, Jorge Luis, 175
Bowie, David, 96
Boyd, Joe, 11–12, 20
Braden, Les, 26–27
"Brain Damage," 103, 107, 109, 112, 116
"Breathe," 103, 107, 114
"Bring the Boys Back Home," 157
Broken China (Wright), 212
Brown, Sarah, 221
"Burning Bridges," 93, 96, 98–99, 101, 103
Byrds, 8

"Candy and a Currant Bun," 11

"Careful with That Axe, Eugene," 42, 47, 51, 70
Carin, Jon, 189–90, 196–97, 200–201, 205–6, 219, 221
Carnal, Charlie, 17
Cars, 155
Chanter, Doreen and Irene, 182
Chapman, Ralph, 65–74, 94–105, 157–73, 178–87
"Chapter 24," 10, 15, 19, 27
"Childhood's End," 94, 101–2, 107
Children of Men, 149
"Cirrus Minor," 38–41, 55
Clapton, Eric, 56, 119, 167–68
Clarke, Vince, 146
Clash, The, 177
Close to the Edge (Yes), 110
Cobain, Kurt, 213
Cohen, Leonard, 20
Collins, Phil, 167, 214
"Comfortably Numb," 159, 166–67, 214
"Coming Back to Life," 211, 214
Committee, The, 38
Cooper, Alice, 13, 16, 193
Corich, Robert, 78–91, 178–87, 221–29
Cornish, Pete, 146
"Corporal Clegg," 23, 26, 29
Council, Floyd, 10
Court of the Crimson King (King Crimson), 149
Cream, 17
"Crying Song," 38–39, 41
"Cymbaline," 38, 41

Daltrey, Roger, 19
Dark Side of the Moon, 48, 63, 66, 70, 72, 77–78, 84, 88, 91, 94–98, 101–3, 105–21, 125, 127, 130, 143, 146, 155, 163, 200, 203–4, 209, 212, 214
Davies, Ray, 19
Deep Purple, 48
Delicate Sound of Thunder, 47, 190, 204
Depeche Mode, 146
Destroyer (Kiss), 194
Dimebag Darrell, 119
Division Bell, The, 35, 197, 199, 201, 204–18, 221–22, 225–26
Doctor Strange, 41
"Dogs," 139, 143, 145–46, 148
"Dogs of War, The," 190, 192, 194, 199–200, 207
Donovan, 16
"Don't Leave Me Now," 173
"Dramatic Theme," 43
Dream Theater, 167
Droste effect, 55–56
Dunaway, Dennis, 10–21, 24–35
Dylan, Bob, 8, 10–11, 68, 179

Eagles, 93, 213
"Echoes," 55, 69, 74, 78–79, 85, 87–91, 96, 98, 107
"Eclipse," 103, 107, 114, 125
Eddy, Duane, 119

Edgar Broughton Band, 48
"Effervescing Elephant," 19
Electric Ladyland (Jimi Hendrix Experience), 110
Ellis, Beggs & Howard, 148
Ellis, Simon, 148
"Embryo," 90–91
Emerick, Geoff, 21
Endless River, The, 48, 53, 139, 202, 206, 211, 218–29
"Entertainment," 59
Ezrin, Bob, 155, 157–58, 163, 171, 177, 189–90, 193–94, 205

Fairport Convention, 20
Falklands War, 175, 179
Fariña, Richard, 20
Farmer, Mimsy, 38
"Fat Old Sun," 65, 70, 72, 89
"Fearless," 77, 84, 93
Fields, Venetta Lee, 132
"Final Cut, The," 180
Final Cut, The, 48, 63, 68, 149, 166, 171, 173–87, 192, 194, 208, 217
Findlay, Heather, 125–37, 139–53
Fish, 133, 135
"Flaming," 10, 20–21
Fleetwood Mac, 177
"Fletcher Memorial Home, The," 185
"Free Four," 93, 95–97, 103, 183

Garcia, Jerry, 103
Gazzarri's, 26
Geesin, Ron, 44, 63, 69, 74
Genesis, 109–10, 121, 142, 161, 165–67, 200, 213–14
Giraudy, Miquette, 93
"Gnome, The," 10, 19, 27, 31
Goblin, 42
Godard, Jean-Luc, 36
"Gold It's in the . . ., The," 93, 102
Gong, 93
"Goodbye Cruel World," 160
Grahame, Kenneth, 13
"Grand Vizier's Garden Party, The," 48, 57, 59
"Grantchester Meadows," 48, 55, 65
Grateful Dead, 8
"Great Day for Freedom, A," 209–10, 214
"Great Gig in the Sky," 103, 115
Green, Peter, 167
"Green is the Colour," 38, 41
"Grooving with a Pict," 48, 55, 65
"Gunner's Dream, The," 180, 183–84
Guthrie, James, 185

Hackett, Steve, 108–21, 157–73, 214
Hall, Lewis, 65–74, 78–91, 94–105
Harper, Roy, 125, 136, 182
Harrison, George, 56, 69, 165,

167
"Have a Cigar," 41, 101, 125, 130, 132–33, 135–36, 182, 200
Hawking, Stephen, 209, 225–26
Hawkwind, 48
Heep, Uriah, 66
Hell Freezes Over (Eagles), 213
Helliwell, John, 199
"Helter Skelter," 40
Hendrix, Jimi, 37, 119
"Hey You," 166–67
"High Hopes," 206, 211, 214, 225
Hipgnosis, 48, 55, 66, 76, 121, 148, 225
Hogarth, Steve, 132–33
"Hollywood," 38
Holst, Gustav, 44
Honky Château (John), 96
Humble Pie, 85

I Ching, 15
"Ibiza Bar," 37–38, 40
Iddins, Damon, 219
"If," 63, 65, 68–70, 97–98
"I'm a King Bee," 11
In the Flesh Tour, 155
In Through the Out Door (Led Zeppelin), 155
Incredible String Band, 11
"Interstellar Overdrive," 10–11, 16–17, 19, 23, 29, 36
"Is There Anybody Out There?" 160
Is This the Life We Really Want? (Waters), 63, 177, 229
"It Would Be So Nice," 39

Jackson, Andy, 190, 218, 222
Jackson, Michael, 190
Jagger, Mick, 165
Jefferson Airplane, 8
Jethro Tull, 94, 165
John, Elton, 96
"Journey, The," 72
Joy Division, 20
"Jugband Blues," 22–24, 28–29

Kamen, Michael, 155, 171, 177, 185, 205
"Kayleigh" (Marillion), 133
Keenan, Maynard, 135
"Keep Talking," 206, 209, 214, 225
Kehayas, Paul, 10–21, 38–45, 78–91
Keltner, Jim, 199
Kent, Nick, 123
King Crimson, 55
Kinks, 72
Kiss, 193–94
Knack, 155
Kossoff, Paul, 74, 167

"Lazy Old Sun" (Kinks), 72
"Learning to Fly," 189, 192, 194, 196–97, 199, 207, 214
Led Zeppelin, 79, 121
Lennon, John, 12, 68, 101, 110, 165, 178–79
Leslie effects, 87, 91

"Let There Be More Light," 23, 26, 32
"Let's Get Metaphysical" (Gilmour), 102
"Levity Ball" (Cooper), 16
Liebezeit, Jaki, 74
Live at Pompeii, 43, 51, 61, 78, 85, 90–91
"Long, Long, Long," 73
Long Run, The (Eagles), 155
Lopez-Reyes, Ed, 190–203, 206–17, 221–29
Lord, Jon, 48
"Louder than Words," 211, 219, 222–25
Love Beach, 180
"Love on the Air," 189
"Lucifer Sam," 10, 15–16

"Main Theme," 42
"Man, The," 72
"Man and The Journey, The," 47
Manzanera, Phil, 219, 222
Marillion, 133, 135, 143, 152
"Marooned," 209, 226
Marvin, Hank, 119, 167
Mason, Lindy, 41
Master of Puppets (Metallica), 114
"Matilda Mother," 10, 20–21, 53
Matthews, Rob, 65
May, Brian, 167–68
MC5, 37
McCartney, Paul, 13, 101, 110, 165
Meddle, 43, 55, 66, 73, 76–91, 93, 95, 98, 105, 127, 146, 184–85
Meddled, 89–90
Mellotron, 55, 74, 97
Misplaced Childhood (Marillion), 133
Momentary Lapse of Reason, A, 35, 78, 101, 135, 188–208, 210, 212–14, 217
"Money," 103, 107, 116–17, 200
Monkees Present, The, 65
Monty Python troupe, 139
Moody Blues, 55
Moon, Keith, 57
Moore, Anthony, 189–90, 192, 197, 199, 209, 221
More, 36–46, 48, 55, 59, 95–96, 98
"More Blues," 42
Morrison, Van, 96
Morse, Steve, 117
"Most Boring Song I've Ever Heard Bar Two . . ., The," 27
"Mother," 165, 167, 171
Mothers in Birmingham, 46
"Mudmen," 99, 101
Mute Gods, 143

"Narrow Way, The," 56–57
"New Machine, A," 198
Nice Pair, A, 21
"Night Light," 225
"Nile Song, The," 37–42
1984 (Orwell), 139
Nirvana, 213
"Nobody Home," 167
Nonsuch (XTC), 16
"Not Now John," 182–83
"Nothing," 78

"Obscured by Clouds," 96, 101
Obscured by Clouds, 38–39, 46, 66, 76, 79, 84, 92–105, 127, 164, 167
Odessey and Oracle (Zombies), 21
Ogier, Bulle, 93
"Omnibus" (XTC), 16
"On Noodle Street," 225
"On the Run," 70, 72, 103, 107, 113
"On the Turning Away," 190, 192, 199, 210
"One of These Days," 77–78, 80–81, 83–84, 89–90, 93–94, 107
"One Slip," 190, 194
O'Rourke, Steve, 94
Orwell, George, 139, 144
Outer Limits, The (Voivod), 39–40

Page, Scott, 199–202, 221
"Paranoid Eyes," 180, 183
"Peace Be with You," 201–2
Pearl Jam, 213
Pet Sounds (Beach Boys), 61
Pictures at an Exhibition, 48
Piece for Assorted Lunatics, A, 103
"Pigs (Three Different Ones)," 101, 139, 143, 149, 151
"Pigs on the Wing 1," 139, 144, 148
"Pigs on the Wing 2," 139, 144, 148
"Pillow of Winds, A," 77, 84
Piper at the Gates of Dawn, The, 8–21, 23–24, 26–27, 31, 35, 38
"Planet Caravan" (Black Sabbath), 41
"Planets" (Holst), 44
Pleased to Meet Me (Replacements), 128
"Point Me at the Sky," 39–40, 51
"Poles Apart," 209
Porcaro, Jeff, 165, 171, 202
"Post War Dream, The," 184
"Pow R. Toc H.," 17
Powell, Aubrey, 76, 225
Pratt, Guy, 205–6, 219
Pretties for You (Cooper), 16
Pretty Things, 21, 59
Prior, Matt, 132
Pulse, 214

Queen, 61
"Quicksilver," 43

Radio K.A.O.S. (Waters), 189
Rainbow Theatre, 116
Ralbovsky, Stephen, 189
Rattle That Lock (Gilmour), 221
"Raving and Drooling," 81, 123
Reed, Lou, 193
"Remember a Day," 23, 27
Replacements, 128
"Return of the Son of Nothing, The," 78–79
Revolver (Beatles), 9, 21
Rhoads, Randy, 119
Richards, Keith, 165
Rodgers, Nile, 164
Rolling Stones, 17, 29, 119, 132, 165
Rothery, Steve, 125–37
Rotten, Johnny, 141
Rudess, Jordan, 108–21, 157–73
"Run Like Hell," 163–64, 209, 214

Rush, 61, 208

Salisbury (Heep), 66
Samson, Polly, 205, 210–11, 221, 223
"San Tropez," 77, 85, 87, 96
Sandinista! (Clash), 177
"Saucerful of Secrets, A," 36, 47, 51, 69
Saucerful of Secrets, A, 17, 22–35, 39, 48, 51, 56, 70, 84
"Scarecrow," 19
Schroeder, Barbet, 36, 38, 92, 99
Scott, Tom, 199
"Scream Thy Last Scream," 23
"Seagulls," 38
"Seamus," 78, 85, 87
"See Emily Play," 16, 29
"See-Saw," 23, 27
"Set the Controls for the Heart of the Sun," 23–24, 26, 31–32, 47, 51
"Several Species of Small Furry Animals Gathered Together in a Cave and Grooving with a Pict," 55
Sex Pistols, 141
S.F. Sorrow (Pretty Things), 21
Sgt. Pepper (Beatles), 13, 21, 61, 65, 112
"Sheep," 81, 136, 139, 143, 152
"Shine on You Crazy Diamond," 101, 107, 109, 123, 125–27, 129–30, 132
"Show Must Go On, The," 167
Shute, Nevil, 184
Shutt, Kyle, 108–21, 125–37
"Signs of Life," 196
Silver Apples of the Moon (Subotnick), 15
Simple Minds, 221
Singh, Vic, 10
"Skins," 225
Smith, Neal, 24, 27
Smith, Norman, 9, 12, 21
Soft Machine, 11, 17
"Son of Nothing," 78
"Sorrow," 197–98, 214
"Spanish Piece, A," 39, 43
Spare Bricks, 174
Squire, Chris, 93
Starr, Ringo, 74
"Stay," 93, 103
Stockhausen, Karlheinz, 15
Stranglers, 142
Strummer, Joe, 139
Styles, Alan, 63
Subotnick, Morton, 15
"Summer '68," 63, 65, 69–70, 95–96, 103, 222
Supertramp, 199
"Sysyphus," 48, 53, 65

"Take Up Thy Stethoscope and Walk," 9
"Talkin' Hawkin'," 225
Tavener, John, 74
Tennille, Toni, 171
"Terminal Frost," 198
Thatcher, Margaret, 175, 179, 183
"Then Came the Last Days of May" (Blue Öyster Cult), 41
13th Floor Elevators, 8
Thorgerson, Storm, 48, 76, 128, 141, 148–49, 194, 197,

208–9, 225–26
Thriller (Jackson), 112
"Time," 69, 93, 95, 102–3, 112, 114, 116, 186, 209
Tool, 135
Torry, Clare, 107, 115
Townshend, Pete, 68, 101
"Trial, The," 171
Turner, Ike & Tina, 132
Tusk (Fleetwood Mac), 177
"Two Suns in the Sunset," 184
2001: A Space Odyssey, 17
Tyler, Bonnie, 132

UFO Club, 11
Ummagumma, 9, 21, 23, 36, 43, 46–61, 63, 65–66, 70, 74
"Unsung," 225
"Up the Kyber," 42, 44
"Us and Them," 53, 103, 107, 112–14

Vallée, La, 38, 92–93
Van Halen, 213
Voivod, 39–40, 49

Wagner, Jeff, 38–45, 48–61, 65–74, 206–17
Wakeman, Rick, 48
Walk Away René (Hipgnosis), 148
Wall, The, 48, 53, 69, 138–39, 146, 149–50, 154–75, 177–81, 188–89, 192, 210, 229
Ward, Bill, 40, 57
Waters, Eric Fletcher, 174, 184
We Can't Dance (Genesis), 213
"Wearing the Inside Out," 209, 212
"Welcome to the Machine," 125, 130, 133, 135
Wet Dream (Wright), 212
"Whale, The" (Tavener), 74
"What Do You Want from Me," 206, 210, 214
"When the Tigers Broke Free," 174, 177–78
"When You're In," 96, 101
White Album, The, 73, 87, 165
Whitehouse, Mary, 143, 150
Whitesnake, 190
Williams, Carlena, 132
Wilson, Brian, 24
Wilson, Jackie, 96
Wind in the Willows, The (Grahame), 10, 13, 41
"Wish You Were Here," 125, 127–28, 130, 132, 144, 214
Wish You Were Here, 28, 61, 66, 80, 122–39, 146, 155, 163, 171, 175, 180, 203, 209

Yazoo, 146
Yes, 200
"Yet Another Movie," 194, 199
"You Gotta Be Crazy," 123
"You'll Never Walk Alone," 84–85
Young, Jimmy, 81
Young, Neil, 93
"Young Lust," 163–64, 167, 171
Youth, 219

Zabriskie Point, 38, 95, 103
Zappa, Frank, 61
Zombies, 21

Inspiring | Educating | Creating | Entertaining

Brimming with creative inspiration, how-to projects, and useful information to enrich your everyday life, Quarto Knows is a favorite destination for those pursuing their interests and passions. Visit our site and dig deeper with our books into your area of interest: Quarto Creates, Quarto Cooks, Quarto Homes, Quarto Lives, Quarto Drives, Quarto Explores, Quarto Gifts, or Quarto Kids.

First published in 2018 by Voyageur Press, an imprint of The Quarto Group, 401 Second Avenue North, Suite 310, Minneapolis, MN 55401 USA. T (612) 344-8100 F (612) 344-8692 www.QuartoKnows.com

Voyageur Press titles are also available at discount for retail, wholesale, promotional, and bulk purchase. For details, contact the Special Sales Manager by email at specialsales@quarto.com or by mail at The Quarto Group, Attn: Special Sales Manager, 401 Second Avenue North, Suite 310, Minneapolis, MN 55401 USA.

10 9 8 7 6 5 4 3 2 1

ISBN: 978-0-7603-6061-3

Library of Congress Cataloging-in-Publication Data

Names: Popoff, Martin, 1963- author.
Title: Pink Floyd : album by album / Martin Popoff.
Description: Minneapolis, MN : Voyageur Press, 2018. | Includes
    bibliographical references.
Identifiers: LCCN 2017054858 | ISBN 9780760360613 (plc)
Subjects: LCSH: Pink Floyd (Musical group) | Rock music--History and
    criticism.
Classification: LCC ML421.P6 P64 2018 | DDC 782.42166092/2--dc23
LC record available at https://lccn.loc.gov/2017054858

Acquiring Editor: Dennis Pernu
Project Manager: Alyssa Bluhm
Art Director: Brad Springer
Cover Designer: Brad Norr
Page Design: Amelia LeBarron

On the front cover: Michael Ochs Archives/Getty Images
On the back cover: AF archive/Alamy Stock Photo

Printed in China